# Power in Capitalist Societies

# Power in Capitalist Societies:
## Theory, Explanations and Cases

**Andrew Cox**
*Senior Lecturer in Politics*
*University of Hull*

**Paul Furlong**
*Lecturer in Politics*
*University of Hull*

**Edward Page**
*Lecturer in Politics*
*University of Hull*

ST. MARTIN'S PRESS      New York

© Andrew Cox, Paul Furlong and Edward Page, 1985

ISBN 0–312–63409–9

**Library of Congress Cataloging in Publication Data**

Cox, Andrew W.
  Power in capitalist societies.

  Includes index.
  1. Power (social sciences).     I. Furlong, Paul.
II. Page, Edward.     III. Title.
JC330.C66     1985     303.3     85–8132
ISBN 0–312–63409–9

# Contents

# Introduction

This book aims at providing students with a guide to some of the major concepts and debates likely to be encountered by researchers in politics. Drawing on material already available in the social sciences, and particularly in political science, we attempt to provide students with an introduction to the different ways in which the nature and location of power in capitalist societies can be understood. Although all three of the authors were trained in traditional political science disciplines, our aim is to show the strengths and weaknesses of the approaches of both political science and other social sciences in the analysis of power.

With this in mind, in Chapter 1 we outline the way in which politics developed as a separate discipline in the social sciences and what its normal focus of study has been. In particular, we chart the massive expansion in political science work since 1945 and try to relate the study of politics to the questions posed in other social science disciplines. It is our contention that all of the social science disciplines are ultimately concerned with the concept of power and that, as a result, the understanding of the nature of power in capitalist societies can only be broadened if we adopt an eclectic approach which draws on insights from the three major disciplines—economics, sociology and politics. This raises a number of problems. Is it possible to develop one theory or explanation of power which draws on insights from all of the social science disciplines? Is it possible to mesh together theories operating from very different epistemological positions? Is any one theory more adequate than other explanations? This problem of the contested and non-commensurable nature of theories of power is addressed in Chapter 2. We take an eclectic view of this problem, arguing that in the absence of an overarching general theory of power useful insights can be gleaned from utilising various theories of explanation rather than opting exclusively for only one method of analysis.

Having drawn this conclusion, in Chapters 3 to 5 we set out in some detail three of the main social science theories of power in capitalist society. Our aim in reviewing and describing the major assumptions of Marxist, elite and pluralist theories is not to commit the reader to any one of these approaches—indeed, the authors themselves would disagree amongst themselves about the relative utility of each of these three theories—but to describe and analyse what appear to us to be their major strengths and weaknesses. It is argued that none of these approaches is, on its own, able to explain the totality of social, economic and political reality. Once the reader is familiar with the nature of these three theories, we then attempt to operationalise them through an application of their explanatory utility in four case studies. In Chapters 6 to 9 we look in turn at four problems common to capitalist societies in general—the growth of military expenditure, the growth of the role of government, the problem of regional decline in the economy and the role of local government. Each of these four case studies is exposed to analysis from Marxist, elite and pluralist approaches, and the strengths and weaknesses of these distinct theories is outlined. In Chapter 10 we conclude with a discussion of the future in the social sciences for theory building about the concept of power.

# PART I

# Power and the Social Sciences

# 1 Politics, Power and the Social Sciences

One might say that the concept 'game' is a concept with blurred edges—'But is a blurred concept a concept at all?'—Is an indistinct photograph a picture of a person at all? Is it even always an advantage to replace an indistinct picture by a sharp one? Isn't the indistinct one often exactly what we need?

Ludwig Wittgenstein[1]

## POLITICS AND THE CONCEPT POWER

As with Wittgenstein's 'game', it is much easier to point to examples of politics than it is to give the term 'politics' a rigid and exhaustive definition. As such, 'politics' seems to defy attempts to encompass its complex set of usages within a single, simple definition. This is what David Easton tries to do in a very influential work with his formal analytic definition of 'politics' as 'the authoritative allocation of values for a system'.[2] This is a definition with many virtues, but it is, as Wittgenstein might have said, 'closed by a frontier'. In order to understand the nature of the academic discipline of politics, it is necessary to ask what such definitions have contributed to the discipline and in what way its study has been changed by them. As we shall see, the term and the studies associated with it have resisted attempts to fit 'the study of politics' categorically into the box designated 'political science'. However, it is also true that while this 'language game' of the study of politics goes on over a wide variety of fields, the subject has developed both a concern for its own ways of going about things and a common orientation towards the notion of 'power'. Some would say that neither of these two developments is altogether healthy. Of course, it may be that 'power', like 'politics', is a concept which cannot be enclosed by stable frontiers. The contemporary nature of political studies in the United States, Britain and Western Europe cannot be encouraging to those who wish to circumscribe 'politics' and 'power'—eclectic, energetic, flexible, even opportunistic, the study is established as a loose, overlapping set of subject areas, united, as it were, by natural kinship rather than by cloning.

At different times and in different places the study of politics has approached a variety of questions. Consider the following, which have individually taxed political writers since the time of Aristotle:

1. What should we do with political power? Should those who exercise political power seek to achieve a good society for their citizens? If so, what form should this good society take?
2. How does legitimate authority maintain itself? How does it function under normal circumstances?
3. What determines the outcome of conflict over material and moral resources?
4. What is the significance of legitimate violence? How should coercive force be exercised?
5. What kinds of society are associated with stable political forms?
6. How does the individual make political choices?

At different times each of these has been espoused as the most important question concerning politics, sometimes even being considered as the *only* important question. Where the questions are different, it may be reliably assumed that the definitions of politics and the methods of investigation are for the most part different also, though they need not be so to the exclusion of all other approaches. But clearly the methods involved in pursuing the questions in the first group, about what we should do, will be rather more synthetic and speculative than will the activity of those who seek to answer, for example, questions about outcomes of conflict or about the conditions associated with political stability, either of which may be more related to observable actions. To identify common themes to such questions as these is a hazardous and challenging enterprise. Yet it does seem that there are common themes to these questions, and one of these, which we take as crucial to the notion of 'politics', is the concept of 'power'. How are these two related?

Earlier we quoted Wittgenstein's description of the concept 'game' as an 'indistinct photograph' and 'a concept with blurred edges'. The metaphors have a wider application than might at first appear, because Wittgenstein goes on to argue that concepts themselves are best seen as games. This is not a reference to game theory such as can be found in the study of international politics and social psychology but rather a complex and subtle point about the blurred nature of concepts, the resemblances among the referents of the concepts and the ways in which every concept (including the concept 'game') has its own rules. As Wittgenstein argues, one of the characteristics of the concept 'game' is the existence of rules specific to each game.[3] There is much that might be said about this controversial line of argument, which has stimulated and spawned a wealth of theories in different fields. To take only the most obvious point, Wittgenstein is arguing that it is a mistake to look for a defining characteristic of any concept which is common to all cases of that concept and to that concept only. But it might be said that this is, in effect, what he is doing with the notion of 'concept' itself, in arguing that all concepts have family resemblances and are like games defined by rules. However, this would not be an indisputable interpretation of *Philosophical Investigations*, since Wittgenstein does return persistently to the question of usage, the flexibility of concepts like 'rules', and the analogous nature of his comparisons (rather than their strict identity).

Whatever the ambiguities of the original analysis, its application to the question in hand is a useful device for clarifying the ways in which 'politics' may be said to have as one of its defining characteristics the structural concept 'power'; the specific rules applying to the ways in which 'power' gives structure to 'politics' will change in accordance with the different forms in which the question relating to the discipline of politics is put.

This notion that 'politics' is a specific language-game does not mean that it is trivial or that it is totally indeterminate.

The first of these caveats is more obvious than the second. To say that usage of the term 'politics' is a large and complex language-game should not be held to imply that the referent of the conceptual usage is in some sense a frivolous recreational activity of second-rate importance. More profoundly, it is not implied that the usage itself—both the everyday use of the term and the academic discipline associated with it—is not ultimately serious, that it is tenuous in its reference to reality or fit business only for amateurs. The importance of the game analogy is *not* that the 'games' of politics or of the study of politics are held to go on at one or even two removes from some supposed real, more valuable world. On the contrary, one of the purposes of the game analogy is to draw out the nature of the rules appropriate to the term, whether it is used as a general concept, or with reference to a particular type of game, or with reference to individual games as they occur. Of course, the rules of the language game of 'politics', as with other language games, are given not by decree but by interaction between the usages appropriate to the different forms of the 'game' in its specific occurrences. To say that the specific rules change is not to say that the terms 'power' and 'politics' have no constant meaning and are therefore indefinitely malleable, for if this were so it would, strictly speaking, be impossible for one individual to use the terms in a way that others could understand. Nor does the reliance on the internal logic formed by other concepts within the language game (such as 'power' within the 'politics' language game) mean that any definition is subject to infinite regress. To believe that to be of use, definitions must be completely free-standing, dependent on no other complex concepts, is to confuse verification with understanding. If the use of concepts is defined by specific rules, then the acceptance of the concept of 'power' as part of a language game called 'politics' does not imply that all usages or definitions of 'power' and 'politics' are equally strong in their logical structure or equally supported by reliable empirical reference. On the contrary, if we really wish to understand what is meant, it becomes important to identify the rules that define the usage, to specify the context within which the usage occurs, the values that inform that usage and the explanatory capacity of the rules or theory within which it occurs.

This is what we try to do with the concepts 'politics' and 'power' in this work. There is, as we have seen, a variety of different questions usually associated with serious studies about politics. Of course, some of the practitioners of those studies might wish to exclude all questions other than their own from the field of politics—to close it off with a frontier or make a sharp photograph of it, in Wittgenstein's terms. In principle, as must be clear by now, this is not the approach that we take here. However, such principled eclecticism does not absolve the researcher from the obligation to analyse, understand and make clear what his or her own usages mean. If necessary, this should be done by means of rigorously applied definitions and an explicit methodology.

The questions referred to earlier about the good society, legitimate violence, conflict over resources, and so on, all imply some common concern with differently conceived notions of power. Broadly speaking, these notions tend to be used at four different levels, with some writers operating at more than one level. First, perhaps the most profound analysis deals with power in the abstract; analyses in this field usually call themselves either political theory or political philosophy, sometimes both. The supposed synonymity between the two terms is significant, as we shall discuss later. Though there may be empirical reference in these works, such reference is often tenuous and usually secondary to the analysis of terms and to the consideration of politics in an ideal form, even where the writers may claim to be adopting scientific methods or offering practical guidance, as in the case of Machiavelli. The concern with politics in the abstract involves operating at a high level of generalisation and often the construction of complex models and theories. The writings of the great political philosophers such as Plato, Aristotle and Hobbes are at this level; a major tradition of political study in Britain (of lesser significance elsewhere) consists of commentary and explanation of the classical texts, often together with more or less explicit normative conclusions. Also in this field are the more

limited attempts at philosophical analysis of political terms
such as justice, sovereignty and equality. Studies of these
kinds derive from the discipline of philosophy and are the
most ancient of the varieties of political study.

Second, there are those who concentrate on formal
authority. Typically in this case one is dealing with the study
of governmental institutions in a relatively empirical manner, investigating the operations of the executive, the
legislature and the judiciary, sometimes without a clear
focus on the question of why such subjects should be
studied. This is the traditional subject of political study as it
developed in the late nineteenth century from the disciplines
of law and history, and in this form it still bears the marks of
its origins. This is particularly so on the Continent, where
politics is sometimes still treated as a category of public law.
Of course, it may be that the real effect of all these
institutions, as opposed to their nominal influence, is
inconsiderable and secondary. Though it is not necessarily
made clear, the implication of traditional institutional
studies is usually that such institutions are important in their
own right, even if only as setters of key values or as agents of
social control.

Third, politics may be studied through the consideration
of the more informal or indirect determinants of power,
most obviously political parties but also societal groups,
economic structure and prevailing cultural norms. Interest in
these areas is often, though not necessarily, associated with
political sociology. This tradition, which in Britain began as
an offshoot of studies of formal institutions, is now
predominant and takes a wide variety of forms. Its assumptions however are that the constitutional forms are inadequate to explain the exercise of power as it actually occurs and
that, to use the term coined by one of its first proponents,
Bagehot, the proper object of enquiry is the 'efficient secret'
of the political system.[4] More recently, the tradition has
extended itself into a wide variety of different concerns,
dealing not only with groups such as political parties directly
connected to the political system, and of course with
elections, but also with more indirect influences such as
interest groups, the effects of class and other social cleavages

and the power of organised elites.

This third line of enquiry, into informal determinants at the group level, was followed historically by the fourth and final level of analysis, which is akin to social psychology in that it deals with the behaviour and attitudes of individuals in so far as they affect politics through public opinion, individual voting behaviour and individual political participation. The similarities in method between this and the previous third level of analysis are close; in particular there can be a shared interest in the use of quantitative methods of investigation, in the importance of rigorous use of empirical evidence and in the need for clear explicit and sophisticated methodological preparation. In principle, however, this shared interest should not obscure the fact that the two approaches operate at radically different levels of analysis, the first considering power as a characteristic of group relationships and the second considering it as properly applied to individuals. Also, there are many who conduct their enquiry into informal political influences without using the methods referred to above. It is these methods however, whose introduction occurred mainly in the United States over a period of thirty years from the 1930s to the 1960s, that are usually described as 'the behavioural revolution'. That their introduction constituted a revolution can be seen by comparing the present state of the discipline's publications with empirical studies of politics prior to their development. The movement is referred to as 'behavioural' on the grounds of its attempts to reach conclusions based on observations of human behaviour as opposed to unverified and sometimes unverifiable conclusions lacking sound empirical support.

## HISTORY OF POLITICS AS A DISCIPLINE

At this point it becomes necessary to explain the historical development of the study of politics, to illuminate the differences within the discipline. It is just as important, however, to show how politics shares its orientation towards the analysis of power with other disciplines in the social sciences, and how it also shares with them many of the

methods associated with modern empirical investigation.
Politics is not the only academic language game which has
'power' as one of its major defining concepts. Paradoxically,
the amorphous state of politics as a discipline and its
overlapping with other social science subjects have become
clearly visible largely as a result of the efforts of behaviour-
ists to establish politics as a cohesive subject distinct and
separate from other social science disciplines.

The original purpose of the first university, founded in
Bologna in the eleventh century, was to train students in the
emerging discipline of law—not for academic purposes but
to equip early medieval courts with competent officials.
Universities are creatures not only of their own history but
also of the society within which they function, of its needs
for trained expertise and of its needs for ideas and research.
This is reflected by the slow development of the subjects
studied at universities and their widening range from narrow
beginnings. Politics did not figure among the traditional
university disciplines even after the clerical domination in
the Middle Ages had ended, and in many places it did not
become a university subject as such until the mid twentieth
century. But, as we have indicated, it was studied under
different names and in different forms and still bears the
stamp of the disciplines of law, philosophy and history from
which it developed. However, in Britain and North America, though not in continental Europe, these disciplines
would not normally go as far as to dub themselves 'sciences'.
The styles of enquiry associated with politics in these guises
was highly pragmatic and at the same time normative,
concerned often with making recommendations about future
policy on the basis of studies made in the appropriate
disciplines. Being unsystematic and lacking any self-
reflective attitude, the conclusions of such studies were often
highly dubious and resulted in politics being treated as a
rather inferior branch of the subject from which it originated. Attitudes of this kind persist even now in the way
historians and philosophers in particular still regard the
study of politics in some seats of learning, even though the
features of politics which these disciplines dislike are ones
which are often derived from the traditional disciplines and

which in some cases are shared with them.

The controversial notion that a science of society is possible did not develop until the capacity of the human intellect to control the physical environment had been established. The origins of social science are associated with the rationalism of the eighteenth and early nineteenth century, with writers such as Bentham, Voltaire, Saint-Simon and Comte. Just as the development of Newtonian physics had been associated with the growing belief in the ability of humanity to exercise ever-increasing and beneficial direction of the natural physical world through the understanding of the positive predictive causal laws of physics, so, or at least in similar fashion, it was believed it should be possible to use the power of human reason to develop just and efficient forms of social organisation. There is therefore a set of ideas and rules—a language game—associated with the idea of a social science which ties it strongly to concepts of explanation and cause derived from positivistic methods in the natural sciences. The crucial change that is signified by the term 'positivism' is that, according to positivism, causality and hence explanation should be understood as referring not to some hidden ultimate mover, as medieval theologians had supposed, but to a regular chronological connection between observable events. A classic and early statement of this argument can be found in the writings of the Scottish philosopher and historian David Hume, who wrote in his *Enquiry Concerning Human Understanding*, 'If we take in our hand any volume; of divinity or school metaphysics, for instance, let us ask; Does it contain any abstract reasoning concerning quantity or number? No. Does it contain any experimental reasoning concerning matter of fact or existence? No. Commit it then to the flames: for it can contain nothing but sophistry and confusion'.[5] The independent disciplines of economics, psychology and sociology developed throughout the nineteenth and early twentieth century with the impetus given to them by positivism, which is not to say that they were ever purely positivistic in their methods or that positivism should be identified as a single, coherent and uniform school of thought.

Social science was thus developing a range of individual disciplines, enabling it to identify itself as a new and worthwhile addition to the established university distinction between natural sciences and humanities. But politics remained largely under the wing of traditional orientations, concentrating on political philosophy or, in so far as empirical study was concerned, on the legalistic study of constitutions and political institutions. So while economists were building quantifiable models of free markets and systems of production abstracted from societal and governmental factors, and while sociologists and psychologists were similarly attempting to derive abstract explanations independent of extraneous factors, studies of politics were still largely concerned with describing what governments do or theorising about ideal societies, in separate modes. In any case, such studies were carried out in university departments of Law, History or Philosophy, on whose goodwill and favour they were dependent. In part at least, the slowness of development can be attributed to the persistence of cultural values of the nineteenth century, among other factors, since economics, the first of the social sciences to establish itself as an academic discipline, had done so with a persistent downplaying of the proper role of government in economic affairs and with an emphasis on the importance of free-market economic systems in the development of industrialising countries. The prevailing liberal view, that academic research should be motivated by the detached, disinterested desire to know permanent truths, had its counterpart in the beliefs that the activity of politics itself was anything but detached and disinterested and that it had little that was permanent or truthful about it.

The development of politics in universities therefore had to wait for a different climate and different societal needs. In Britain, despite academic unease about the status of the subject, the increasing need for trained public administrators, the interest of Fabian Socialists and Liberals in methods of welfare provision and the development of mass political parties with the onset of universal suffrage had resulted by 1928 in the establishment of chairs of Political Theory or Political Institutions in three major universities,

Oxford, Cambridge and London. This occurred however without any clear break with the traditional disciplines. The relatively fragmented structure of these universities militated, with other factors, against the development of the subject as a completely separate discipline, and even where the term 'political science' was used, as in the London School of Economics, it was never implied in practice that politics was anything other than a part of the humanities. The British tradition of the study of politics, which was established in the period up to 1939, predominates in British universities even now and involves research mainly into political philosophy and into political institutions, broadly defined. As such, the traditional product, as it were, varies between the normative and the descriptive. Some of the work done in the founding period has certainly not lost its vigour and quality over the years, and particularly in the fields of theory and public administration the British method, such as it was, proved capable of producing original and very useful research. The undoubted virtues of this way of going about the study of politics are that the method is flexible, the language clear and the research comprehensible to a relatively wide audience.

This contrasts very sharply with the development of political science in the United States. Under the influence of logical positivism, researchers like Harold Laswell were concerned to show the irrationality of the language of everyday politics and to develop an elite understanding of the dynamics of mass politics through the study of language as a political instrument.[6] But the change was not only at the level of language. It involved a radical shift in the practice of research and was constituted mainly by the convergence of three lines of investigation—voting studies, policy sciences and social and political enquiry into general conditions of stability. Each of these had its different source: in the case of voting studies, the interest and effort came initially from the attempt to apply social psychology to electoral behaviour in a quantitative manner; with policy sciences, there was a very strong impetus from the increasing involvement of academics in American government service in the 1930s, which led among other things to a demand for professional-

ism and a new rigour within the discipline; and in the growth
of more general political enquiry, apart from the influence
on political sociologists of German developments in the
field, the rise of Fascism and onset of the war stimulated an
enduring interest in the problems associated with the
collapse of democratic systems and, in the post-war period,
in the conditions under which democratic systems could be
rebuilt in a more enduring form.

The behavioural revolution, which came to its peak in the
1950s and 1960s, had at its centre the attempt to establish
political science as an independent discipline. The traditional approach was criticised for its amateurish methods, its
naive or commonsense empirical assumptions and its inconsistent approach to the procedures of research. Practitioners
of the new political science aspired to develop the study of
politics away from pure theory dissociated from empirical
research, away from the mere description of what governments do, towards the new predictive science of political
behaviour. This would establish a proper positive relationship between theory and practical research, based on
systematic scientific and rigorous study, and of course
deriving its mode of explanation and its definitions of
causality from the natural sciences and from positivism. An
immediate target had to be to define the subject matter of
the new discipline in such a way as to make it amenable to
positivist methods—to make it observable, quantifiable and
if possible subject to repeated investigation. Hence there
emerged the emphasis in the literature on 'power' as the
central concept which united the discipline and on definitions of power which fitted the new methods.

## POLITICS AND THE SOCIAL SCIENCES

In the chapters that follow, we go on to discuss the substance
of the changes in theory and practice that made up the
behavioural revolution. In the remainder of this chapter we
will consider some of the other components of the social
sciences and their relationship to the study of politics. It is
important to observe here that there are distinct positive

aspects associated with the developments described, whatever may be said about the narrowness of vision associated
with them. In particular, there is now a much greater
concern with clarity and consistency of definitions, with
accuracy and rigour in the use of data and with the
importance of a positive relationship between theory and
research. This latter point, however, is one of the most
suspect in the whole of the methodology, in that behaviourism in politics does not at times provide theories at all; that is
to say, its supposed theoretical explanations of its welters of
empirical data may amount to nothing more than empirical
generalisations about associations which have been observed
to occur between events rather than genuinely abstract
theories which provide causal links. Criticism of this kind
amounts to a rejection of positivism. Other criticisms
levelled at behaviourism are that it encourages a methodological fetishism in researchers, an obsessive concern with
justifying one's method which inhibits practical research and
that the insistence on using only directly observable evidence leads to an unnecessary narrowing of the scope of the
study of politics.

Implicit in criticisms of this kind there is a difference of
opinion not only about the nature of causality but also about
the significance of human values and intentions in giving
meaning to action. For positivists, human value and intentionality are irrelevant since to explain a fact means to
attribute regular association with other known facts, in
which case a theory is a complex set of such associations.
Others hold that the restriction to such limited conclusions
inevitably favours an uncritical attitude towards existing
social organisation, whereas a willingness to seek explanation in the wider significance of actions within a social and
political framework allows for more profound abstractions
and for genuine social explanations of social causes. This is
not the only division over method, but it does serve to locate
the changes within politics inside the more general
framework of the development of the social sciences, since
similar disagreements occur particularly in sociology and
economics. Also there is a crucial line of distinction which
separates 'politists' from those who follow a more interdisci-

plinary approach. Whether operating at our second or third level of analysis, that is on formal or informal determinants, practitioners of political study ('politists' is Hayward's term, while continental Europeans refer to 'politologists') tend to argue that in principle the 'polity' should be regarded as a determinant of societal structure and of societal change. On the other hand, practitioners of other disciplines, particularly of economics and sociology, are much more inclined to view the relationship the other way round: society determining the polity. A radical version of this (such as traditional Marxist analysis) would deny the polity any autonomy at all, arguing in the Marxist case that power is in principle an economic relationship deriving from the forms of control associated with particular means of production.

In practice the changes in method and direction associated with the behavioural revolution have not made the relationships with other disciplines in the social sciences more clear-cut or categorical. On the contrary, questioning of the relationships and concern over the ambiguity of the social sciences is now more widespread than ever, though one should not exaggerate the vulnerability of the traditional British pragmatism to self-doubt of this kind.

The approaches adopted by other disciplines may give some indication of the directions and methods politics ought to pursue or perhaps avoid. There is a strong tendency in sociological writings to argue that social institutions, groups or values determine political action; this may be either with an emphasis on cohesion and consensus, as in the cases of Talcott Parsons and Durkheim, or in a conflictual manner, as Marxists argue. In either case, power, however it is defined in specific terms, is likely to be seen not as determined in a political manner but ultimately as residing in relationships between social and economic groups, and as determined by factors such as integration into particular groups (class, elite, religion, locality) or by exclusion from social or economic resources (control of the means of production, control of values). Undoubtedly there are strengths in sociology that researchers in politics cannot ignore—in particular, the analysis of the logic of sub-institutional groups such as elites and interest groups; the emphasis on the way attitudes, beliefs and values may independently affect political choices; the importance of the constraints on autonomous political action imposed by social and economic conditions; and the two areas where the behavioural revolution most drew from sociology, which were the concern for theoretical support in research and, in a much more practical vein, the significance of social cleavages such as class in electoral behaviour. Indeed, one might argue that the interest in the internal dynamics of significant political groups, which is a fundamental part of the pluralist methods associated with behaviourism, has its origins in the early political sociology of writers such as Mosca, Pareto and Weber—even though, as we shall see, Mosca and Pareto are categorically elitist not pluralist.

The contribution of economics to the development of politics is much more varied in its range and also more equivocal. The theoretical assumptions both of orthodox economics and of Marxist approaches are close to being anti-political, in the sense that in their different ways they would deny the apparent contingencies of politics any significant role in determining human action. Orthodox economics has traditionally been narrowly scientific in its orientation, in that it treats economic systems as autonomous markets subject to ascertainable laws and therefore operating in a predictable manner. Historically, of course, the relatively early development of economics in the writings of Adam Smith and David Ricardo was associated with the end of mercantilism and the emergence of free-market principles in international and national economic organisation.[7] Economics relies on important and limiting theoretical assumptions; in particular, economics might be characterised as a set of theories about the rational distribution of resources in which 'rationality' is taken to mean maximisation of material benefits. Within the constraints of availability of resources, of information and of alternatives, the individual economic actor is assumed to be a utility-maximiser, in such a way that whatever the particular contingencies, the behaviour of the individual economic unit of analysis can be predicted. The other major doctrine of classical economics, enshrined in Say's Law, was a theoretical assumption of general equilibrium under conditions of perfect competition.

In the post-war period, the growth of state economic intervention, broadly on Keynesian principles, significantly reduced the confidence of economists in the optimality of free markets; in a separate trend there developed in the writings of Downs, Beular and others a line of argument which attempted to apply economic rationality to political behaviour—the so-called 'economic theory of democracy'.[8] Though this had some success for a period, the resurgence of free-market principles in the Chicago school, the adoption of monetarist policies by major Western governments and the retreat of academic economists into heavily statistical econometrics have all contributed to a widening of the gap between the disciplines of politics and economics. On the positive side, however, it must be said that economics provided an important impulse in shifting politics away from the traditional, relatively formal analysis of the question 'Who governs?' towards the more empirical analysis of 'Who gets what, when and how?'—towards distributional outcomes, in other words. Other themes that made their way into politics by this route are the idea that political institutions may be considered to be artefacts, social constructs which are not fundamentally dissimilar from other such constructs; similarly came the far-reaching notion that politics can be understood as transaction or as a set of exchange relationships founded on rational choices in which the individual voter or citizen is the basic unit of analysis and is regarded as a maximiser of utility (however that utility may be understood).

Marxism operates on very different bases. Though it certainly is a theory of economic determination, its direct implications have a very wide social and political range. Denying the validity of utility-maximiser assumptions, Marxists argue that economic determination occurs not in accordance with consumer or producer preferences but rather in accordance with the relationship to the means of production. According to Marxism, all societies are differentiated in this way, and the different ways in which this relationship occurs give rise to the variety of class structures which are also basic characteristics of all societies. Thus, under early capitalism the aristocracy have that class identity because of their ownership and control over one of the earliest and most important economic resources—land. The bourgeoisie on the other hand control the technological capital of industry, while the labour class have nothing but their labour power. Power in Marxist economics is a function of class, and political and social action are held to be determined by the inevitable conflict between classes. Though there have been attempts to develop a Marxist science of politics by Poulantzas and others,[9] the degree of determinism which Marxism entails is a serious obstacle to such efforts: Marxism generally allows the polity only a secondary role at most in the determination of social and economic change. Researchers into politics who rightly take Marxism seriously would derive from it a wide concern for the ways in which social and economic changes, particularly those based on technological development, affect general political strategy and direction. Such changes are usually seen as forming a major constraint of autonomous political action, not as providing an opportunity for choice, since the state form is regarded as subject to materialist laws in which it has no independent function.

Psychology as a discipline played a major part in the development of political science, but its input is still controversial, mainly because of the categorical individual-ism with which it is associated in politics. It usually falls unambiguously on the other side of the argument from holists, for whom groups not individuals are the unit of analysis. Therefore the emphasis in psychology tends to be either on individuals in decision-making (as in James Barber's *The Presidential Character*) or on mass public opinion treated in a relatively undifferentiated manner. In any case, psychology is concerned with elements of subjec-tive behaviour—perceptions, values, attitudes, beliefs—which are frequently absent from disciplines such as sociolo-gy and economics, where the causality is objective in character. Psychology's input into politics is less controver-sial and more widely accepted where it deals with the effects of socialisation on political behaviour and the psychology of mass elections.

The weaknesses and limitations of other social science disciplines in investigating politics are not hard to find. Though there are close links between sociology and politics, sociology tends to be apolitical both in its assumptions and in its practice. In its assumptions, as Sartori has observed, sociology argues along lines that are determinist in the sense that they seek objective social institutions or groups which shape human behaviour; politics may be reduced to a matter of social cleavages or social integration, with the effective denial of the autonomy even of political institutions such as parties. With economics, as we suggested above, the assumptions of general equilibrium and of optimality of free markets, apart from lacking empirical proof, would rule out of the argument a host of questions usually associated with politics by imposing a theoretical rationality on free markets and the individual components of them. The application of this rationality to political goods, as well as to economic goods, requires a considerable leap and would demand assumptions about equality of resource, freedom of competition, and complete information, which are not tenable in politics. Ideological factors, economically irrational behaviour, inconsistency of response to identical events, all would be excluded from an analysis in which power is considered either as a characteristic of individual economic resource-holders or as a feature of overall markets operating in an objective manner. These may be aspects of political power, but they are not its sole manifestation.

In all of this the enduring relationship of politics to the traditional disciplines is rendered more ambiguous. In the case of history and law, the anti-theoretical perspectives associated with their British practice have meant a greater separation from them, even though historical data is still of profound importance for politics. The study of political tradition is crucial to an understanding of contemporary politics, but this is much more than 'contemporary history' because of the wider range of disciplines involved, the different methodologies involved and the more theoretically based focus of attention. The problem of political philosophy and its relationship to political theory is, however, one that has a persistent and direct relevance to the development of the discipline.

By 'philosophy' we mean to refer loosely and generally to non-quantitative methods of abstract reasoning without immediate reference to empirical data, while 'theory' we take to refer to a coherent set of principles which purport to explain empirical data in abstract terms and which usually produce or are the source of empirical generalisations and hypotheses. By these definitions philosophy is properly a method of enquiry, and theory is the product of enquiry. The most important feature of philosophy for our purposes is its abstraction, while the relevant feature of theory is its capacity for explaining hard facts systematically. It should be obvious (but apparently is not) that the two are different, that they are not mutually exclusive and that theories must have a philosophical content in them to be properly explanatory. In a misleading fashion, however, even major and highly distinguished authors sometimes fail to distinguish them properly.[10]

Traditional political philosophy, to which we referred earlier, engages in four kinds of activity. First, there is theory building—the construction of models which explain, justify or criticise existing conditions or which propose new political values or political organisations. This is the tradition of Plato, Aristotle and other major political thinkers, as well as of many other much less successful model-builders, a tradition which is more or less explicitly evaluative and normative in its approach. Second, a favoured pursuit of erudite scholars is commentary on the texts written by thinkers in the first mode. Such commentary takes the form of description, analysis and criticism of the texts, often reaching normative conclusions. Some very successful and enduring works have been written on this basis, by Sabine, Wolin and Plamenatz for instance. Third, a relatively recent development consists in commentary on major modern ideologies such as socialism, liberalism, conservatism and fascism. This third kind of activity is really a continuation of the operations in the second category, only carried out on modern political thinkers who have not yet achieved sufficient status to warrant the respect implicit in such textual investigation. It is these commentaries on texts and ideologies which constitute the bulk of the political philosophy taught in British and North American universities; the relationship with empirical research, particularly for studies of modern ideologies, might not be difficult to find, but partly because of traditional divisions and partly because of behaviourist disregard for such academic activities, their theory-generating potential is largely untapped.

Fourth, at some distance from the other activities there is a much more limited political philosophy which consists of the analysis of particular political terms in common use, such as 'sovereignty', 'representation' and 'obligation', usually with proposals for their clearer definition and more coherent use. This is a relatively new method which derives ultimately from the British tradition of so-called 'empirical' philosophy and derives immediately from the overwhelming predominance of linguistic philosophy in British universities. Typically, philosophers in this mode ask questions such as 'What do we mean when we say "x"?', and 'Can the question "x" be answered intelligibly?' Philosophers operating exclusively in this mode claim not to be evaluative, not to have words of wisdom for practising politicians, but rather to be clearing the ground, sharpening the analytical tools, making words more precise.[11] The first three kinds of political philosophy might be thought of as the 'master builder' approach (the term is originally John Locke's),[12] while the fourth and narrower conception is sometimes referred to as the 'under labourer' style.[13]

These differences cover a wide range of issues and call into question the nature of social science itself. The traditional position would be that because of the difficulties inherent in social science data, the social sciences cannot be regarded as scientific in any meaningful sense of the term. The difficulties would be, briefly, that social data is indefinitely complex and multi-factored, that it is not subject to experimentation or repetition, that it is difficult to quantify and that it lacks any established theory to tell researchers what is relevant. The certainty of the natural sciences is therefore unattainable in the social sciences, and there is a dualism in epistemology between the two. Karl

Popper adds a further string to this by arguing that human history is significantly determined by the development of human knowledge, which is by definition unpredictable; therefore social sciences cannot claim to predict social events in the same way as natural sciences do.[14]

Empiricists, however, argue that what traditional philosophy does cannot be regarded as theory properly so-called, and they attempt to achieve a more integrated relationship between theory and research by establishing a sub-discipline known as political theory (as David Easton aspires to) which has the central function of serving political science. It does this both by building empirically based theoretical models and by linguistic analysis. In principle, empiricists argue for the unity of methodology of all natural phenomena; in other words, that the notion of causality inherent in the natural sciences is also applicable to the social sciences. While some disciplines in the social sciences, such as economics and psychology, readily accept natural science notions of causality, others are distinctly uneasy or even hostile to the idea of unity of methodology. Though the subject matter of the disciplines overlaps and the raw data may even be identical, there are profound differences between disciplines over methodology as well as over subjects of enquiry.

In this introduction we cannot do more than indicate some of the larger obstacles scattered across the path, though it should also be clear by now where our own propensities would take us in the search for solutions to these problems. The function of the intellectual is never an easy one and is more difficult for those who have to exercise it in an Anglo–Saxon culture, which decries intellectual effort and which associates the term with pedantry or impractical idealism. Nevertheless, the attempt to understand political reality has to begin with an understanding of one's own function in that reality; this entails in particular the development of a critical awareness of one's own values and of a willingness to learn from the insights of others. Within an academic environment, the effects of theoretical myopia can be exacerbated by institutional demarcations which may be artificially heightened by needs having little to do with the demands of understanding. The most obvious examples in terms of the discussion in this chapter would be the relationships between philosophy and politics or between economics and politics, where the urge to preserve academic identity has led to the creation of linguistic and technical barriers between the disciplines, ensuring in some cases that the results of research on a subject in one discipline may be useless or even unintelligible to interested researchers in cognate disciplines. In this work we try to emphasise the potential utility of theories drawn from other disciplines and to avoid theoretical short-sightedness, while at the same time developing concepts of 'power' which may give an identifiable character to the discipline of politics.

# NOTES

1. Ludwig Wittgenstein, *Philosophical Investigations* (Oxford, Basil Blackwell, 1967), p. 34, para. 71.
2. David Easton, *The Political System* (New York, Knopf, 1953), pp. 129–40.
3. Wittgenstein, *op. cit.*, pp. 150–1, para. 567.
4. W. Bagehot, *The English Constitution*, Intro. by R.H.S. Crossman (London, Collins/Fontana, 1963).
5. David Hume, *Enquiry Concerning Human Understanding*, L.A. Selby-Bigge, ed. (Oxford, Clarendon Press, 1902).
6. *See*, in particular, H. Lasswell, N. Leites, *et al.*, *Language in Politics: Studies in Quantitative Semantics* (Cambridge, Mass., MIT Press, 1965).
7. *See*: A. Smith, *An Enquiry into the Nature and Causes of the Wealth of Nations* (London, Routledge, 1880); D. Ricardo, 'Notes on Malthus' in *Principles of Political Economy* (Baltimore, John Hopkins, 1928).
8. *See*: A. Downs, *An Economic Theory of Democracy* (New York, Harper and Row, 1957); J.M. Buchanan and G. Tullock, *The Calculus of Consent* (Ann Arbor, Michigan University Press, 1962).
9. *See* Poulantzas, N., *Political Power and Social Classes* (London, Verso, 1978); but *see also* R. Miliband, *Class Power and State Power* (London, Verso, 1983).
10. *See*, for example, the apparently unconcerned substitution of the one term for the other in I. Berlin, 'Does Political Theory Still Exist?' in P. Laslett and W.G. Runciman, eds., *Philosophy, Politics and Society*, 2nd series (Oxford, Basil Blackwell, 1962), pp. 1–33.
11. Examples abound, but *see*: T. Weldon, *The Vocabulary of Politics*

(London, Penguin, 1953); J.L. Austin, *How to Do Things with Words* (Oxford, Clarendon Press, 1962).

12. John Locke, *Essay Concerning Human Understanding*, A.D. Woozley, ed. (London, Fontana/Collins, 1964), p. 58.
13. As in P. Winch, *The Idea of a Social Science* (London, Routledge and Kegan Paul, 1963).
14. Karl Popper, *The Open Society and Its Enemies*, 5th edn (London, Routledge and Kegan Paul, 1966); but *see also* A. O'Hear, *Karl Popper* (London, Routledge and Kegan Paul, 1980) among the many critiques of Popper's philosophy.

# 2 Power and the Problem of Contestability

We saw in the last chapter that in the social sciences the study of political action is approached from various directions and with a range of different assumptions. This complexity of approach is also true for concepts like 'power', which are of concern and interest to sociologists, psychologists, economists and politists alike. As a result, different explanations of social, political and economic change and continuity have been developed, based on approaches operating from very different levels of analysis. Historically, traditional political science explanations confined their analysis to formal office holders and their activities. Sociologists have tended to concentrate on social structures, groups, values and culture to explain the cohesion of society. Economists eschewed interest in human actions and concentrated on notions of rational action based upon market analogies of choice. Finally, cutting across these disciplinary boundaries, Marxists have traditionally argued that thought and action are determined by the objective requirements of the impersonal workings of systems of production.

We also saw that the approach of each of these disciplines makes, before commencing research, implicit or explicit value judgements about the nature of how society does operate. This is another way of saying that all explanations of the workings of society are in some sense theory dependent. Social scientists develop hypotheses about how society ought to, or does, function before conducting research. These hypotheses are usually part of a researcher's implicit or explicit theory of power in society. Research is, then, but an attempt to see if the hypotheses, which contain embryonic theories, are corroborated by empirical reality. Any aspiring novice to the social science profession must be aware that all explanations are in some sense ideologically based. But is this true? There is a long and continuing debate within the social sciences about the possibility of conducting objective, non-value dependent research. This is particularly apparent in the debate concerning the nature of power in capitalist societies. There are at least two broad lines of thinking on this issue. On the one hand, some writers argue that it is possible to identify in rigorous terms the meaning of the concept 'power'. Other writers, however, argue that all key concepts in the social sciences are evaluative, lacking undisputed empirical content and being based on non-rational assumptions. For these writers 'power' is an 'essentially contested concept'. In this chapter we look at different theories of power in capitalist society and ask the question 'Is power an essentially contested concept?'

## THE ESSENTIALLY CONTESTED NATURE OF CONCEPTS

What do we mean by the idea that concepts are essentially contested? Think for a moment about the following ideas: socialism, democracy, art and Christianity. What do these ideas, words or concepts mean? It may well be that you believe that all of these concepts have meanings which everyone agrees upon. But is this really the case? Take, for example, the concept 'socialism'. The Conservative government in Britain led by Margaret Thatcher has used this word to label anything that post-war Labour governments have done. This means that any form of intervention by the state in economic and social affairs is to be seen as part of a move towards the creation of socialism. But is this the correct or the only definition of the meaning of socialism? A strong theme in European social thought has been that socialism refers to the creation of a stateless society, an ideal which is not apparent in any present-day society. How would writers in this tradition label the decisions by Labour governments since 1945 to expand the role of the state into social and economic affairs? They might describe this activity, especially as it was also supported by most Conservative post-war governments, as an extension of the ideas of the economist

John Maynard Keynes (Keynesianism) or, because it involves the creation of a mixed public and private economy
based upon notions of social justice and welfare, social
democracy.[1] To confuse the issue further, the Thatcher
government and Reagan administration in the United States
would clearly see the state–society relationship in the Soviet
Union as an example of a socialist society in practice.
Indeed, the leaders of the Soviet Union might well agree
with them. But Western socialists and others might describe
the Soviet Union as a totalitarian rather than socialist
country. They would mean by this a country dominated by a
single party or elite, with very limited forms of direct
democratic representation and a state structure which
dominates the whole of society. This label would clearly
have a closer approximation to the reality of life in the
Soviet Union than a label like 'socialism'; especially if
'socialism' was used, as it also often is, to refer to a society in
which people were to live on the basis of the maxim 'From
each according to his abilities, to each according to his
needs'.

Clearly, then, once we start to look beneath the surface of
key concepts, we discover that they are merely labels of
convenience, simplifying complex relationships and phenomena the interpretation of which is widely disputed. The
notion of democracy is a similarly contested concept. While
it might well appear to the reader that democracy means
simply 'one man one vote' or universal suffrage, the actual
meaning given to democracy by political philosophers has
meant very different things in history. Take, for example,
the Greek city states. These were seen as democratic states
in which all of the citizens were allowed to have a direct say
on issues which affected the state. Was this then a
democracy? On the face of it there would appear to be little
doubt, but when one is informed that this right of participation was denied the bulk of the inhabitants of the Greek city
states because they were slaves and that only the non-slave
minority were allowed to vote, then it is clear that by our
modern conception of democracy they were not democracies
at all.[2] The problem does not, unfortunately, end here.
Even in more contemporary times political philosophers

who have argued for democracy have had a very limited conception of its meaning. Rousseau, one of the first thinkers to question the undemocratic and non-representative power of the absolutist monarchs in the eighteenth century, limited his notion of democratic representation to property owners. Even John Stuart Mill, a leading liberal thinker of nineteenth-century Britain, called for the extension of the franchise but with limits based upon property ownership.[3] Democracy means different things to different people, as the suffragettes and people under the age of twenty-one in Britain would have testified to before 1928 and 1969, when women and eighteen year olds, respectively, were first granted the vote.

We could provide numerous examples of similar concepts which have been subject to various interpretations. Art and Christianity are clear examples of this. How many different churches and faiths are there which claim to be the true Christian faith? Would you agree that a pile of car tyres laid end to end is art in the same way that the Mona Lisa is art? What all of these examples do is to indicate that most of the important concepts we use to describe reality are *evaluative*. By this we mean that there is no single or irreducible meaning on which everyone agrees; value judgements or normative assumptions intrude to leave us with very little agreement. This occurs because individuals can defend their understanding of the meaning of complex concepts by perfectly reasonable argument and evidence about their proper use which cannot be resolved by rational argument alone. This fact is shown by W.B. Gallie in the classic example of the meaning of 'the champions'.[4] Gallie argues that the commonsense notion of the concept 'the champions' is normally associated with a competition in which 'the champions' are indisputedly the team which scores the most points at the end of the year. But this is not the basis on which most key social science concepts function. Rather, most social science concepts can normally be equated with competitions in which teams are involved in continuous and on-going games in which 'the champions' is a concept which is awarded to the side which plays the *best* game. Once this evaluative element is added into our judgement, it is clear that there will never be agreement amongst rival groups of supporters about which team are 'the champions'. This is because, even though a team may have lost the game, judged by the criteria adopted by its own supporters, that team may well be the moral champions for having played the game best.

When concepts can have this meaning Gallie refers to them as 'essentially contested concepts' to differentiate them from words or concepts which are capable of formal and rational verification. Examples of non-contested concepts or words would be 'concrete', 'brick' and 'wood'. Thus it is possible to verify formally, empirically and rationally whether a building is made of brick, concrete or wood. Normally there is perfect agreement about the meaning of these words or concepts because they do not involve a normative or evaluative element. But, Gallie argues, concepts like 'socialism', 'democracy', 'Christianity', 'art' and 'the champions' are evaluative and not capable of rational verification. As a result, these concepts are essentially contested. Gallie has constructed an idealised schema of what a concept must include for it to be labelled as essentially contested:[5]

1. It must be *appraisive* in the sense that it involves some valued achievement.
2. Its achievement must be *internally complex*.
3. It must be capable of being *variously described* in terms of style, method, tactics and strategy.
4. The accredited achievement must be capable of *modification* with changing circumstances.
5. Different groups or individuals accept *different uses of it and defends their own use of it against all others*.
6. It is developed from an *original exemplar* which all agree upon.
7. The *original exemplar is sustained* despite debate.
8. There is *no way of testing* empirically which is right or wrong.

# IS POWER AN ESSENTIALLY CONTESTED CONCEPT?

What is the purpose of this discussion? While it may seem at first a very abstract debate, the notion of 'essential contestability' is of crucial importance in discussions about power in capitalist societies. As we shall see, there are very different approaches to the analysis of power which are drawn from competing theoretical and disciplinary traditions. Each of these approaches operate from discrete levels of analysis and therefore makes very different assumptions about the meaning and nature of power. Each of these theories, furthermore, makes claims to be the proper and correct method of analysing power in capitalist societies. Now, if power is not an essentially contested concept, then it should be possible to discover which of these theories is the correct method for analysing power or, if all of them are inadequate, to formulate an alternative theory of power which everyone can agree upon. On the other hand, if the concept of power is essentially contested and evaluative, and not capable of formal and rational verification, then it means that it will never be possible to arrive at a single or all-inclusive analysis of power. If this is the case then there is little point in trying to arrive at an all-embracing general theory of power, rather we should concentrate upon understanding the different insights which alternative theories of power can provide from their competing levels of analysis. In this way, while a general theory may have to be rejected, a more sophisticated and revealing insight into social reality may be possible by adopting a sceptical and eclectic approach to research. It is our view that the latter approach is the best method to adopt because power is an essentially contested concept. However, before we can go on to look in more detail at the theories that can be used to analyse power in capitalist society, we must first explain why we believe power to be an essentially contested concept.

What is power? A commonsense approach might define it as the ability of an individual or group (we shall call them A) to influence another individual or group (we shall call them B) in a non-trivial, significant manner. We may all agree on this definition but, when we use the concept of power in relation to the question 'Who has power in capitalist society?', we must be aware that we are concerned with politically relevant decisions. Thus we are concerned not just with whether A can influence B but whether or not A can politically influence B in a non-trivial, significant manner. But this raises a further problem, which we touched on in Chaper 1 when we discussed the different ways in which politics has been perceived. What do we mean by 'significantly' and what do we mean by 'politically'? D.M. White has argued that, because these two questions can be answered variously in terms of their scope, range and content, then the meaning of power must be essentially contested.[6]

This view has been further elaborated by Steven Lukes in a classic book on this problem. Lukes has argued that there are at least three broad dimensions or ways of analysing power in capitalist societies which are based on very different answers to the questions of what 'significantly affect' and 'politically' mean.[7] The first dimension Lukes defines as 'the ability of A to prevail over B in formal political decision-making (normally in government) on one or more key issues, when there is a direct and observable conflict between A and B over outcomes'. The second dimension is defined as 'the ability of A to prevail over B in determining the outcomes of observable conflicts of interest in formal decision-making and also in determining what is to count as a formal issue, where there is a conflict of interest over policy preferences and observable grievances over these preferences outside the political system'. The third dimension is defined as 'the ability of A to prevent B from realising his "real" interests or from articulating them effectively due to the mobilisation of bias resulting from the institutional structure of society'.

Lukes argues that these three dimensions operate from competing theoretical, disciplinary and normative backgrounds and that, as a result, power is treated so differently that it is bound to be evaluative and essentially contested. Let us look at each of these dimensions in turn to assess the various ways in which they deal with the concept of power.

In the first dimension it is clear that theorists operating within this approach are concerned with discovering *who decides* about policy in the formal decision-making structure of capitalist society. Power is taken to mean the ability of one formal office-holder to shape the final outcomes of government in observable conflicts of interests over that policy. Thus researchers operating within this level of analysis would be concerned with who was formally in a position to decide the key issues for society and what conflicts of interest were apparent over the choices which had to be made. Researchers would look at the major social and economic policies of the government and ask who decided, for example, to raise or lower public expenditure; who decided on housing policies; or who decided to spend more on primary as opposed to higher education? In looking at these questions the researcher would limit his or her analysis of power to a specification of who decides about those policies which emanate from the formal political system. All other decisions would not be of interest because the key decisions in capitalist societies are taken to be those which governments make. In assessing these decisions, great emphasis would be placed on the conflicts between different groups, individuals and interests in society to discover who was gaining most from the authoritative and binding decisions which governments impose on society.[8]

Lukes is himself unhappy with this approach as an adequate analysis of power in capitalist society, and he argues that some theorists have formulated alternative definitions which broaden the scope and meaning of 'power'. This is Lukes second dimension.[9] He argues that it is debatable whether there is an objective test of what is and what is not a key issue. If this is the case, then all decisions are likely to be of importance to some group or interest in society. Since theorists operating at the first level of power have no way of differentiating between issues, and because all issues in the political system must be key issues for the people concerned, then this approach to power must lead to the conclusion that power is plural in distribution. By this we mean that there is no significant concentration of power and that no one group or interest could perennially influence or shape all the issues on which governments have to decide. Lukes argues, however, that this is inadequate because it takes no account of the ability of some strategically placed actors in the political system to ensure that all issues which threaten them are resolved in their favour (other issues can be left to a pluralistic struggle) or are never allowed to enter the political agenda for discussion.

This is clearly a very different way of conceptualising power in capitalist society. While first-dimension theorists see power operating only within the formal political system, second-dimension theorists argue that some interests (either social or economic elites) outside the political system can continuously use their influence or presence in the political system to determine the outcomes on those issues which are of most importance to them. The way in which this is achieved is through what is known as agenda setting or non-decision-making. In other words, power is not confined to the decision-makers in the political system; it is also manifest outside the political system, and the strategic position of some elites in society can be used to determine the nature of choices within the political system.[10] The important point here is, of course, that the nature of what is meant by 'politics' is much broader in this formulation than in the first dimension. In this dimension what is to count as of political importance (and therefore of importance to power) is the social and economic structure of society outside the political system and the way in which its stratification gives opportunities to elites to exert a disproportionate influence on formal political decision-makers and their policies. This dimension also adds something else to the meaning of power because it introduces the idea that power is manifest not just through *overt* acts of conflict but can be exercised by *covert* means through denial and closure of access to the political system.

However, Lukes argues that even this approach misses something which third-dimension theorists have brought to the analysis of power.[11] Lukes argues that while second-dimension theorists do concentrate on conflicts outside the political system, they do not take this insight far enough. Some theorists, particularly those operating within a Marxist world-view, have argued that the focus of first- and second-dimension theorists is still largely confined to observable conflicts in society. Marxists, however, go further; they are concerned to explain how it is that people come to believe the things that they do, not just with who wins out in observable conflicts of interest or who sets the agenda of political debate. Third-dimension theorists are therefore less concerned with conflict and more interested in suppression and social conditioning. For them, power in capitalist societies is equated not just with who decides in the political system or which grievances are not discussed there (although these are clearly important elements of power) but with the way in which the economic and social structure of capitalist society conditions human thought and action, so that individuals never understand their 'real' interests. In this formulation, power can never be analysed merely by studying observable conflicts; it can only be fully comprehended by first asking the prior question of where people's ideas of reality and their desires, which lead to observable political demands, come from. For third-dimensional theorists the answer to this question is that the underlying structure of the capitalist economic and social structure predetermines individual thought and action such that fundamental threats to the system are not only contained but that people are incapable of realising that they should want to change the system.[12]

Having outlined these three very different conceptions of power in capitalist society, Lukes concludes that since the third dimension recognises both the overt and covert forms that power can possess, it is capable of including the insights of the first and second dimensions and of taking them further, and is, therefore, the better theory of power. Yet Lukes still maintains that power is an essentially contested concept. The reason for this is that while Lukes prefers the third dimension, he also concedes that anyone accepting this approach must first accept the Marxist theory of economic and social change. This involves an acceptance that people are capable of having 'real' interests which are continually suppressed and never articulated effectively in the political system. The problem here, of course, is that the definition of what those 'real' interests are is derived from Marxist theory of what man would be like in a state of nature if capitalism had never existed. The difficulty is that we have no way of knowing what man would have been like without capitalism, and any specification of 'real' interests must be value dependent and determined by the personal proclivities and preferences of the researcher. Lukes recognises this fact and yet, somewhat confusingly, he then attempts to outline a method by which his definition of 'real interest' can be empirically tested. This is confusing because, while one can accept that all theories of power are contested and have different strengths and weaknesses, Lukes' attempt to argue that his third dimension can be empirically verified leads him to contradict his original and beneficial insight that all theories are value dependent.[13] As a result, his useful survey of the theoretical debate has merely served to further cloud the issue as to whether or not power is an essentially contested concept.

Lukes's view has been criticised by theorists who argue that the meaning of power should be verifiable by rational argument and empirical analysis. Perhaps the leading exponent of this view is the American exponent of the first-dimensional approach, Robert Dahl. Dahl has contended that although there are very different approaches and theories of power, so long as we can subject the hypotheses contained within these theories to falsification by exposure to empirical investigation then it will be possible to arrive at an all-embracing definition of power.[14] But, Dahl argues, because Marxist theories rely on 'false consciousness' and the researchers specification of 'real' interests, it is impossible to falsify these theories empirically. This leads Dahl to reject Marxist explanations as empirically unfalsifiable because the theory can be continuously rewritten to justify and incorporate any empiricist critique of it. On these grounds Dahl argues that power must be confined to cases of observable conflict.

While this is a powerful argument and one which, no doubt, led Lukes to attempt to find an empirical test for his own third-dimensional approach, it would seem that if we accept Dahl's view, we are severely limiting our conceptualisation of what power might be in capitalist society. There is little doubt that useful insights into the operations of capitalist societies and how its resources are distributed are to be gleaned from an appreciation of the way in which individual and group perceptions of reality are conditioned and shaped. Nor does one have to adopt a crude determinist or anti-empiricist approach to the formulation of political preference to accept that 'Men make their own history, but they do not make it just as they please; they do not make it under circumstances chosen by themselves, but under circumstances directly encountered, given and transmitted from the past.'[15] This means that our conception of power must go beyond the purely observable conflicts in society (important as they are) to comprehend the nature of the constraints within which political decision-makers and individuals operate when they come to make choices.

This empiricist line of criticism has not, however, been confined to Robert Dahl. More recently John Gray has criticised Lukes on similar terrain.[16] Gray concludes that the debate over the meaning and scope of power must be capable of resolution by rational argument and empirical tests. In particular, Gray argues that pluralist theories have thrown up empirical evidence to refute their own theories. He points to the fact that pluralists, like Dahl, have discovered that political parties have their own oligarchic organisational structures and that elites dominate decision-making in some circumstances. The problem with this is, of course, that Gray's position is confusing. While it may be possible to support the argument that empirical evidence must be used to refute any theory of power, once that theory has been falsified, Gray's approach does not tell us how to go about constructing a theory to replace the discredited one. In other words, Gray's evidence only serves to reinforce the argument that first dimensional analyses of power are refutable and that there is more to power than they assume. Perhaps Gray's original view that in liberal, non-closed societies all concepts with an appraisive content must be essentially contested is his most useful insight.[17] If this approach is adopted, then it would leave the way clear for us to adopt an eclectic perspective on power. This would allow us to draw on the insights to be gleaned from various approaches without having to adopt any one as the exclusive, and only, way to understand the concept.

Another line of argument against this view is that power cannot be essentially contested because it does not meet Gallie's strict criteria of tests of contestedness. It has been argued that Lukes accepts that power is not appraisive and that it has no original exemplar.[18] Furthermore, it is contended that the real debate is not about power but about *values* and *interests*. From this position it can be argued that power can be limited conceptually to the ability of A to force B to act contrary to B's interests, and that debates about A and B's interests are those which will be essentially contested. Lukes's response to this would seem to confirm the view that power will remain essentially contested.[19] He argues that even though power is not appraisive, any attribution of power must be evaluative. Further, while there is no original exemplar of power, we all agree that there are standard cases of the possession and exercise of power. What is in dispute is not the possession or exercise of power but the boundary of the concept. In saying this Lukes would seem to reaffirm his original assertion that there are various ways of viewing the concept and that each one sets the boundary of power at very different points in the relationship between the political, social and economic systems.

On the other hand, you may accept the position taken by those who argue power can be identified. If you do then you will probably believe that it is possible to define once and for all the concept of 'power'. But, and this is perhaps the most damning criticism of this viewpoint, to achieve this it may well be that the concept has to be confined only to a very narrow focus related to the observable conflicts within the formal political system. Even more worrying, perhaps, is the fact that the first-dimension approach has been refuted by its own reliance on empirical research. If this is so then it behoves researchers to formulate alternative theories which accommodate these weaknesses and inadequacies. But if this is done then it leads to the problem of theory building before research and the same charges of subjectivism and value dependency which Dahl and others have traditionally levelled at second- and third-dimension theories. It may well be that there is no way out of this impasse. Either one relies on the first-dimension approach and its bias towards systematic empiricism (with all its attendant problems of description rather than analysis)[20] or one chooses between the two remaining approaches. But it would appear that the use of either of these approaches is likely to lead to an over-concentration on only some aspects of the reality of power to the exclusion of others. Perhaps, then, the solution is to adopt a more eclectic and detached perspective, which would involve keeping an open mind to the insights which competing theories offer and recognising that some concepts are likely to remain essentially contested.

## LEVELS OF ANALYSIS IN THE STUDY OF POWER

It may well be at this point that the reader throws up his or her hands in despair and wonders what the point of the social sciences is. The reader will be familiar with the fact that in the natural sciences there have often been conflicts between competing perspectives or theories of reality. These disputes, it will be argued, have normally been resolved in favour of one or other viewpoint, and research has proceeded on the basis of this agreed theory until alternative, competing theories are thrown up in the future, when further conflict will ensue. This means that natural scientists normally operate within a disciplinary framework which possesses a dominant theoretical perspective which, it is believed, is leading gradually to the formulation of a more complete understanding of the natural world.

The problem with the social sciences is that there is no agreed theory which best explains social reality. But should one be overly concerned by this? Richard Little has argued that all theories perform specific functions in the social science; these include selection, evaluation, explanation and prescription.[21] What Little means by this is that within the social sciences there are various theories about how society is organised (and therefore what we mean by 'power') and that each of these operates at different levels of analysis and that each makes a valuable, if very different, contribution to our understanding of the major causal forces of change and continuity in society. What each perspective or theory does, even if from different levels of analysis and concentrating on distinct actors, is first, to allow the researcher to *select* and discard from the totality of information that exists in the world. In the absence of a theory of how society functions, the individual would face an immense and almost impossible task of making some sense and order out of the myriad of relationships and events in the world. Theories help to simplify reality. But having put some order on the world, theories then allow the researcher to go beyond a description of events to *explain* social reality. In other words, individuals wish to have some idea of causality in society and they need an explanatory model of how the world functions. The process of explanation must, however, also involve us in a process of *evaluation*. By this we mean that any theory of explanation will have chosen some relationships or events as the most significant. If this is the case, it must also be true that our values will shape our choice of what is significant. In this way all theories must, ultimately, be value dependent. Furthermore, if our evaluation is value dependent, it is likely that our theory will also contain, whether implicitly or explicitly, some *prescription* about how society ought to function.

If Little's position is correct, it is doubtful that the social sciences can operate on the same basis as the natural sciences. In the social sciences there is no single reality which is being explained, because the theories which are used to explain social reality are built on competing and incompatible ideological foundations. In the natural sciences the theories developed do not operate from different ideological perspectives; they are competing explanations of the same complex reality which are, ultimately, capable of empirical verification.[22] The fundamental difference with social science theories is that there is no agreement as to what the proper object of analysis should be. Disagreement occurs over the meaning of 'power' because each theory has a distinct interpretation of where the boundary of the 'political' begins and ends. As we saw, pluralists tend to confine their analysis of power and politics to the formal policy-making process; elite theorists take it beyond this to look at social and economic stratification systems, while Marxists argue that power and political action is manifest in every aspect of social and economic life. In other words, these theories are in competition: they have different bases of selection, evaluation, explanation and prescription.

If this is so then it is debatable whether a 'supra' or 'meta' theory of power in capitalist societies will be developed. We should, however, not worry too much about this because the function of theories in the social sciences is not necessarily to provide us with a general theory of social action. Rather, as Little has argued, comparing different theories is a useful heuristic exercise because 'there is always a danger of absorbing values unconsciously and uncritically, the task of examining divergent perspectives, therefore, should help to sensitize . . . [us] to the role played by values in the analysis of reality'.[23] To put the same point in a slightly different way, it is arguably better that the aspiring political and social analyst is aware that there is not one but various ways of selecting information to place order on a complex social and political reality. It is also desirable that individuals should be able to appreciate that there are different ways of explaining and evaluating the world and the way in which society functions. Given this, we might hope that individuals trained in the social sciences will be aware that any prescription that they or others proffer will be irrevocably value dependent and ideological. If this assists in cultivating a sceptical, rigorous, critical and informed populous, then theories will have served their function.

A simple example of the benefits of utilising different perspectives or theories operating from different levels of analysis may serve to reinforce this point. Take, for example, the case of a car crash at a road junction in which you, the observer, are sitting in a car which has collided with another car. You have tried to turn right but a car from your right has run into the side of your car. Now, from the point of view of the law, strictly speaking, you must be the guilty party because you must give way to cars on the main road. But from your perspective the other car driver is in the wrong because he was indicating to turn left at your junction. Thus, you would argue that you only turned right because you thought the other car was about to turn left. Is your view of reality the correct or only explanation of events? Perhaps, but what if the driver of the other car did not know that he was indicating to turn left because there was a fault in the car's electrical system? What, also, if this fault had been caused the day before by an incompetent mechanic who had not known how to do the repair job asked of him? Is then the accident due to the mechanic's incompetence? Perhaps, but why was the garage owner employing an incompetent individual? It might be because the employer did not want to pay the proper market rate for qualified labour in order to make more money for himself and because he had an ideological antipathy to employing trade union workers. Is the culprit then the garage owner? Perhaps, but did the car owner have to take the car to this garage? Isn't he culpable for not ensuring that the car was properly serviced?

Obviously we could take this discussion much further and end up delving into the individual psyche of the unfortunates involved, the state of the road surface or even the weather conditions. The point of the discussion, however, is to indicate what we have been trying to say in a more abstract way. There are various ways of explaining reality, evaluating causality and laying blame and responsibility for actions; each of these will concentrate on selecting different phenomena as the key factors to explain the same complex reality, and while none of them will capture the whole of that complex reality on their own, none of them will be totally invalid either. We should therefore be careful of assuming that there is any one best way of explaining reality. If this is so, then by analysing problems at various levels we may well broaden our understanding of that complex reality. This realisation should also sensitise us to the limited and value-dependent nature of most of the theories offered to explain the nature of power in capitalist societies. It is to the task of indicating in more detail the strengths and weaknes-

ses of three major theories of power in capitalist society that
we now turn.

## NOTES

1. For a discussion of the role of Keynes *see* Michael Stewart, *Keynes and After* (Harmondsworth, Penguin, 1972); on the issue of social democracy and Keynes *see* Andrew Cox, 'The Instability of Liberal and Social Democratic State Forms in British Society', *Parliamentary Affairs*, Vol. XXXV, No. 4 (Autumn 1982), pp. 381–95.
2. For a discussion and presentation of the various approaches to democracy and the good society from a range of political philosophers *see* David Held *et al.*, eds., *States and Societies* (Oxford, Martin Robertson, 1983), pp. 59–132.
3. *Ibid.*, pp. 97–100.
4. W.B. Gallie, 'Essentially Contested Concepts', *Proceedings of the Aristotelian Society*, Vol. 56 (1955–6), pp. 170–1.
5. *Ibid.*, pp. 171–80.
6. D.M. White, 'The Problem of Power', *British Journal of Political Science*, Vol. 2 (1972), pp. 479–90.
7. Steven Lukes, *Power: A Radical View* (London, Macmillan, 1977).
8. For a classic presentation of this approach *see* R.A. Dahl, *Who Governs?* (London, Yale University Press, 1961).
9. Lukes, *op. cit.*, pp. 16–20.
10. Peter Bachrach and Morton S. Baratz, 'The Two Faces of Power', *American Political Science Review*, Vol. 56 (1962), pp. 947–52; and 'Decisions and Non-Decisions: An Analytical Framework', *American Political Science Review*, Vol. 57 (1963), pp. 641–51.
11. Lukes, *op. cit.*, pp. 21–5.
12. I. Balbus, 'The Concept of Interest in Pluralist and Marxist Analysis', *Politics and Society*, No. I (1971), pp. 151–77.
13. Lukes, *op. cit.*, pp. 46–56.
14. R.A. Dahl, 'A Critique of the Ruling Elite Model', *American Political Science Review*, Vol. 52 (1958), pp. 463–9.
15. Karl Marx, 'The Eighteenth Brumaire of Louis Bonaparte', in D. Fernbach, ed., *Surveys from Exile* (Harmondsworth, Penguin, 1973).
16. John Gray, 'Rationality and Relativism in the Recent Work in the Theory of Power', *Hull Papers in Politics* (Hull University, 1980).
17. John Gray, 'On the Contestability of Social and Political Concepts', *Political Theory*, Vol. V (1977), pp. 331–48.
18. I.K. MacDonald, 'Is Power Essentially Contested?', *British Journal of Political Science*, Vol. 6 (1976), pp. 380–2.
19. S. Lukes, 'Reply to MacDonald', *British Journal of Political Science*, Vol. 7 (1977), pp. 418–19.

20. D. Willer and J. Willer, *Systematic Empiricism: Critique of a Pseudo–Science* (Englewood Cliffs, NJ, Prentice Hall, 1973). This provides an extensive critique of empiricist approaches to theory building.
21. This discussion relies heavily on Richard Little, 'The Characteristics of a Perspective' in *World Politics in Perspective* (Paper I, Open University Course, D233, Open University, Milton Keynes, 1981), pp. 18–24.
22. Richard Little, 'Retrospective Reflections on Perspectives' in *Reflections on World Politics* (Paper 16, Open University Course, 233, Open University, Milton Keynes, 1981), p. 35.
23. *Ibid.*, p. 37.

PART II

Theories of Power in Capitalist Societies

# 3 Marxist Approaches to Power

In this chapter we deal with one of the oldest theories of power in capitalist societies. The writings of Karl Marx and Frederich Engels in the nineteenth century provide one of the earliest critiques and explanations of the structure of power in capitalism. Indeed, it might be argued that subsequent elite and pluralist theories are nineteenth- and twentieth-century reaction to this analysis. As we shall see in subsequent chapters, elite and pluralist theories locate power in areas of social and political life very different from those put forward in Marxist accounts. In this chapter we will outline the two main schools of Marxist writings—instrumentalist and structuralist—before assessing the overall strengths and weaknesses of this school of thought.

## INSTRUMENTAL EXPLANATIONS

The first point to recognise is that there is as much debate within Marxism as there is between Marxists and non-Marxists as to the exact meaning and location of power. This intra-Marxist debate arises out of four problems.

1. There is a debate about discrepancies between the writings of Marx as a young man and his later output. It is argued that in his later life Marx was heavily influenced by Engels and his writings were much less determinist as a consequence. In his later writings, it is argued, Marx reveals far more concern for the political level of society and the freedom for human beings to act independently of the laws of motion of capitalism as a system of economic production. If this is so, there is a central confusion in Marx's writings about the freedom of action of individuals and the state at the

47

political level. This is compounded by point 2 to 4 following.

2. There is a disagreement about whether Marx's classic account of capitalism, *Das Kapital*, was an idealised statement about how a perfectly functioning capitalist system ought to function or whether it was a statement about how such societies, economies and states do function in practice.

3. Also, Marx did not write a book about the state and the political level. One can piece his ideas together from his mammoth output, but there is no single source from which to develop a definitive statement of the role of political action in capitalism.

4. This is exacerbated by the fact that capitalism has developed and been maintained throughout the twentieth century and is a very different system from that when Marx and Engels were writing. The role of the state, the improvement of material living standards, the rights to welfare and popular representation were not fully apparent and require explanation.[1]

Obviously this had led to considerable controversy between Marxists and non-Marxists as to whether Marx had fully understood capitalism and whether or not subsequent developments have invalidated his account of its structure of power. More interesting, in the context of this chapter, is the fact that these developments and the confusion in Marx's own writings have generated an internal debate amongst Marxists over what he really meant and how his initial insights ought to be understood in modern times. In this section we set out one broad school of thought—the instrumentalist explanation—which draws its inspiration from the early writings of Marx.

Traditional Marxist writings—and particularly contemporary Soviet and Stalinist accounts—have normally taken the early writings of Marx, plus *Das Kapital* and *The Communist Manifesto* to be the definitive statements of Marx's theories of power in capitalist society. In other words, these writings explain how capitalist societies and their state structures do in fact operate; they are not idealised constructs. According to these accounts, the structure of power in capitalism is based upon a state which acts as a mere instrument to serve the interests of those (the ruling class) who own the means of production.

Starting from the base upwards, instrumental explanations contend that the economic base (the mode of production and who owns it) will determine the political superstructure (governmental and social institutions) of that society. From this formulation change in society will flow, not from the autonomous actions of individuals acting subjectively but from fundamental and objective changes in the economic base of society. Individuals acting as politically relevant actors will therefore have very little scope at all to shape the economic base of society or its political and social superstructure. For instrumentalists this is what Marx meant by his classic statement about men making history but not in circumstances of their own choosing.[2]

This account is clearly an attempt to develop an objective theory of how society functions, and it delimits the scope for autonomous action by individuals. Unlike pluralist and elitist accounts, this Marxist theory denies that individuals choose freely and that political action can be based upon their subjective and value-free preferences. This account emphasises, instead, the structural and objective determinants shaping human action and relates change in society to the transformation and development of the economic mode of production. Such Marxists are arguing that whatever people may believe subjectively about their own freedom to make choices which will shape their society, the true locus of change can only be understood in terms of the objective laws of motion and requirements of the capitalist mode of production. It does not matter very much what people believe; what they will do will be determined by the requirements of the economic base. Any action which contradicts these laws—whether it is the working class believing that parliamentary reform can eradicate the exploitative nature of capitalism or capitalists believing that reform can eradicate the ultimate demands for fundamental and revolutionary change from the working class—is defined merely as an expression of false consciousness. People may misperceive the objective laws of motion of capitalism and

their own objective 'real' interests within it; but their scope
for subjective, autonomous action is ultimately constrained
by the workings of the objective laws of history. But what
are these objective laws?[3]

For Marxists these are the historical working-out in
human society of the laws of dialectic materialism. By this
Marxists mean that change and power in all human society
can be explained as the result of the struggle between
contending classes. Classes are defined in terms of whether
one owns or is a servant of a particular means of production.
Change occurs as one particular means of production (and
the classes to which it gives rise) comes into conflict with an
alternative means or mode of production (and with the
classes which this in turn generates). As one mode of
production is superseded by another, then the ruling class
which own the newly dominant means of production will
reshape the state structure to serve its own ends. This state
will repress all other classes in society until it is questioned
by an alternative mode of production. This can be shown
schematically:

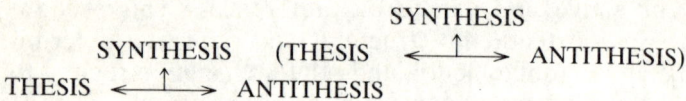

*Figure 1*: **The dialectic in Theory**

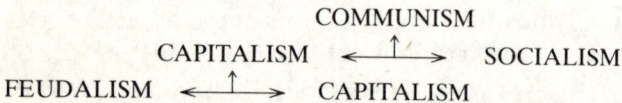

*Figure 2*: **Dialectic Materialism in Practice**

What these figures illustrate is the underlying explanatory
and predictive thesis of the Marxist account of power and
change. In general, what the theory of dialectic materialism
states is that every society is structured around its material
basis of production. Once that original structure (thesis) is

questioned by an alternative mode of production (antithesis), conflict will ensue until the new mode of production becomes dominant. This will give rise to a particular social and political system (synthesis) which will, as the dominant structure, throw up its own antithesis, and so on. In practice, Marxists argue, this process (derived from changes in the mode of production or the economic base of society) explains the historical questioning and transformation of the feudal mode of production and the state structures it gave rise to. This feudal system was replaced by the capitalist mode of production, which created its own state system to serve the interests of the owners of the means of capitalist production. Ultimately, and this was what Marx and Engels were trying to encourage in *The Communist Manifesto*, this capitalist system of power would be challenged by the working class which capitalism created. The people, exploited economically, socially and politically by capitalism would rise up and seize the state for themselves (socialism) and then replace it (after the withering away of the state) by a system of communism. Under communism there would be no exploitation, and society would be run by and for everyone on the basis of equality and community. Let us look in more historical detail at how Marxist accounts deal with these changes.

Under feudalism, Marxists argue, the dominant mode of production was based on the ownership of land. Surplus was generated by the working of this land (using fairly primitive tools and labour power) to produce food and raw materials (e.g. wool) for consumption and a surplus for conspicuous consumption. In this society, while trade in bullion and material commodities (clothing, jewellery and household effects etc.) occurred, the perpetrators of this trade—a merchant and skilled artisan class living in cities and towns—lacked ownership of land and, therefore, any direct social and political representation in society. The dominant class in feudal society consisted of the landowners who owned urban land, from which they extracted rents, and non-urban land, from which they usurped the surplus generated by peasants. This expropriation took the form of tithes, taxes and labour in kind in return for the physical protection of the people living on the land by the noble landowners. Under this system of economic production, even though a merchant class was able to find a niche for itself by providing loans and commodities for kings, princes and noble landowners, this class was largely excluded from control over the state, which was dominated by increasingly absolutist kings and their royal entourge of lords and nobles.[4] Wealth and position in society derived largely from land ownership, and the prominent position of this landowning class was reinforced by their ability to people and dominate the state—the judiciary, military, bureaucracy and legislature—with their sons and relatives. This dominance of the political level ensured that the state and its policies were always an instrument of class rule. The state was a repressive instrument to ensure class domination. The feudal state achieved this by, amongst other things, stopping popular elections, protecting agricultural rents by excluding cheaper competition from overseas and maintaining punitive laws against theft of property.

For instrumental Marxists, however, a change in the power structure of society arose, not because of conscious efforts by committed individuals at the political or social levels of society, but because this feudal mode of production was fundamentally challenged by an alternative and technically more efficient mode of production. Once this new mode of production began to replace the old, it threw up a new class of owners. These new entrepreneurs—the bourgoisie—relied for their accumulated economic wealth on the ownership of machines and factories rather than upon land. But they were not content merely to question the economic rule of the landowners, they also began to question the social and political structure of power in feudal societies. Many of the policies which protected landowners (limited enfranchisement and protective trade tariffs) were inimical to the economic interests of the rising middle class. Thus, as the capitalist mode of production ousted the feudal mode, its owners gradually came to shape and control the organs of the state (the superstructure) in order that the policies which were formulated within it served their interests. Eventually the state came to be a repressive tool or instrument serving the interests of a new ruling class based upon the ownership of capital not land. The state became, according to Marx, but 'a committee for managing the collective affairs of the bourgeoisie'.[5]

But why was the capitalist mode of production more efficient than feudal landownership, and why does this generate social and political change leading to a new power structure in society? To understand all of this we need, according to Marxists, to understand the laws of motion of capitalism.

Under feudalism, wealth or surplus was created by extracting either crops, as food or raw materials, labour in kind or, later with the introduction of money economies, taxes from those working on the land. Merchants and artisans in the towns normally contributed to the material wealth of the landowner in the form of the rents they paid for their places of domicile and work. This economic system, which allowed the landowning classes to take a dispro-portionate share of the productive capacity of the economy, was based upon traditional craft skills using fairly primitive tools and it was labour intensive. Such surplus as was created was used not for the accumulation of more wealth but, instead, was used for conspicuous consumption (courts, fine clothing and castles) or for wars against foreign foes. But, in the eighteenth century—as a direct result of the Enlighten-ment and scientific revolutions[6]—there was the gradual application of scientific discoveries to the process of agri-cultural production on the land. This use of technology (like Jethro Tull's seed drill) increased agricultural productivity: by replacing men by machines or giving men machines to work with more crops were produced and with less labour power. This had the effect of raising the efficiency of land and creating a greater surplus. at the same time there was a realisation that economic benefits could be had by replacing the old common-land system of peasant agricultural produc-tion with a system of enclosed lands. The stimulus for this came from the desire by some landowners to raise the efficiency of sheep rearing to take advantage of the wool trade with the Netherlands. These twin processes led to the gradual displacement of people from rural areas. Labour was no longer as efficient as machinery and new systems of agricultural organisation and, as a result, the peasantry (who had owned or had common rights to work the land in their villages) were gradually forced off the land to become wage labourers.[7]

There were a number of related reasons for this revolution in economic organisation. The increase in agricultural production increased the living standards of everyone. There were fewer famines and a greater agricultural surplus which allowed people to live longer and increase their fecundity. As people lived longer and the death rate fell, a larger population was able to persist. Since there was a higher population and a greater surplus of output people had a higher disposable income; this led directly to a desire for more than just food and a demand for material commodities for the household (pottery, cutlery, more and better clothing in cotton and wool). This increase in effective demand was a crucial factor in encouraging the application of technology to the production of material commodities. This application of technology to domestic systems of commodity production was to have a profound effect on the old feudal merchant and artisan classes and lead, eventually, to their challenging the dominance of the landowning class. It is not surprising, either, that the cotton industry of Lancashire should be the first industry to feel the full effects of the application of machinery to production. The cotton industry was relatively new compared with the older and more protected and restricted woollen trades and was therefore more open to innovation. It also had a cheap supply of raw materials from the slave-based American colonies and required only a radical increase in output for cotton to oust wool from its dominant role in clothing production. This increase was achieved by cotton entrepreneurs who used new technology in the form of spinning jennies, water frames, power looms and fly shuttles. This new economic process, assisted by an increasing effective demand, was to have the same impact on feudal manufacturing structures as it had in agriculture—it destroyed the old order of things.[8]

The old systems of production based on the 'putting out' of work to domestic workers using rudimentary technology was replaced by factory production with steam-powered engines massively increasing the output of a single operative.[9] Compared with the older production system, this new process, in which workers owned no machinery but were paid wages, was able to produce more and at a cheaper price. It is hardly surprising that it replaced the old 'putting out' system, nor that it led displaced domestic workers and artisans to smash machinery in a wave of 'Luddite' outbreaks.[10] This, then, was a new mode or system of production, and one which was very different to the old feudal economic system. In the past, society had maintained a degree of stability and hierarchy. The peasant might be at the bottom of the pile, but he still had rights to own or work common land and thus the certainty of providing some food for the survival of himself and his family. If he was exploited by landowners and the merchant and artisan classes, this did not result in total dependence on them. Furthermore, the society was based in the principle of *noblesse oblige*: the landowners had an obligation to protect the destitute and unemployed in their areas.

Compare this with the capitalist system. Under capitalism, market relationships replaced feudal ties of obligation and exchange. Increasingly labour was forced off the land, and the only right workers had was the right to sell their labour for a money wage. The old ties of obligation were replaced by pursuit of self-interest and the pursuit of capital accumulation. This was a profound change from the feudal economy. Urban centres and factories geared to the production of commodities for sale in order to augment the wealth of the factory owners (capital accumulation) became the driving force of the economic system. Conspicuous consumption, foreign wars and protectionism gave way to the saving of monetary wealth, free trade and the search for additional overseas and domestic markets to exploit for economic gain. This profound change in the structure of the economy and society led also to the growth of a new class of people. This class, known by Marxists as the bourgeoisie, were the owners of the means of production associated with this system of capital accumulation and commodity production. It did not matter whether they had been far-sighted landowners, former artisans or merchants in feudal society; what is crucial for Marxists is the belief that their ownership of the new and increasingly predominant mode of production led them to have common interests and goals. These interests of defending and sustaining the capitalist mode of production led them to act collectively against both the old landowning ruling class and the new working class (proletariat) of landless factory workers created by this profound change.[11]

In terms of Marxist theory, a thesis (feudalism) had been fundamentally questioned by its antithesis (capitalism), and eventually this mode of production would replace it with its own social and political system. Thus in Britain in the late eighteenth and early nineteenth century the new capitalist ruling class (often supported by the proletariat) challenged the economic and, eventually, the social and political supremacy of the landowning aristocracy. By 1846 the repeal of the Corn Laws—which ended the protection of corn and the underwriting of agricultural rents by the exclusion of cheaper foreign competition[12]—spelt the death knell of the aristocracy's dominance of the economy and society. After this date the leading elements of the landowning class and the bourgeoisie were to merge to form a new ruling class, based firmly on Britain's international primacy in trade and manufacture. The symbols of this were the crushing of the demands for equal rights to enfranchisement for the working classes, as espoused by the Chartist movement, the maintenance of the repressive Combination Acts which suppressed workers trades unions and the gradual dismantling of feudal protectionism and social welfare measures as enshrined in the repeal of the Navigation Acts and the Elizabethan Poor Laws.[13]

This, then, was the basis by which Marx and Engels could argue that the state in capitalist society was but an instrument for the exploitation and repression of the working class. The profound changes in the economy and society which had swept the old feudal practices away were for Marx and Engels merely an expression of the profound changes which had first taken place in the mode of production. Whatever workers and capitalists might believe subjectively, the state served the interests of the class which owned the means of production. This power over the working class was achieved at the economic level, through the extraction of surplus value at the point of production,[14] and politically, through the enactment of repressive legislation by the state.

From their historical perspective Marx and Engels could be forgiven for arguing that late-nineteenth-century Britain had a repressive capitalist state. It is understandable, therefore, why they should also believe that this harsh and exploitative system—a fact noted not just by Marxists but also by social reformers like Dickens, Rowntree, William Booth, the Webbs and Edwin Chadwick at the time[15]— would ultimately be questioned by the class of people who were at once both the most numerous and the most exploited by this mode of production. For Marx and Engels the working class had nothing to lose but their chains of false consciousness. Once the truly exploitative nature of the system was revealed to the proletariat, they would rise up and replace capitalism with a system based upon common ownership and collective action.[16] The problem for modern Marxists, however, is that the objective laws which Marx had developed to predict the way in which the capitalist system would develop do not seem to have fully explained what has happened in the twentieth century. True, there have been revolutions in the name of socialism and communism, but these have never been in highly industrialised but in agricultural and industrially backward countries like Russia, China and Cuba. Furthermore, Marx and Engels did not foresee the twentieth-century transformation of capitalism as a social, economic and political system. These changes, which were just beginning to develop at the end of Marx's life have thrown into question much of this original Marxist theory and account for the modern debate about whether or not the capitalist state is always (or ever) an instrument which defends the interests of the ruling class in a repressive way.

The list of changes in modern capitalism which have been seen as fundamentally questioning the original Marxist theory are too numerous to mention in detail, so we will

confine ourselves to the major changes which have fuelled
debate amongst Marxists. First, Marx and Engels argued
that one of the reasons why capitalism would be destroyed
was due to the internal contradictions of the system itself.
The major contradiction was the tendency of the rate of
profit to decline.[17] Marx argued that to compete in the
market for commodities, capitalists had continually to
increase their productivity and efficiency. The only methods
available to do this were either to find cheaper sources of
raw materials, squeeze labour's wages or increase the
technological composition of the productive process. The
first two solutions were difficult to achieve. Eventually the
supply of raw materials would become finite and alternative
and cheaper sources of supply would not be found. While
labour could be paid poor wages they must also survive and
be able to work efficiently. This meant that there was a limit
beyond which wages could be reduced without harming the
industrial process or generating such misery that the workers
would rebel against the system. The only effective solution,
then, was to raise 'the organic composition of capital'. It was
machinery which had led to increased efficiency and output.
In order to compete, firms would therefore have to seek
ever-increasing technological innovations to raise productivity, increase output and reduce prices. This would mean, on
the one hand, replacing men with machines and, on the
other, tying up more and more of capital in the form of
machines. Marx argued that the former might lead, through
unemployment, to working class unrest and the latter would,
in tying up capital and removing it from the circulation of
capital, reduce the rate of profits made in production. This
was because the circulation of capital slows down and the
process of exploiting labour power is hindered. With more
and more money tied up in investment and machinery, firms
would be unable to buy off workers during slumps and class
conflict would be raised.

Marx and Engels did not foresee that it was possible for
capitalists to find new markets or cheaper supplies of raw
materials and labour in the colonies of the Third World.
Imperialist relationships increasingly replaced reliance on
domestic markets at the turn of the twentieth century and

provided a temporary breathing space for capitalism.[18] Today, capitalism is not just a domestic economic structure; it is international in its ramifications and based upon large multinational or monopoly capital firms located in the centre of the industrial world, but with outlets in most parts of the globe. This expansion of international capitalism and its attendant massive increase in output and productivity, especially between 1945 and the world slump of 1974, was also not predicted by Marx. Since his death the workers of the industrial world have experienced (despite severe dislocations in the 1920s, 1930s and 1970s) a fairly continuous increase in their material standards of living, a massive expansion of social welfarism and have also been given the right to vote for their own governments in relatively pluralistic political systems with competitive political parties and regular elections. These changes have, of course, encouraged non-Marxists to argue that Marxist theory is now invalid because power is no longer concentrated in the hands of a few economic owners and their friends. Workers have their own organisations which can bring pressure to bear on governments and make demands on the state. Workers can also finance and create their own political parties, which often become the government of the day and direct the executive and legislative power of the state. As a result, such theorists argue, the structure of power is no longer in the hands of a capitalist ruling class; it is pluralistic and will change depending on the issue and the circumstances.

There is no doubt that these profound changes in modern capitalism have questioned Marx's and Engel's general formulation of the relationship between the economic base of society and the political superstructure of power. But, as we shall see, in Marxist scholarship there are those who have modified Marx original theory so as to accommodate these changes in a way which is consistent with the original insight about the determined nature of the locus of power in capitalist societies. In this school we include Lenin and other state monopoly capitalist theorists (whether class-theoretical or capital-logic accounts) of modern capitalism. All of these theorists conclude that the state still serves the interests of the ruling class, even if the mechanisms of that instrumental relationship have changed since Marx wrote.[19]

Lenin, in two works, *State and Revolution* and *Imperialism: The Highest Stage of Capitalism*, was the first major theorist to update Marx's writings in line with modern conditions while seeking to maintain his original determinist insights. In these two works Lenin laid the base for a modern reworking of Marx which is normally referred to as the theory of state monopoly capitalism. This theory holds that, since Marx wrote, capitalism has metamorphosised from its early liberal, freely competitive market base. Today (i.e. from the end of the nineteenth century to today) the competitive market base of nation states has been superseded by the concentration of capitalist markets and the internationalisation of large monopoly and oligopoly capitalists firms. There were a number of reasons for this. First, the logic of private competition was to replace small firms by larger firms which could dominate and control markets. This came about because enterpreneurs realised that they could maintain higher profits by not indulging in fierce competition which forced them to pass on benefits to consumers. Rather, if they bought up smaller firms, they could rig markets in their favour by creating cartels, trade agreements and trusts with similar-sized competitors. This concentration of the market also came about because of the increasing tendency of the rate of profit to decline. As the technological composition of industry increased, only the largest firms could afford to invest in and run large-scale factories requiring heavy research and development costs. The increase in the scale of operation also led to a search for further sources of raw materials and safe markets for corporate products. This led to the internationalisation of capitalist companies and the protection of their markets by national governments in the service of capitalism. This Lenin called—following J.A. Hobson, a liberal economist[20]—'imperialism', or the highest form of capitalism. For Lenin firms had to move overseas because this was the only way they could guarantee the cheap raw materials and the effective demand for their commodities once international competition had increased and the costs of innovation had reduced the rate of profits to be made at home.

There are other reasons why capitalism needs to exploit the Third World, according to Lenin.[21] Following Marx and Engels, Lenin argued that capitalism was an objective system for the exploitation of the working class. As a result, exploitation led them to organise and, through militancy, question the logic of power in the system. To preserve the system, Lenin argued, concessions had to be granted to the proletariat at home. Thus, in order to maintain the stability of capitalist regimes at home, social welfare concessions were granted and, slowly, popular representation was allowed. This was not a threat to the capitalist class, however, because the leaders of the trade unions and workers parties were normally incorporated into the political system and educated to the imperatives and requirements of capitalism. The social welfare and material benefits which the imperialist state could grant to workers in Britain and Germany at the turn of the twentieth century allowed capitalism to survive because it divided Third World workers from their similarly exploited, if differently rewarded, working-class brethren in the industrialised centre of the world economy. Not until rising nationalism and socialism ousted capitalism from the Third World would capitalism be destroyed.

In more recent times this theory (which has been the orthodoxy of post-war European Communist parties and Stalinist accounts of modern capitalism) has been further refined to take account of the ever-increasing directive interventions of the state into the private economy, on top of earlier moves to provide social welfare concessions. These interventions, associated with the Keynesian revolution in economic thinking which called for the state to become involved in maintaining the level of aggregate demand in the economy through the use of budgetry policies, have been seen not as a triumph of democratic struggle but as a further example of the use of the state as an instrument of the interests of the ruling class. A ruling class, it must be pointed out, which is no longer defined as individual enterpreneurs but in terms of the fusion of large monopoly and oligopoly joint-stock companies with financial institutions (banks, insurance companies, pension funds, merchant banks) and the state. Thus the post-1945 intervention of the state into an increasingly regulative and directive role for the economy is seen as the high point of state monopoly capitalism. But, while this new Keynesian role may result in greater material benefits for the workers of the industrial world, it is always perpetrated in an economic system in which the state is acting to defend the interests of capital accumulation and the objective exploitation of the proletariat, whether at home or abroad. Within this still broadly instrumental Marxist approach, two major lines of argument, emphasising different causal phenomena for this development, have been developed. These are, respectively, capital-logic and class-theoretical accounts.[22]

Capital-logic accounts contend that the shift from small- and medium-scale industries owned by individual entrepreneurs and their families to larger-scale units, with a high scientific and technical content, has resulted in the concentration of the market. This objective change in the market has also generated a logical change in the role required of the state by capitalism. The state now has to intervene to guarantee demand, protect markets, set up state monopolies, regulate foreign trade, control credit and fight imperialist wars. French studies have argued that this full state monopoly capitalist system did not come into operation until the 1930s. Simple monopoly replaced liberal capitalism in the period between 1873 and 1918 as a result of a severe slump and depression. After the crisis of the 1930s, when Keynesian ideas were fully developed, the state's role changed remarkably. According to these accounts, as the structure of the economy became more concentrated, in order to defend the logic of the capitalist mode of production, the state had to fuse with the monopoly sector and act against the interests of both the working class and the non-monopoly sectors of capitalism. The state's bureaucracy came to be staffed by the monopoly capitalists and their friends so that the state could co-ordinate the interests of the monopolies. Working-class political parties also came to serve a useful integrative function for monopoly capital. By incorporating the working class into the state structure on the basis of social democratic politics, the increasingly centralised and bureaucratised party structures were incapable of mounting a serious challenge to the capitalist system. Functional pressure-group activity has also increased, which has allowed the state to bypass legislatures and which will eventually lead to the creation of corporate state structures dominated by the monopolies. As the functional role of the state in the economy expands, the executive can develop its role and begin to question the rule by dictat and administrative fiat. Finally, the monopolies come to dominate the educational system, the media and other social institutions so that they can control social values.[23]

This interpretation of the structure of power and the role of the state in modern capitalism has been questioned because it is overly determinist and descriptive. For example, this account does not discuss the conflicts which occur between different sectors of capital and the conflicting political pressures this will generate. Nor does this account explain why it is that the state must act to serve the interests of the monopolies. The political rationale for this logic is never explained. Furthermore, it assumes that monopolies have a single or unitary interest which the state can follow without question. What this might be, other than the preservation of capital accumulation, is never properly explained. Finally, and perhaps most importantly, this account fails to explain why it is that the forms of state intervention have shown tremendous variability in capitalist economies and why it is that not every country had the same welfare and interventionist economic policies.[24] As a result, some Marxist writers, who wish to argue that the state is ultimately a repressive tool of the capitalist ruling class but recognise the weakness of simply reading off the role of the state from what is happening in the economy, have formulated an alternative class-theoretical account.

This account contends that the structure of power and the role of the state in capitalist societies will be crucially conditioned by the political forms which exist. While in the long run the requirements of capitalism determine the actions and the role of the state, the form of the state has varied across countries and over time. This fact needs to be explained and cannot be assumed, or read off, in terms of the logic of capitalism. The system of production may have become international and concentrated, but the form of the state and its role in particular economies has been extremely varied. This, it has been argued by a group of German and British Marxists in the 1960s and 1970s, means that the form of the state must be shaped by the nature of class conflict and struggle in society.[25] For writers like Altvater, Muller and Neususs, Holloway and Picciotto, Hirsch, Offe, and Gerstenberger, while the role of the state is limited by the laws of capital accumulation (the state can only redistribute wealth once profits have been made) and the imperatives of capital that must be maintained, the role of the state in modern capitalism is not to defend the interests of a ruling class on every specific but to provide for the interests of capital 'in general'. Capital competes for itself economically and, therefore, only requires that the state's role is facilitative of general market conditions by reproducing labour power (underwriting welfare and education for a proficient labour force) and providing a political safety valve for capitalism (through the apparent neutrality of the bourgeois, liberal democratic state based upon universal suffrage). In this formulation, while working-class struggle and political action may allow the state to act in ways which are inimical to the interests of specific sectors of capital, it is unlikely that any policies pursued will be inimical to capital in general. If the working class push their action too far, the apparent neutrality of the state will disappear and the state will act against them. In the absence of economic crises, and given the apparent political neutrality of the state, class conflict may well lead to very different compromises bewteen the classes in each capitalist country and very different state forms and economic and welfare policies. In crisis, however, the state must act to defend the imperatives of the capitalist system and, in this conditional sense, is still an instrument of class rule and repression.

This formulation clearly has greater insights than the capital-logic account. It shows that the nature of political power in capitalist societies is very different under monopoly capitalism than under liberal capitalism, and it indicates that the state can act as a political force in its own right against both capital and labour.[26] But, insofar as it argues that the state, notwithstanding its apparent neutrality and the inherent variability of state forms and interventions, still serves the interests of the owners of the means of production, this account still maintains that at all times the state acts to defend capital. The apparent neutrality of the state is seen as functional for capitalism because it masks the exploitation in society, and in crisis situations the state's truly repressive nature against the working class and marginal sectors of capital in favour of monopoly capital is always revealed. In this sense, despite the greater sophistication of this analysis, it is still centrally located within an instrumentalist account of power in capitalist society and suffers from an over-reliance on defining the state as an object for class rule.

Jessop has argued, we think correctly, that this view is invalid because it ignores the central truth of the state in capitalist societies; namely, that it is a field of political struggle. Jessop argues that what instrumental Marxist writers fail to grasp is that the state does not respond to the economic crises of capitalism. Rather the individuals within the state (beset by their own subjective awareness and myopia) perceive the *political* repercussions of economic crisis. Thus it is the balance of political forces which shapes and determines state intervention in any society; economic movements are only represented indirectly in state interventions.[27] Class-theoretical accounts, however, persist in arguing that even in crises the state will always use repression to discipline the working class to defend capital. But this assumes that individuals within the state have some prior and superior knowledge of what the interests of capital (and its monopoly sectors) are in a crisis. Jessop argues that this is highly unlikely and that in a crisis we cannot say in advance whether the state—now divorced from any one-to-one relationship with the ruling class—will assist capital, labour or (as seems to be the perennial case in Britain) pursue policies to the mutual ruin of the contending classes. The point here is that what the state will do will depend on the balance of political forces in the state.[28] This is, however, to run ahead of our discussion. Jessop's viewpoint is informed by a structuralist critique to which we now turn for further elaboration of modern Marxist interpretations of power in capitalist society.

## STRUCTURALIST EXPLANATIONS AND THE CONCEPT OF RELATIVE AUTONOMY

Most Marxists would accept the thrust of the economic arguments presented by instrumental theorists. While the increasing concentration and internationalisation of capital is not in question, there is, however, serious debate over whether the state is always dominated by the ruling class and whether it is always repressive. Instrumental theorists ultimately conclude that while the state may have a degree of political neutrality, this is just a sham to mask the dominance of the state by the interests of the dominant class. Structuralist Marxist writers, taking their lead from Antonio Gramsci, an Italian Marxist,[29] have doubted this and have contended that the state may have a degree of autonomy from the interests of the ruling class. This autonomy is however conditional—a relative autonomy—because the capitalist ruling class are able to ensure their dominance over society and economy through the unequal competition between different ideologies. In this way, thought and action are conditioned to serve the interests of capitalism through an ideological hegemony. It does not matter very much which interests run the state, they will always act in the interests of the preservation of the capitalist mode of production. Thought and action is then structurally determined.

This school of writing allows the pluralistic nature of politics and the control of the state by the representatives of the working class to be explained, while at the same time outlining why it is that capitalism persists. For Gramsci, class domination is not achieved through the state being dominated by the ruling class; it is achieved through a complex process of coercion and consent. This is achieved via the use of force (individuals being coerced into accepting the capitalist mode of production) and hegemony. Hegemony implies the mobilisation of the active consent of those dominated by a ruling class through the use of intellectual, moral and political persuasion and leadership. This might involve the granting of concessions to the subordinate classes or political forms which allow a real degree of choice, in order to maintain an overall world view which preserves capitalism by distorting beliefs, values, common sense assumptions and popular culture. The mechanisms of transmission are the 'so-called' private institutions of civil society—the church, the trade unions, the schools, the media and the political parties.[30]

This view of the structurally determined nature of thought and action, and the difficulty this posed for the representatives of the working class when using a formally neutral state to serve ends other than those of capitalism, was one of the major insights which underpinned Ralph Miliband's seminal book of the 1960s, *The State in Capitalist Society*.[31] Miliband's book is important because it contains within it a bridge between instrumentalist and structuralist accounts of the state and power in capitalist society. It also fuelled a major controversy in the 1970s with Nicos Poulantzas over the meaning of 'relative autonomy'. This book and debate assisted in the further elaboration of a structuralist Marxist school of writing based on the notions of 'hegemony' and 'relative autonomy'.

Miliband accepted that the economy had become monopoly capitalist, but in recognition of the pluralistic nature of the politics in modern capitalism he tried to draw a distinction between *state power* and *class power*. By making this distinction, Miliband sought to account for the fact that the state is not always an instrument of the ruling class, even though, in terms of ownership and control of the economy, a ruling class clearly existed.[32] To arrive at this viewpoint Miliband argued that society was stratified by a number of elites—social, economic (including managers and not just owners), bureaucratic and political—each of which had its own basis of power. In this way Miliband argued that power was derived not just from ownership of the means of production but might also derive from position as a politician or bureaucrat in the state's institutions. Miliband argued, however, that this apparent plurality of interests was a sham because all of these elites together constituted a ruling class serving the interests of capitalism. The problem for capitalism was that this rule was always problematic because of the pressure from the working class and non-monopoly capital for policies which would question the interests of monopoly capital. In this way, out of the competing power bases of the different elites and the pressure for change, the state in modern capitalism had to become a 'field of political struggle' with a degree of autonomy in its own right. Under certain conditions the balance of class forces, plus the conflicts within and between different elites in the state system over state power, might result in opportunities for interests opposed to monopoly capital to seize the state and pursue policies antithetical to its interest.[33]

However, this victory would only be short-lived because state power was not as powerful as class power due to the structural constraints embedded within the nature of capitalist society. In this light Miliband followed Gramsci and discussed the way in which ideology and culture are formed by the media, the church and the educational system to prop up the capitalist system in general. At the same time Miliband argued that these hegemonic powers would also be supported by the economic constraints (crises of business confidence and runs on currencies) possessed directly by the ruling class.[34]

Miliband's position led to serious criticisms, not just from traditional instrumentalist Marxists but from other structuralists who recognised the importance of updating Marxism to take account of ideological hegemony and the pluralistic nature of politics in modern capitalism. The leading exponent of this structuralist critique was Nicos Poulantzas, who had been influenced by the French structuralist Marxist Louis Althusser.[35] Poulantzas's main critique of Miliband was that by introducing the notion of elites and subjective choice and free will into Marxism, Miliband was no longer a Marxist. By allowing the individual to choose freely,

Miliband rejects, according to Poulantzas, the underlying logic of Marxist thinking that thought and action is determined and shaped by the logic and requirements of capitalism. This lead Poulantzas to accuse Miliband of arguing that the state in capitalism could do whatever it desired. If this was so, then, the state must, following the pluralist critique he was trying to challenge, be seen as independent and autonomous. Poulantzas' own position was to argue for the development of a Marxist, structuralist account which provides for the state to have only a relative autonomy and never a true autonomy.[36] Let us look at this position in more detail.

Following Gramsci, Poulantzas argued that the dominant class relies on the complex use of coercion and consent. The state is then a complex 'institutional ensemble' which functions to organise the hegemony within the power bloc of the dominant class by mobilising the active consent of the dominated.[37] Thus for Poulantzas there are no elites or subjectively motivated individuals deciding on the role of the state. Different groups exist within the power bloc of any society, but this power bloc and the groups within it are there because of their objective/structural position in relation to capital. Since capital is divided between different sectors (monopoly, non-monopoly, productive, commercial, financial and merchant), and because the state itself is a complex ensemble of different agencies responding to these divisions and the class struggle, there is bound to be conflict of interest over state policy. In the end, however, the power bloc is working to maintain the hegemony of the dominant class and any policies which appear to question these interests are in fact nothing of the sort. The relative autonomy which the state appears to possess is in fact functionally necessary because of the institutional separation of polity and economy in capitalism. True autonomy could not be possible anyway because, like Miliband, Poulantzas argues that thought and action are conditioned by ideological hegemony.[38]

This formulation, while recognising the separation of the political and economic levels in capitalist economies and emphasising the crucial role of ideology and hegemony, was not really much of an advance on the class theoretical accounts we discussed earlier. Unlike Miliband, who was trying to argue that there was scope in the short term for autonomous state action, Poulantzas (while recognising that policies against the dominant class and other sectors of capital was possible) was still insisting that when this did occur it would always be functional for the long-term survival and hegemony of the monopoly sector. In other words, by insisting on the dominance of the ruling class in the last instance, Poultantzas's approach retained within it the central tenet of all reductionist instrumental accounts: namely, the state must be functioning to defend and protect the interests of the dominant class all of the time.

However, Jessop has shown in his later writings that Poulantzas began to move more closely towards Miliband's approach.[39] Just before his death Poulantzas did come to accept that the state could be a field of political struggle and that this 'institutional ensemble' was not unified but was subject to conflict and disunity. In this sense, even though they did not fully agree, Poulantzas and Miliband came closer together. But both Miliband and Poulantzas were unprepared to accept that what came out of this conflict over, and within, the state would be against the long-term interests of the ruling class. In the short term, Miliband and Poulantzas argue, the dominant class might lose out to reformist political movements, or even genuinely revolution working-class movements, but in the end these attacks on the nature of the capitalism by a reformist and pluralistic state would be defeated due to structural and ideological constraints operating to preserve capitalism. By this, structuralists (Miliband and Poulantzas alike) mean that short-term concessions might be given to, or seized by, interests antithetical to capitalism, but once these interests pushed their demands beyond what was safe for the continuity of the capitalist mode of production and accumulation, then economic crisis would arise to constrain choice and force policy-makers to recognise that they operated within a capitalist world economic system. Furthermore, the scope for truly radical action would be undermined through the unconscious acceptance of an ideology which limits the range of alternatives that political leaders might conceive of, or sustain popular support for. Thus power in modern capitalism might be more fractionated and pluralist than in the past—it might also be based on non-class political divisions—but in practice the use that was made of the state and its scope of manoeuvre would be conditional on whether it threatened capitalism as a system. If it was not used to preserve, bolster and enhance capitalism and its leading sectors in the long term, then severe economic crises would ensue. This is, then, the meaning structuralists give to the 'relative autonomy' of the state. While they reject the instrumentalist accounts of power, which assume that any and all actions by the state must serve the interests of the ruling class directly, in the last instance the constraints imposed upon the state by the private ownership of the means of production severely limit the long-term freedom of manoeuvre of the state.

## STRENGTHS AND WEAKNESSES OF MARXIST EXPLANATIONS

It is obvious from our previous discussion that when we come to assess the utility of Marxist explanations of power and the state, we have to be careful to differentiate between instrumental and structuralist accounts. It is, however, useful first to provide a general methodological and epistemological critique of Marxist theories in general. It should be apparent that the critiques presented here will depend to a large extent on the very different insights which are gleaned from theorising about power from the pluralist and elitist perspectives to be studied later in this book.

What strengths do the Marxist approaches contain, whether they be structuralist or instrumentalist? First of all, Marx's theory of historical materialism was one of the very first theories of society and change to be formulated which provided a historical overview and, at the same time, attempted to mesh together the workings of social, economic and political phenomena. While pluralists and elite theorists might dispute that an analysis of power should start with the workings of the mode of production in any society, they have been less successful in providing lasting and interdisciplinary accounts of the changing nature of economic, social and political forms in the last two centuries. Pluralist accounts, in particular, which treat the political system as an independent sphere of social action in which power can be isolated, are particularly weak on explaining how it is that the pluralist framework of policy-making in many capitalist societies has arisen. To argue as they do that it was because individuals and groups wanted it so is hardly an explanation. To say change is always due to individual preferences smacks more of faith or simple assertion than concrete analysis of the changes in the distribution of power and the forms of political representation in capitalist societies. This indicates a further strength of the Marxist approaches. While they do not exclude analysis of the 'who-whom' of power (which individuals are involved in decision-making and what do they want?), they go beyond simply relying on the subjective preferences of individuals as the causal factor in power relationship; they look as well at the impersonal forces and arrangements in social and economic life which shape human perceptions of reality and the formulation of their preferences and wants. It is taken as axiomatic by Marxists that wants do not appear out of the air as God-given endowments but are directly related to the social and economic circumstances which men experience.[40]

Marxist approaches also make claims to scientific enquiry because they are abstractive theories. What we mean by this is that, like natural scientists, Marxists consciously formulate a theoretical framework of analysis which is said to define the objective laws of motion of capitalist societies. These abstract theoretical constructs are then tested in the 'real' world to explain political, social and economic change. If the theory does not fit that reality then the theory is redrawn and reformulated to take account of aberrant cases. It has argued that this process is the one which is used in the natural sciences and it is a very different approach to that adopted by pluralist and, to a lesser extent, elite theorists. Such theorists operate within a methodological approach based upon systematic empiricism.[41] By this we mean that researchers collect by observation numerous pieces of evidence about the same observable relationships and phenomena in society. Having observed these relationships systematically, broad descriptive generalisations can be made about society. Marxist writers, and their supporters, argue that this latter approach can do nothing more than describe reality; it can never explain and analyse the complex causal relationships of human existence, because research only concentrates on what is observable. In this way, researchers can never explain why it is that wants or preferences manifested by individuals in social and political action are originally formed. Issues like suppression and conditioning and the role of ideology and hegemony are non-observable and cannot be brought within any empiricist explanation of power. But common sense tells us that the most important aspects of power are not always situations of observable conflict between visible, politically relevant actors (first and second dimensions of power). Rather, the most powerful individuals are often those who do not have to engage in conflict but who obtain what they desire because everyone accepts unconsciously that they should benefit (third dimension of power). Only Marxist accounts fully tap this element of power, and this is one of their strengths. Furthermore, because the approach is abstractive, only Marxist approaches can allay claims to being able to predict how capitalist societies will develop. All of the other theories to be discussed here can only describe what has happened; they have no real conception of what the motive force of power or change is in society over time other than to rely on describing the eclectic, indeterminate behaviour of subjective and free individuals. Marxists clearly reject such notions of voluntarism and begin their analysis of change and power from a starting point rooted on the changing relationships between different modes of production. One may not like or agree with the theory, but it does contain a theory of history, change and power which other social science approaches often lack.

But Marxist approaches also have weaknesses, depending on one's interpretation of proper social science enquiry. Perhaps the most glaring epistemological critique levelled at

Marxist approaches is that they contain no counter-factual. What this means is that there is no way that any hypothesis drawn from Marxist theory can be disproved by empirical investigation.[42] For social scientists trained in empirical inquiry this means that the whole theory is invalid because it can never be invalidated by exposing it to analysis in the 'real' world. Let us take a simple example. Most Marxists (certainly instrumentalists) believe that the state is a repressive tool of the ruling class. Empirical studies show that the working class has been granted the vote, the material living standards of most workers have increased and social welfare benefits have been won. For non-Marxists this is evidence that power is not located in the hands of a capitalist ruling class and that society is pluralistic, open and democratic. Marxists however doubt this. As we saw, modern Marxists have reworked their theory to account for these changes while still maintaining the centrality of Marx's original insights. Thus pluralistic political representation is a sham which masks the structural and ideological limits of reformist political action. True, material living standards have risen but this has only been granted either to increase the overall rate of exploitation of the workers or because the workers of the Third World are being exploited even more rapaciously to 'buy off' subordinate classes at home. Furthermore, politicians and workers always work for goals which—due to ideological hegemony—never fundamentally question the logic of capitalism. For non-Marxists, then, Marxist theories can never be disproved empirically because the theory can always be reworked or 'false consciousness' invoked to explain any apparent aberrant behaviour which appears to be inconsistent with the general logic of the objective laws of change which Marx originally formulated.

But, although Marxists have been able to refute empiricist critiques of their theories by these methods, it has been the case that the original theory has come under severe strain, and this is one reason for the development of the modern structuralist approaches. The fact that this has occurred indicates that Marx's and Engels's original formulation probably does not do justice to the nature of power in a modern capitalist society. It is worth remarking again on some of the issues with which instrumentalist accounts have had difficulty in coming to terms with before turning our attention, finally, to structuralist accounts.

The main problem for instrumental Marxist accounts is that they have great difficulty in explaining the eclecticism and indeterminancy of events in the world under a single reductionist or economist explanation which relates all actions by the state to the desires and power capabilities of a ruling class based on economic ownership. Events such as the extension of the franchise, the seizure of power by working-class parties, the fractionated and conflictual basis of state institutions, the crucial mediating role played by state bureaucracy, the higher material and social benefits granted to the working class and, perhaps most importantly, the fact that the forms of political representation and state intervention in different countries have shown remarkable dissimilarities over time and space, have all been difficult to accommodate within Marx's and Engels's original formulation about the nature of power in capitalist societies. This has led, since the turn of the century, to a number of interesting attempts to reformulate the original theory with a new appraisal of the role of the state in monopoly capitalism. Jessop, however, has argued that while there are important insights to be gleaned from this approach, the instrumental reappraisal falls somewhat short of giving an adequate theoretical account of the state in capitalism. Jessop's critique rests on the following grounds. First, it is difficult to account for the very different forms of state intervention and political representation if one follows the instrumentalist position, and it is also difficult to explain how it is that the whole capitalist system coheres and is reproduced if the capitalists do not control and dominate the bureaucratic and political levers of the state, as modern instrumentalists now accept.[43] Second, this account rarely encompasses the conflicts within and between different sectors of capital, whether they be monopoly/non-monopoly or commercial, productive, financial or merchant divisions. Third, the political rationale of state interventions is often ignored in favour of economic explanations only. There is a lack of discussion of the complex institutional conflicts

*within* the state and their impact on policy formulation and
implementation. The approach also assumes, without showing what it is, that monopoly capital has a single and unitary
purpose and goal.[44] Finally, even more sophisticated class-
theoretical accounts rely, ultimately, on the repressive role
of the state and ignore the role of hegemony and political,
non-class, forces in shaping the actions of the state.[45]

It is not surprising, therefore, that recent Marxist explanations of power in capitalist society have tried to explain the
more pluralistic modern forms of representation and policy-
making in terms, not of some devious desire by the ruling
class and their friends but as a limited freedom for actors and
forces opposed to capitalism, which is constrained and
limited in the last instance by the economic structure of the
capitalist mode of production and its ideological hegemony.
This allows for a far greater sophistication of analysis
because it recognises that the state and the policies it pursues
may well be a result of internal conflicts *within* the state or
due to conflicts between fractions of the capitalist class or
from struggle by classes opposed to capitalism. Even these
more sophisticated attempts to elaborate where power lies
and to allow for some freedom of manoeuvre for the state in
capitalism can between, however, as reductionist. This
arises because they rely not on 'false consciousness' but on
the 'last instance' to sustain the belief that the ruling class
always has power over other classes and that it will always
dominate the state. But, as Jessop shows, by insisting on the
plurality of forces around the state and also arguing that the
ruling class must always win out in any politics which flow
from this conflict, structuralists are misguided. At best their
analysis is tautological; at worst it is meaningless because
from their analysis any and all state forms (apart from
socialist ones) must, by definition, work in the interest of
capitalism. This is patently absurd.[46]

Since the death of Poulantzas there have been one or two
attempts by Marxist and neo-Marxist theoreticians to
accommodate some of these substantive criticisms. Indeed,
as we shall see in our concluding chapter, Jessop has
developed an approach to the analysis of power and the state
in capitalism which brings together insights from Marxist

and non-Marxist accounts. Since this approach is not clearly within mainstream Marxist explanations, it is not analysed in detail here.[47] It is, however, worth stressing what Jessop has said in support of his own neo-Marxist approach to the analysis of power and the state, because it emphasises both the strengths and weaknesses of the Marxist school of writings: 'an adequate theoretical analysis of the state [and power] must consider not only economic determinations but also those rooted in the distinctive organisation of the state as well as in the social division of labour between officialdom and people'.[48] But:

the exercise of power is not the unconditional outcome of a mechanical clash of wills but has definite social and material conditions of existence and is circumscribed through its links with other determinations in a social formation. This is why politics can be justly described as 'the art of the possible'. The analysis of these limits and constraints is therefore logically prior to the study of the actions of the agents involved in a power relation.[49]

No further testament is needed to illustrate both the strengths and weaknesses of Marxist accounts of power and the state. It is to an analysis of alternative theories, which specifically emphasise the 'who-whom' of power and the nature of the political system (if not the socio-economic constraints within which this game is played) that we now turn.

## NOTES

1. For a discussion of the debate about the early and later writings of Marx *see*: Lucio Colletti, *Karl Marx, Early Writings* (Harmondsworth, Penguin, 1975), especially the Introduction; Robin Blackburn, 'Marxism: Theory of Proletarian Revolution', *New Left Review*, Vol.97 (May–June 1976), pp.3–35; Bob Jessop, *The Capitalist State: Marxist Theories and Methods* (Oxford, Martin Robertson, 1982), pp. 1–31. Jessop in particular denies that there is such a distinction in the early or later writings. Jessop's position is to argue that Marx and Engels might have had an instrumentalist view in general, but in practice this was always heavily qualified when they analysed concrete events. For a similar critique of Marxist accounts

which are reductionist *see* E.P. Thompson, *The Poverty of Theory and Other Essays* (London, Merlin Press, 1978) pp. 193–398.

2. For this quote *see* Ch. 2, p. 42.
3. For further discussion of Marx's and Engels's theories *see* W.H.C. Eddy, *Understanding Marxism* (Blackwell, Oxford, 1979).
4. Perry Anderson, *Lineages of the Absolutist State* (London, New Left Books, 1974), pp. 15–42 and 428–29.
5. Karl Marx, *The Communist Manifesto* (Harmondsworth, Penguin, 1970), 1982.
6. R.M. Hartwell, ed., *The Causes of the Industrial Revolution in England* (London, Methuen, 1976), pp. 17–23.
7. This insight is understood by Marxists and non-Marxists alike. For a non-Marxist account *see* John A. Hobson, *The Evolution of Modern Capitalism* (London, Allen and Unwin, 1928), pp. 1–29. For a Marxist account *see* Karl Marx, *Capital: A Critical Analysis of Capitalist Production*, Vol. 3 (London, Lawrence and Wishart, 1894), pp. 617–20.
8. Hobson, *ibid.*, pp. 66–112; Marx, *ibid.*, Vol. 1 (1897), pp. 359–65.
9. Marx, *ibid.*, pp. 360–62.
10. Luddism basically referred to the act of smashing machines by displaced workers. For further details *see* Harold Perkins, *The Origins of Modern English Society*, 1780–1880 (London, Routledge & Kegan Paul, 1969), p. 81.
11. Marx, *The Communist Manifesto*, *op. cit.*, pp. 79–94.
12. E.J. Hobsbawm, *Industry and Empire* (Harmondsworth, Penguin, 1969), pp. 106–7.
13. *Ibid.*, pp. 106, 120–26, 179.
14. By 'surplus value' Marx meant the value that was added to any commodity over and above the cost of employing workers and paying them wages which the enterpreneur kept for himself as profit once the commodity was sold. For further elaboration *see* Marx, *op. cit.*, Vol. 1, Ch. 7.
15. Derek Fraser, *The Evolution of the British Welfare State* (London, Macmillan, 1975), pp. 115–34.
16. Marx, *The Communist Manifesto*, *op. cit.*, passim.
17. Marx, *Capital*, Vol.3, *op. cit.*, Part III.
18. V.I. Lenin, *Imperialism: The Highest Stage of Capitalism* (Moscow, Progress Publishers, 1968).
19. For an extended discussion of this and for a more elaborate and inclusive analysis of modern Marxist theories, on which this discussion relies, *see* Jessop, *op. cit.*, pp. 32–43.
20. J.A. Hobson, *Imperialism: A Study* (London), Allen and Unwin, 1961).
21. Lenin, *Imperialism*, *op. cit.*, pp. 73–74.
22. This distinction is taken from Stuart M. Hall, 'The Representative Interventionist State: The British Case' (Block IV, Unit I, Open University Course, *States and Societies*, 1983), pp. 21–78.
23. Jessop, *op. cit.*, pp. 32–59.

24. *Ibid.*, pp. 63–76.
25. *Ibid.*, pp. 78–115.
26. *Ibid.*, pp. 140–1.
27. *Ibid.*, pp. 117–25.
28. *Ibid.*, pp. 126–7.
29. Gramsci was an Italian communist who worked against the development of fascism in Italy in the 1920s and 1930s. He was imprisoned, and during that time he wrote what was to become his most famous book on Marxist theory: Antonio Gramsci, *Selections from the Prison Notebooks* (London, Lawrence and Wishart, 1971).
30. Jessop, *op. cit.*, pp. 142–50.
31. Ralph Miliband, *The State in Capitalist Society* (London, Weidenfeld and Nicolson, 1970).
32. *Ibid.*, pp. 53–5.
33. Ralph Miliband, 'The Capitalist State—Reply to Nicos Poulnatzas', *New Left Review*, Vol. 59 (1970), pp. 53–60.
34. Miliband, *The State in Capitalist Society*, *op. cit.*, pp. 179–264.
35. For the writings of this French structuralist *see* Louis Althusser, *Essays in Self Criticism* (London, New Left Books, 1976).
36. Nicos Poulantzas, 'The Problem of the Capitalist State', *New Left Review*, Vol. 58 (1969), pp. 67–78; 'The Capitalist State—A Reply to Miliband and Laclau', *New Left Review*, Vol. 95 (1976), pp. 63–83.
37. For a fuller discussion of this position *see* Jessop, *op. cit.*, pp. 153–207.
38. *Ibid.*, pp. 181–2.
39. *Ibid.*, pp. 183–207.
40. Isaac Balbus, 'The Concept of Interest in Pluralist and Marxist Analysis', *Politics and Society*, No. 1 (1971), pp. 151–77.
41. D. Willer and J. Willer, *Systematic Empiricism: Critique of a Pseudo-Science* (Englewood Cliffs NJ, Prentice Hall, 1973), passim.
42. This critique can be found in G.W.R. Smith, 'Must Radicals be Marxist?', *British Journal of Political Science*, Vol. II, No. 4 (October 1981), pp. 405–25.
43. Jessop, *op. cit.*, pp. 211–240.
44. *Ibid.*, pp. 63–76.
45. *Ibid.*, pp. 117–41.
46. *Ibid.*, pp. 153–4.
47. Jessop's approach is discussed in detail in the concluding chapter but can be found on pp. 211–59 of his book.
48. Jessop, *op. cit.*, p. 30.
49. *Ibid.*, p. 255.

# 4  Elite Approaches to Power

We have seen that theories in the social sciences often appear to have irreducible value-components which may render them fundamentally incompatible with one another. In spite of the increasing sophistication and complexity of many middle-range theories of social action or behaviour, these value-components may introduce confusing elements of ambiguity and illogicality, as well as weakening the empirical reference of the theories. A flight from positivism has been witnessed in recent years in the social sciences, and the argument appears to be now widely accepted that since knowledge is never the direct product of experience, all observation is to some extent determined by theory—a very old theme in a not-so-new guise. But it is worth noting that though the problems this produces for validification of theory are still not resolved in the social sciences, some researchers comfort themselves with the argument that different theories may agree at least on common working definitions, while a significant body of methodological writers has learnt to love the thorny creature by arguing (after Max Weber) that the theory- or value-component is a crucial positive factor in social-science explanation. It is not the case that social science theories, once their value-components or culture-boundedness have been revealed, are for that reason relegated to the local museum of the social sciences to become an object of quaint curiosity. On the contrary, few aspects of the social sciences show quite so clearly the importance of value in explanation as the capacity of social science theories, whether middle range or general, to return in modified guises after apparently destructive attack.

On the grounds of its ancient lineage and apparently perennial vigour, the 'grand survivor' of all general theories might be said to be elite theory. The term covers such a wide array of diverse explanations that the survival might have been bought at the cost of radical change to its empirical and normative content. In this chapter we analyse some of the common factors in this family of theories.

## THE FOUNDING FATHERS OF ELITE THEORY

Concern with the functioning of elites in politics is as old as the study of politics itself, and in its earliest forms relied on commonsense assumptions, which are still the starting-point of much research, about the inevitability of the appearance of select groups of dominant individuals wielding political power in any given society. Much political theorising was therefore restricted to explicitly normative, though often very sophisticated, comparisons of different forms of elite rule. In these forms of academic reflection on politics, empirical observations and explanations of the origins and survival of actual elites tended to take second place.

The development of an elite theory which dared to call itself such came about in the late nineteenth century as a reaction particularly against the radical egalitarian democratic ideals of Karl Marx and the Western European socialist movements. It was particularly strong in France, Italy and Germany, where it represented an attempt by the established liberal groups to counter the political and intellectual challenge of socialism. But it also represented an important stage in the development of the science of politics, since it relied heavily on positivistic assumptions both about the nature of societal development and about the capacity of human intelligence to achieve objectivity. Thus many elite theorists, particularly the early ones, do provide abstract explanations, models which differ in style and method from the scientific pretensions of the much later and much less theoretical pluralists. Elite theorists who dominated political studies as an academic discipline before 1939 enriched and advanced the study of politics even if their empirical assertions may now appear naïve or gross. The strength of their conviction both in the inevitability of elites and in the certainty of their own demonstration is both a limitation and on occasion a source of penetrating insights.

Often regarded, even if misleadingly, as the modern founder of elite theory, is Vilfredo Pareto, a writer of intense conviction and categorical inclination.[1] By profession an economist, Pareto builds up a complex model on the basis of the argument that just as material resources (in particular wealth) are distributed skewly in an economy, so are human resources (moral and intellectual abilities) in society. This apparently unexceptional contention is of central importance in the development of elitist theory, since Pareto uses it, in effect, both to attempt to provide a firm empirical and scientific basis for elitism and to explain the predominance of elites. The axiom underlying the contention is the far from unexceptional one that in the long-term wealth, power and moral and intellectual superiority are closely and positively linked together in the maintenance of stable elites. Pareto calls up an inevitably partial selection of historical evidence to support the view that elites are always present in any social system.

We will not linger over the fiction of popular representation . . . let us rather see what is the substance beneath the various forms of power in the governing class. Discounting exceptions, which are few and of short duration, there is everywhere a governing class, not large in membership, which maintains itself in power partly by force and partly by the consent of the governed.[2]

These assertions, which would of course be very difficult to demonstrate in a literal or historical sense, are justified as part of Pareto's general scheme of the equilibrium of social systems, which rests on a social-psychological basis: 'The principle of my sociology rests precisely upon separating logical from non-logical actions and in showing that in most men the second category is far larger than the former'.[3]

This division enunciated in 1897 stayed with Pareto in a variety of forms for the rest of his work, and is the source of his later arguments about the importance of 'residues', the common basic sentiments which determine human conduct and which are the basic unit of analysis. The power of the elite is held to derive from the greater intensity and quality of the sentiments or residues of its members which give its members the will and the ability to maintain their own rule either by force or by consent (but not usually both, according to Pareto). The methodology supporting Pareto's analysis is individualistic, resting on a view of human nature rather than directly on assumptions about society. Pareto's initial training was as a civil engineer; he always seems to have regarded the natural sciences as superior to the social sciences, and he consistently attempted to apply models of equilibria derived from mechanics to society. His vision of society was of a set of individuals subject to a wide variety of forces, some of which such as economic forces are relatively well understood and for others of which the science is 'extremely backward'. Pareto does not consider politics or government as subjects separate from sociology, and he has little to say about the concept of power as such. His particular ideas of politics and government are an application of his more general theory about the interaction of various forces on individuals. Political power is therefore seen as a result of greater capacity to manipulate residues or to impose coercion, as a quality inherent in the individual rather than as a characteristic of societal relationships.

Like many elite theorists who came after him, Pareto is peculiarly ambiguous about the concept 'governing elite', which is often taken to be his most important contribution to sociology. For Pareto himself, as we have seen, it was an inevitable conclusion of his general reasoning rather than a central explanatory concept. The concept of 'elite' derives from the notion of inequality of distribution of 'qualities, good or bad as may be, which guarantee power'.[4] Again like many who followed him, Pareto uses the term 'governing elite' sometimes to mean those who actually do govern and sometimes to mean those who are most qualified to govern. Pareto also argues that in practice the distinction between elite and non-elite is blurred and that within the elite a governing and a non-governing group can be discerned. Sometimes, particularly in his later writings, Pareto refers to the governing class or governing classes. Granted his contention that in the long-term or ideal equilibrium, wealth and power are inevitably associated with one another, it is coherent with his general model that he reduces class analysis to elite analysis, but again this is a problem which recurs in later elitists in more potent form.

The control which the elite exercises is ensured by their moral and material superiority, and the distinction between the elite and the powerless majority results from this. Pareto's economic theory began with free competition, and his theory of society similarly seems to argue that in ideal conditions of free competition between elites the individuals in the elite groups will be slowly but continually replaced by the free circulation of elites. The mechanisms by which elites maintain their rule is a matter of great interest to Pareto, and he discusses in some detail how the differing kinds of elite (predominantly those relying on force or consent) interact and replace one another. This leads to a famous metaphor which comprises for many among the non-political the sole sliver of political theory of which they acknowledge possession, namely Pareto's distinction between 'lions' and 'foxes' in ruling elites:

> A small group of citizens, if prepared to use violence, can impose its will on governing circles which are unwilling to meet violence with equal violence . . . If the authorities refrain from using force because they think it wiser to use other means, the effect is often as follows: . . . to prevent or resist violence, the governing class may use guile, cunning, fraud and corruption—in short, government passes from the lions to the foxes.[5]

These two types are directly associated by Pareto with one or other of the two main types of 'residue' or basic sentiment—Class 1, that of combination, predominant in the 'foxes', and Class 2, that of persistence of aggregates, predominant in the 'lions'. The cycle of rise to power and decay of elites is held by Pareto to be inevitable and is explained by the alteration in elites of the proportions of these residues, both of which are necessary for the maintenance of rule. The masses are usually characterised by Class 2 residues, which the governing elite has to be able to manipulate for its own purposes. The failure properly to deal with troublesome residues among the masses, such as by allowing circulation of elites or by meting out violence where appropriate, may lead to the growth of 'Paretian tension' in the masses, civil unrest, revolution and ultimately the entire replacement of the decadent elite by a new governing elite. The problem of how the several self-seeking individuals may combine to form an elite group is one of many loose ends in Pareto's writings.

Another element of Pareto's attack on classical democratic theory is in his contention that the governing elites, whether characterised by the residue of combinations or by the residue of persistence of aggregates, are motivated not by morality or reason but by these common basic sentiments which are in themselves morally unspecific and illogical. Pareto is clear that political activity is not necessarily a moralising activity; on the contrary, the governing elite has to be able and willing to use violence, corruption, guile and deceit to ensure public order, national independence and social conditions for the growth of national prosperity. His perspective is therefore utilitarian, in a broad sense. He also seems to go further than this and sets the pattern for future elite theorists in distinguishing between maximum utility *for* a community and maximum utility *of* a community. The former is made up of the utilities of the various classes or groups in society, while the latter is the utility of the community as such, discussed by Pareto in terms of maximisation of national military and political power.[6]

Pareto is in no doubt that the two types of utility, for and of a community, do not necessarily coincide. Though their decline is inevitable, and must usher in a period of unrest for the community, the maintenance of their own power adds of course directly to the utility of the governing elite and is a necessary condition for the order and stability of the community. The maximum utility of a community may often involve, says Pareto, 'a sacrifice for the subject classes'[7] though it also entails an increase in the utility of the governing elites. Hence the need for non-logical factors to influence the subject classes so that they will allow themselves to neglect their own utility and pursue what is in the interest of the governing elite and therefore of the community as a whole. As an economist, Pareto was well aware of the further dimension to social phenomena which the concept of interest introduces, and he acknowledges its significance without, however, dealing with it in great detail in his sociological work. When he is criticised by later elite theorists such as Suzanne Keller for neglecting the relationship of elites to the moral order of society, or by Marxists for failing to analyse the specific material interests involved in the maintenance of their own power by elites, both these two gaps in his theory are at least in part due to the disproportionate attention given to non-logical factors, such as residues, to the detriment of factors, such as interest, associated with rationality or logic. But the questions on which he focused attention—in particular, the permanence of a restricted group of personnel in power, and the tendency of this not to be related directly and specifically to economic structure—remain a central part of modern critiques of Marxist analysis.

It might be argued that other missing concepts in Pareto's elite analysis are those of 'ideology' and 'organisation'. The concept of 'ideology', though not made clear, is in fact of crucial significance in Pareto's discussion of how elites maintain themselves in power. The independent status ascribed to this concept by elite theorists, as opposed to the reflective and subordinate quality it has in late Marx and early Marxism, is an important characteristic of elite theory. The idea of autonomous organisation of elites is similarly important and contrasts with the class-determined power analysis of Marxism. Organisation of elites is not a significant feature of Pareto's analysis, but is of central importance in the elite analysis of Pareto's contemporary Gaetano Mosca.

Mosca, like Pareto, had at one stage of his writing career some sympathy for the socialist parties of the period, and like Pareto he is more remembered for his argument that socialists should be seen as dangerous purveyors of an illusory hope of democratic participation. Also like Pareto, he saw positivist science as a means of combating the socialist illusion. Mosca uses the term 'ruling class' to denote the permanent group of organised rulers in society, but his use of the term 'class' introduces an element of confusion in that his 'ruling class' is very different in its functions and internal characteristics from those of the Marxist usage. The control exercised by Mosca's 'ruling class' is held to be assured by the organisational capacity of the ruling minority: this is the basis of their power and the characteristic that best distinguishes them from the disorganised and powerless majority.[8]

Within the disorganised majority, however, there occur random interests and forces, the result both of human volition, of social pressures and of economic developments. The capacity of the ruling class to adapt to these haphazard destabilising phenomena is another essential element in their control and is another way in which the rational long-term approach of the elite contrasts with the more short-term sporadic characteristics of the majority. But the emergence of new interests, capacities and forces within the majority provides dynamism in the political system and stimulates the circulation of elites from the majority to the ruling class, and vice versa, whether as individuals, as groups or as entire elites. Mosca, like Pareto, is concerned to demolish democratic illusions about the altruism of the elite, but he recognises a positive dynamic relationship between rulers and ruled, and implies that the elite has an ideological function in that it expresses in a coherent rationalising way the moral unity of society through the rule of law. This is one way in which the stark anti-democratic arguments of Pareto are modified to allow for a more consensual perspective. Similarly, Mosca develops the concept of a political class, made up of organised minorities who occupy an intermediary position between the ruling class and the majority, which is clearly a precursor both of the functional elites of Keller and Aron and of the pluralistic elites who make up Dahl's polyarchy.[9]

There are important developments on Pareto's analysis in that Mosca identifies in a more concrete and specific manner how it is that elites arise, maintain themselves in power and are replaced. But this greater specificity carries with it a price in terms of relevance and verifiability. Pareto has a very broad usage of the term 'elite'—the minority who rule—such that his concept has a plausibility and, superficially at least, some claims to general application, even if the empirical reference is distant. This definition suits the highly abstract nature of Pareto's model very well. Mosca is less abstract, more specific, and his usage is appropriately more narrow. It therefore comes up against the problem that the inevitability of Mosca's specific type of elite is less immediately plausible and more easily disproved. This vulnerability was readily seized on by critics of elite theory, in particular by Harold Lasswell in its application to the United States and by J.H. Meisel in a more general sense.[10]

Meisel's criticism centres on the notion that the ruling elite is claimed to be a class; this is already an important point in Pareto's theory, and with Mosca the flaw becomes a fatal one, for he founds the power of the elite precisely on their greater organisational capacity, with necessary implications for their internal characteristics. It is therefore possible to operationalise Mosca's definition and to provide counterfactuals in a way which was not possible with Pareto. Meisel identifies three functional characteristics which Mosca's elite has to have—group consciousness, coherence and conspiracy. This can be expanded to provide a relatively clear theoretical conformation for an elite which might fit Mosca's model. Such an elite should, in these terms, be able to maintain itself in power by means of its organisational capacity, its ability to adapt to new forces and its dynamic positive relationship with the moral unity of society expressed through the rule of law.

A salient characteristic of the internal structure of the elite is that it is rational, in the sense that it is structured so as to achieve in a purposeful and conscious manner the objectives of the elite as a whole. This demands, among other things, that the group should share opinions and attitudes on issues that specify those objectives. The argument here is not that the group shares a common material objective interest which unites them, though they may well do so; such an argument, if framed in a strict manner, might take elite theorists perilously close to Marxist positions, in which the material interests related to the appropriate mode of production specify the class. Elite theorists have tended to concentrate not on the material interests but on a common ideology, whether broadly or narrowly defined. From propositions expressing arguments of this nature it is a relatively short step to the notion that a shared ideology, which is usually regarded as a product of social forces, is the inevitable result of common social origins, education and recruitment processes. Wright Mills took this to its logical conclusions in assuming that to demonstrate the existence of an elite it was not necessary to prove the existence of group consciousness but rather to show, among other things, that members of the supposed elite share a common social background, from which the group consciousness and shared objectives then follow.[11] In the morass of detail Mills brings forward to describe his 'power elite', it is easy to ignore this fundamental assumption which precedes his empirical work: 'In so far as the power elite is composed of men of similar origin and education, in so far as their careers and their styles of life are similar, there are psychological and social bases for their unity, resting upon the fact that they are of similar social type and leading to the fact of their easy intermingling'.[12] A precursor of this line of reasoning is Max Weber, for whom the shared ideal and material interests of groups are primary analytical components. But as Weber is more concerned with explaining the meaning of social action than with analysis of political power (though he is also interested in power), his concept of 'elite' is altogether broader, more analytical and more flexible than either Wright Mills's or Mosca's.

To return to the internal structure of Mosca's elite, it must also be emphasised that this organised elite should not only share attitudes on significant issues but should also be aware of doing so, otherwise they cannot properly manage the affairs of state in a responsible and decisive manner. Mosca, like many other positivists in politics, is a moraliser, a sceptic about the human condition who seeks salvation in technical expertise and the liberal circulation of talents. Though the elite may have to use 'political formulae' (Mosca's term) to preserve popular illusions about their rule, they must nevertheless be clear-sighted and purposeful about themselves and their own capacities and, of course, about their own membership of a group holding power and united in this way. From Wright Mills's position that one does not need to demonstrate directly the existence of the shared ideology

and shared objectives, it might also be argued that the
corollary is also unnecessary; that is, that the members'
awareness of the shared ideology is not a necessary
condition either. In plain terms this means that one may be
unwittingly a member of an elite group, on Wright Mills's
argument. Since this effectively precludes the existence of
internal organisation as a source of elite power, this line of
explanation has to find other such sources and other unifying
characteristics. In Wright Mills's case, the power elite
appears to be united by its hold on power (derived largely
from institutional office and property rights) and by a variety
of common social characteristics. Therefore one would have
to say either that the power elite is a mere statistical
phenomenon, a category, an aggregate of disparate individuals who happen to share some socially relevant resources, or that it is united by its objective interest. In the
first case, elitism does not provide an explanation, being
merely a loose term to describe a social category about
which other features rather than the elite characteristic
provide what explanation there is; in the second case, the
power elite looks remarkably like a social class, and elite
explanation has come back full circle to its point of
departure.

Thus we see that in the narrow sense of the term 'elite', as
used by Mosca, group consciousness entailing a sharing of
attitudes towards relevant issues, and an awareness of so
doing, is a necessary characteristic of the elite. Meisel's
second functional characteristic is coherence, which is rather
more straightforward. If a group wittingly shares an attitude
over a relevant issue but does so only for a limited period of
time before falling into disarray, it would be difficult to refer
to the group as an elite in any meaningful sense since the
outcomes would be insignificant. A group is coherent in so
far as it has a certain continuity in its consciousness, its
organisation and its action; but its coherence also implies
that its members do actually support one another in practical
ways that are consistent with the objectives of the group.
The coherence is therefore not only a coherence over time
but also a consistency or cohesion in action.

Finally, Meisel argues, the elite, in Mosca's sense of the

term, must exhibit the last of the three Cs—conspiracy. This does not mean that the group is clandestine but rather that it has other characteristics of a conspiracy; in particular, common purpose and internal communication on significant issues. Without internal means of communication the group cannot be united in its performance, and without the common objective the group lacks the rationality and purposive control that would unite the actions of the elite in its efforts to establish, maintain and strengthen its own power. 'Conspiracy' is crucial to organisational capacity of the elite; without it the group's consciousness and coherence are ineffective and directionless. Each of these three features is essential to the narrow sense of 'elite', and Meisel's schema, deceptively simple in appearance, in fact constitutes a problem for elitist theory. Two at least of the features—consciousness and conspiracy—are difficult to operationalise and rarely demonstrated satisfactorily by empirical means; direct empirical evidence for common objectives and awareness of group consciousness is not easy to envisage, because of the nature of the referents, and it is not surprising therefore that elite theorists such as Wright Mills have tended to use their sociological imagination to provide a plausible construct of indirect evidential demonstration.

## MODERN ELITE THEORISTS

Thus the narrow strict sense of elite, though sometimes used misleadingly as if it had been demonstrated satisfactorily, is rarely applied consistently throughout an argument in modern elite theory. The term is now used more commonly in a broad sense in which it connotes a looser grouping of individuals, each exercising power and united by one or more of a number of features such as wealth, social origins or pre-eminence in achievement in a particular field. Though such groups are considered by writers such as Mannheim and Keller to have central roles in organised society, their unity as elites is not usually emphasised and neither is their internal communication or common purpose.

Modern elite theorists are more concerned to analyse the role played by elites in society than to use their internal characteristics as unified elites to explain their predominance. The predominance is assumed to follow in a Paretian manner from inequality in the distribution of the relevant power-related resources. So Keller states that elites are 'fundamental features of organised social life'.[13] As Meisel observes correctly, merely to state that the number of those who hold power in any given society is fewer than those who do not, is to state a truism which has rarely been sensibly denied, but which explains little.[14] Elitism has to mean more than this—even in its modern, broader sense—for it to be of analytical use, so modern elite theory has tended to argue for a plurality of elites which may interact or compete in a variety of ways. Few elitists now hold to the notion of a single dominant elite effectively exercising or directing the exercise of all important functions, and few now use the term 'elite' as the all-embracing explanatory concept which it is for the classical theorists.

The transition from classical elite theory to modern variants of elitism and to its mutant offshoot pluralism is best illustrated by reference to the work of Joseph Schumpeter, whose most important contribution to modern political theory is to provide the template for many theoretical efforts to reconcile the 'fundamental fact' of elitism with democratic theory. This is not the principle aim of *Capitalism Socialism and Democracy* (written in 1942),[15] but it is the longest-lasting element of that work, which actually Schumpeter wrote to demonstrate the inevitable and regrettable emergence of socialism (as he defined it) after the Second World War. 'But History sometimes indulges in jokes of questionable taste', the last sentence of the book, captures the sceptical Paretian 'Don't say I didn't tell you so' flavour of Schumpeter's analysis.[16]

Schumpeter's main substantive target is what he regards as the nonsensical idea of classical democratic theory that the people can exercise a rational choice on individual questions and can give effect to this by choosing representatives. In typical elitist manner Schumpeter describes these notions as both unrealistic and dangerous; but a major difference from classical elite theorists is that Schumpeter wants to redefine democracy so as to preserve some recognition of the fact of popular participation and to take account of the inevitably limited nature of this participation. Such a definition should enable us to provide fresh, more realistic descriptions of functioning democracies. Schumpeter produces at least two definitions, closely similar in spirit to one another: 'Democracy means only that the people have the opportunity of accepting or refusing the men who are to rule them'.[17] Schumpeter immediately qualifies this by observing that free competition among would-be leaders for the vote of the electorate is the democratic method of exercising this choice, though of course there may be other non-democratic ways of accepting or refusing. Thus we arrive, via the epithet 'Democracy is the rule of the politician' to a complete formal definition: 'The democratic method is that institutional arrangement for arriving at political decisions in which individuals acquire the power to decide by means of a competitive struggle for the people's vote'.[18]

This definition, according to Schumpeter, is a summary or basis of a revised theory of democracy which 'is much truer to life and at the same time salvages much of what the sponsors of democratic method really mean by this term'.[19] Schumpeter builds up a definition of the modern political system in the West, which he claims 'to try out on some of the more important features of the structure and working of the political engine in democratic countries'.[20] So, though Schumpeter's claim to be able to predict the future course of capitalism is certainly ambitious and extremely controversial, the route by which he reaches his prediction is marked by rather more modest and specific conclusions. Schumpeter is still prone to lapses into Paretian historical generalisation, but on the whole his methodological self-consciousness, though unobtrusive, ensures a constant and intellectually stimulating interaction between criticism and historical detail, between definition and reality. His implicit model of 'the political engine' is a complex one, containing leaders, their agents (the parties), sectoral interests, group volitions and an amorphous public opinion. It should be noted, however, that already with Schumpeter we have moved away from models based on the distinctiveness of the elite characteristic as an explanatory factor, to a lower-level operation which explicitly refers to realistic definitions rather than to explanations, and in which the model, such as it is, looks remarkably like a composite description of liberal democracy. Such explanation as there is tends to rely on 'competition' as the major factor rather than on the elitism.

According to Schumpeter, his definition improves on classical democratic theory in a variety of ways. First, 'the Common Good' is held to be an illusory concept, which in practice is rarely used to refer to any aim that can fairly be called 'common' and which might not even refer to a 'good' at all; pursuit of 'the Common Good' is therefore not useful as an identifying objective of democracy, and Schumpeter prefers to identify democracy not by its objectives but as a method. The particular method associated with democracy is electoral competition. Second, the revised theory of democracy in this version includes 'the vital fact of leadership', by which Schumpeter means mainly competing individual leaders who use elite groups to manipulate or, as he puts it, to manufacture the collective will. The leaders are important also because they are an essential factor in making effective political forces in this way out of more general group interests, referred to by Schumpeter as 'group-wise volitions'. Schumpeter also recognises that individual freedom is not an absolute good—it is obviously important for the proper exercise of competition, but the stability of procedures necessarily limits it. Unlike Weber, therefore, who argues that in advanced industrialised societies representative democracy is for a variety of reasons the best available method by which to recruit political leaders,[21] Schumpeter has little interest in recommending political participation for any reason. He is concerned rather to redefine democracy so that the crucial role of elites (broadly understood) is recognised. Whether or not his redefinition of democracy salvages what classical theorists meant by 'democracy' is one of the points on which his work has been most criticised. Democratic theory as an ideal construct may recognise the existence of elites in real polities which are to be explained; a democratic theory which accepts the existence of elites, describes democracy as a set of institutions and builds them into its descriptions as a central restraining factor, is arguably not in the democratic school and might not even be properly called theory.

In general, elitism in analyses of this kind tends to explain elite power through both the social function of the group, the success of the group in carrying out that function and the particular contingent demands of the society for that function. Within this framework, differentiation can be made between strategic elites, which may have power over society as a whole, and segmental elites (the terms are Keller's), which are predominant or which vie for predominance in restricted fields. What remains from classical elite theory is the theme of the powerlessness of the masses and the rational unifying capacities of the minority groups, but modern elite theorists, perhaps surprisingly, are more concerned than their precursors to argue that the elites function not only in their own interest but also in the interests of society as a whole—an inevitable concomitant of the functional elitism now prevalent.

## ELITE THEORISTS AND COMMUNITY POWER STUDIES

As we discussed in Chapter 1, it was after the Second World War that the behavioural revolution which had begun in the inter-war period swept the Faculties of Social Science, and the reaction to Schumpeter's work was one of the instrumental features in the attempt by the pluralist researchers to reassert the enduring values of the American way of politics in a robust and authoritative manner. Early empirical researchers in the United States such as Berelson produced results which startled and dismayed academics wedded to the conventional normative assumptions about the nature of American democracy. Nowhere was this more strongly felt than in community power studies, and it was in this field that the pluralists most persistently attempted to combine empirical methods with assumptions which, if they were not entirely Madisonian, at least fitted prevailing norms rather better than the emerging stark elitism. The pluralist approach in the community power debate, it is argued in Chaper 5, is only the most visible and coherent strand of an approach which has much wider ramifications, some of which appear in the case studies later.

Even on what became its own home ground, however, the pluralist approach was not unchallenged, nor of course was it the first chronologically. Elite studies preserved for some time their emphasis on stability and survival of political rule rather than on the visible exercise of power. This difference of perspective and lack of immediate concern with definitions of power and with empiricist rigour result in research methods which may appear to be more approximate in their conclusions than are the pluralists, at least as far as the distribution of power is concerned. Floyd Hunter, in one of the classical community power studies, states his assumptions about power clearly in the form of postulates:

1.  Power involves relationships between individuals and groups, both controlled and controlling . . .
2.  Power is structured socially, in the United States, into a dual relationship between governmental and economic authorities on national state and local levels . . .
3.  Power is a relatively constant factor in social relationships with policies as variables . . .
4.  Power of the individual must be structured into associational clique or institutional patterns to be effective . . .

These postulates seem to the author to be self-evident propositions.[22]

In this case, though the term 'power' is 'used to describe acts',[23] there are important areas outside the realms of 'acts' which are also associated with power but about which there is less certainty. These are referred to by Hunter as 'residual categories', and they cover historical aspects of power, psychological motivations and value considerations. Methods of this kind necessarily begin by assuming that there is something mysterious, arcane or difficult about power which makes it ultimately an elusive concept. A commonsense method of finding out about elites in politics might be to look at formal membership of political institutions and of social or economic organisations known to be active in politics. Much political research still relies on this approach to explain how government is maintained, but immediate problems that present themselves are that it cannot be assumed either that the institutions or organisations themselves do really exercise power or that their nominal members are all equally active in such exercise of power as there is. The method used by Hunter, often referred to as the reputational method, is also one that has come to be associated typically with elitist studies. This method begins with four specific and usually implicit assumptions:[24]

1. Power is to be found in individuals in the community which is to be studied.
2. Within the community there will be identifiable groups which have connections with powerful individuals.
3. The recognised or nominal leaders of such groups may be relied on to produce an initial list of individuals who are presumed to have power in community affairs (leaders).
4. These 'leaders' may be assumed to be aware of each other's power and reliably to report it.

By a process of mutual choice, referral back and elimination a number of names is arrived at of individuals who by reputation are assumed by those who should know to have power in the community. One important objection made against this method is that even at its best it provides evidence not of the actual exercise of power but of potential power, and presumed potential power at that. However, by asking members of the elite group questions such as 'How many members of the group have you worked with on committees?', and 'How well do you know each member of the group?' and 'Whose support would be necessary for a major project to get substantial community backing?', some elite studies of community power have revealed remarkable consensuses about the existence of elite groups, and about their power, and have supported such findings with demonstrations of the interaction of members of the supposed elite groups. Though ultimately the methodological bases of such findings must induce caution in the researcher, nevertheless the findings may lead to plausible conclusions about the workings of elite groups in local communities, in particular about the economic base of the members and the support given to their power by specific cultural norms.

Apart from the other limitations referred to here, such community power studies also suffer from the constraint imposed by the non-applicability of reputational methods to national politics. Where highly decentralised systems of local government (such as in the United States) are not found, the methods are limited in their applicability even in the field of local government, since they assume a significant degree of autonomy on the part of the specific communities within which power is exercised.

However, between Floyd Hunter and later elitists there is a wide gulf, which is fashioned by the community power debate and which has put Hunter's elaborate methods and those of others like the Lynds[25] into semi-retirement. The responsibility for this lies very largely with the emergence of pluralism, after which elite studies would never quite be the same.

Pluralism we discuss separately in Chapter 5, but before concluding this chapter we must briefly refer to the subsequent history of elitism. There is now a clear distinction between two strands of modern elite theory. Mainstream elitism is now represented by writers such as Keller and Aron, as we discussed earlier; this refers mainly to the interactions and functions of ruling and strategic elites, and though it differs in emphasis from earlier writings, these writers appear to have normative assumptions not radically removed from those of the classical elite theorists. The second strand of elite theory, sometimes referred to as 'neo-elitism', is highly critical both of traditional elite theorists and of the pluralist school, which it regards essentially as a revision of democratic theory. This neoelitism took issue with pluralism initially in reaction to the voting studies of Berelson and others, but the major battleground was the community power debate, where the revision of democratic theory had practical implications for research methods and theoretical implications for the definitions of power.

The notion of power referred to here is that which Lukes

referred to as the second dimension of power (see Ch. 2). Usually associated with the work of Bachrach and Baratz,[26] this line of argument rejects both the earlier reputational approach to community power, and also pluralist methods based on observation of decisions on key issues. There are many criticisms made of pluralism by writers who object to its normative implications, and some of these, as we argue in Chapter 5, give a distinctly strawlike quality to their description of their target. A good example of a pluralist straw man can be found in Jack L. Walker's attempted broadside, in which he constructs a version of pluralism which patently is unattributable to any individual writer.[27] In reply, Robert Dahl had no difficulty making it seem that Walker was pinning arguments to him and to others in an arbitrary manner,[28] but in the process some of Walker's stronger points were diminished—in particular the argument that 'political scientists . . . have overlooked the importance of broadly-based social movements, arising from the public at large, as powerful agents of innovation and change'.[29] More sophisticated and telling critiques of pluralist theories were provided by Duncan and Lukes[30] and by Bachrach and Baratz. Though they adopt the confusing and misleading distinction between normative theory and empirical theory, Duncan and Lukes argue cogently against Dahl that classical democratic theory is not invalidated by modern sociological findings since 'their ideals can logically contrast with facts without being invalidated by empirical research, which does not in any *obvious* way call for their general revision'.[31] Duncan and Lukes therefore have a much broader view of the function of theory than does Dahl, for whom the separation of fact and value appears an obvious and readily attainable objective. Hence Dahl argues against Walker that 'he insists upon interpreting as if they were normative or deontological certain writings that were mainly if not wholly intended to set out descriptive empirical theories'.[32] Other criticisms of pluralist democratic theory rely less on episte-mological differences and more on inconsistencies and omissions. Pluralist community power methods are held to assume a state of equilibrium in the society under investigation and, finding apathy and low participation, make a functional connection; but no specification is made by pluralist writers of what this balance, harmony or equilibrium consists of; though other elements of the model may be carefully defined and rigorously quantitied, the conditions within which the equilibrium operates are generally neglected. Hence, for example, there is little indication of precisely how much dissent or cleavage will throw the system out of balance.

The arguments of so-called radical democrats like Bachrach and Baratz had rather more direct impact than did disagreement over the nature of theory, partly because they shared some important ground with the pluralists. An immediate and obvious problem with pluralists' methods is that in the effort to achieve falsifiability, only major visible issues reaching decisional status are used, yet of course it is possible for pre-decisional power to be used to keep grievances from becoming observable issues. Dahl tends to view elites as a species of potential conspiracy against the public interest; this is one reason why he rejects the accusation that he himself is a surreptitious elitist and why he prefers to refer to 'polyarchy'. More analytically, pluralist methods might in theory uncover conspiracy by an elite by investigating observable decisions, and the fact that in various studies they did not find evidence of narrow conspiratorial elites led pluralist community power researchers to conclude that a more flexible competitive and open system prevailed. Bachrach and Baratz argue that pluralists ignore or neglect that 'face of power' which consists in confining the scope of decision-making to safe issues; they go on to make the less convincing point that an elite may exist without actually being aware of its own dominance since this may never have been challenged.[33] As we have seen, it is difficult to know in what sense one may talk of an unselfconscious elite, and Bachrach and Baratz's more limited point is the more cogent. What this does point to is the need for community power studies which look at what they describe as real and important issues—those in which the established values are challenged.

While Bachrach and Baratz must be recognised to have identified a major problem in pluralism, there are serious limitations to their analysis. Most obviously, despite their efforts to provide an analytical framework for the observation of this second face of power, no fully successful effort has yet been made to operationalise their analysis. They assert that though their 'non decision-making situation' ('preventing certain grievances from developing into full-fledged issues')[34] is not observable, being a non-event, nevertheless, the non-decision-making process is indeed observable since it consists of the mobilisation of bias around a latent issue, both of which are discernible. In practice the difficulty of rigorous identification of a latent issue and the looseness of the concept 'mobilisation of bias' have made this an unrewarding line of enquiry. In particular, indirect attempts to uncover the phenomenon have been made by Crenson and others, but these have tended to founder on the difficulties of separating the notion of a 'latent issue', for which one relies on observation of declared but otherwise undeveloped wishes of significant actors, from that of 'real interests', which introduces altogether different problems of method, and of course takes one completely out of the field of behaviourism.

## STRENGTHS AND WEAKNESSES OF ELITE THEORIES

In principle, elite theory is still opposed to class analysis at several different levels, arguing as it does that the interests and power of elites are not based on economic factors and that elite differentiation is inevitable even under socialism. Broadly speaking, elite analysis directs the researcher's attention towards socio-political determination as opposed to economic determination. Though associated to a certain extent with the advent of behaviourism in the study of politics (because of its positivist claims to scientific status), elitism actually lends itself easily either to a concentration on institutional or organisational identifications of power, as in the traditional study of politics, or to a concern with socio-political cleavages and integrative factors more associated with political sociology than with political science.

These differences of orientation are what serve to separate elitism from pluralism, rather than a mere argument over numbers in the distribution of power. Since elitists tend to begin by assuming that power is located within the minority, they offer a different perspective to that of behaviorists who begin by questioning the term 'power'. 'Power' is not central to orthodox elite analysis; structures, constraints, functions and ideology all may play their part in elite theories, but 'power' (except in self-confessed revisionists of pluralism like Presthus and Bachrach), if not quite the grand absentee, is understood as given in a particular way. The often-repeated criticism made of elite and traditional theorists that they assume what they should be proving—namely the distribution of power—may from this perspective be seen to miss the point of elite analysis, since it is not typically concerned with the question of whether the minority that exercises power is a significant proportion of the entire population. As we shall discuss in the next chaper, this is a question that has concerned pluralists much more. What concerns traditional elitists is not so much 'Who governs?' as 'How is government maintained?'.

Neo-elitists such as Bachrach and Wright share with traditional elite theoreticians a concern to demonstrate the real persistence of elites in modern society. But in other ways they differ very strongly. Neo-elitists have contradictory normative beliefs to those of the traditionalists, arguing for the persistent significance of classical democratic ideals, and in this sense could be said to have turned traditional elitism on its head. The strength of neo-elitism is best seen against the background of pluralism; as a critique of pluralism it introduces the concept of non-decision-making and points up the failure of pluralist methods to define properly what is meant by the term 'key issues'. Analysis of political power in terms of 'agenda-setting', with distinctions between 'institutional' and 'systemic' agendas, derives largely from the non-decision-making approach and is the nearest neo-elitism has come to producing general models of the kind favoured by the traditional elitists.

Elitism, either in its traditional or in its recent form, appears profoundly critical of the pretensions of modern liberal democracy, though in different ways in each case. Many elite writers such as Burnham and Weblen have taken up the issue of technological advance and argued that the increasing division of labour and sophistication of the practical instruments of government are associated not with greater participation by the newly enfranchised masses but with concentration of political power in the hands of those who control the technological resources. In other words, it might be argued that wealth, whether inherited or earned, is not sufficient to give real power, and neither are the traditional status groups such as the clergy, the military and intellectuals able to command as before. The concern of elite theorists with the circulation of elites, their changeability and development, leads to the modern argument that the new elites are based on ability to exercise strategic control over the technologically sophisticated instruments of mass society, and as a consequence of the increasing diversity and rapidity of development of these means, elites are themselves increasingly unstable. But arguments of this nature, often plausible and just as often highly speculative, give some indication of the enduring characteristics of elite arguments that make such arguments readily comprehensible, and convincing in a synthetic manner, but lacking either the pretensions to analytic rigour of behavioristic pluralism or the steam-roller systematic explanations of Marxism. Elitism will survive because of its suggestiveness, its plausibility and its capacity for generating explanatory insights; whether it will be able to provide exhaustive convincing theories is another matter. It was in part dissatisfaction with the methods of elite theories as well as with its conclusions that led to the development of pluralism in political science; this we now go on to consider.

## NOTES

1. The best approach to Pareto's work for English speakers is through the selection contained in V. Pareto, *Sociological Writings*, selected and introduced by S.E. Finer (London, Pall Mall Press, 1966).
2. Pareto, *op. cit.*, pp. 266–7.

3. *Ibid.*, p. 20.
4. *Ibid.*, p. 131.
5. *Ibid.*, p. 257.
6. *Ibid.*, p. 253–5.
7. *Ibid.*, p. 255.
8. *See*, in particular, G. Mosca, *The Ruling Class*, ed. A. Livingston, (New York, McGraw Hill, 1939), pp. 50–3.
9. *See* S. Keller, *Beyond the Ruling Class: Strategic Elites in Modern Society* (New York, Random House, 1963); R. Aron, 'Social Structure and the Ruling Class', in *British Journal of Sociology*, Vol. 1, No. 1 (March 1950) pp. 1–17; *British Journal of Sociology*, Vol. 1, No. 2 (June 1950) pp. 126–44; R.A. Dahl, *Who Governs? Democracy and Power in an American City* (New Haven, Yale University Press, 1961).
10. H. Lasswell, 'Agenda for the Study of Political Elites', in D. Marvick, ed., *Political Decision-Makers* (New York, Free Press, 1961), pp. 264–88; and J.H. Meisel, *The Myth of the Ruling Class* (Ann Arbor, Michigan University Press, 1962); but *see also* J.H. Meisel, ed., *Pareto and Mosca* (New Jersey, Prentice-Hall 1965).
11. C. Wright Mills, *The Power Elite* (New York, Oxford University Press, 1956).
12. *Ibid.*, p. 19.
13. S. Keller, 'Elitism', pp. 26–9 in *International Encyclopaedia of the Social Science*, Vol. 5 (New York, Collier/McMillan, 1968).
14. In the Introduction to Meisel, *The Myth of the Ruling Class*, *op. cit.*
15. J. Schumpeter, *Capitalism, Socialism and Democracy* (London, George Allen and Unwin, 1943).
16. *Ibid.*, p. 375.
17. *Ibid.*, p. 285.
18. *Ibid.*, p. 269.
19. *Ibid.*
20. *Ibid.*, p. 273.
21. *See* 'Politics as a Vocation' in H.H. Gerth and C. Wright Mills, *From Max Weber: Essays in Sociology* (London, Routledge and Kegan Paul, 1970), pp. 77–128; also in D. Beetham, *Max Weber and the Theory of Modern Politics*, (London, George Allen and Unwin, 1974) pp. 95–118.
22. F. Hunter, *Community Power Structure* (Chapel Hill, University of North Carolina Press, 1953, p. 6
23. *Ibid.*, p. 2.
24. *Ibid.*, passim, and particularly 'Appendix—Methods of Study', pp. 262–71.
25. *See* H.M. Lynd and R.S. Lynd, *Middletown in Transition—A Study in Cultural Conflicts* (London, Constable, 1937).
26. P. Bachrach and M.S. Baratz, 'Decisions and Non-decisions: An Analytical Framework' in *American Political Science Review*, Vol. 57 (1963) pp. 632–42; Bachrach and Baratz, 'Two Faces of Power' in *American Political Science Review*, Vol. 56 (1962), pp. 947–52;

Bachrach *The Theory of Democratic Elitism: A Critique* (Boston, Little Brown and Co., 1967). *See also* S.W. Rousseas and J. Farganis, 'American Politics and the End of Ideology' in *British Journal of Sociology*, Vol. 14 (1963), pp. 347–60; C. Bay, 'Politics and Pseudo-politics' in *American Political Science Review*, Vol. 59 (1965), pp. 39–51; H. Kariel, *The Decline of American Pluralism* (Stanford, University of California Press, 1961); R. Presthus, *Men at the Top* (New York, Oxford University Press, 1964).

27. J.L. Walker, 'A Critique of the Elitist Theory of Democracy', in C.A. McCoy, and J. Playford, *Apolitical Politics: A critique of Behaviouralism* (New York, Crowell, 1967), pp. 199–219; first published in *American Political Science Review*, Vol. 60 (1966), pp. 285–95.

28. R.A. Dahl, 'Further Reflections on "Elitist Theory of Democracy" ' in *American Political Science Review*, Vol. 60, (June 1966), pp. 296–305; to which Walker replied in the same volume, 'A reply to "Further Reflections on 'The Elitist Theory of Democracy' " ', pp. 391–92.

29. Walker, *op. cit.*, (1967), p. 214.

30. G. Duncan and S. Lukes, 'The New Democracy' in McCoy and Playford, *op. cit.*, pp. 160–84; first published in *Political Studies*, Vol. 11 (1963), pp. 156–77.

31. *Ibid.*, (1967), p. 173. Emphasis in original.

32. Dahl, *op. cit.*, p. 298.

33. In Bachrach and Baratz, *op. cit.* (1962).

34. Bachrach and Baratz, *op. cit.* (1963), p. 641.

# 5 Pluralist Approaches to Power

At a relatively high level of abstraction it is simple to draw a distinction between pluralist, elitist and Marxist approaches to the distribution of political power. Marxist approaches argue that economic relations more or less determine who has political power and how this political power is exercised, with power being concentrated in the hands of the bourgeoisie. Elite theories argue that there is one class that dominates in a political system, although which class actually dominates is not necessarily determined by the economic system. Pluralist approaches argue, in contrast to Marxist approaches, that political power can and should be regarded as analytically distinct from economic power and that, in contrast to both elite and Marxist approaches, power is not concentrated in the hands of a single group, but relatively widely dispersed among a variety of groups and actors.

From some authors it may be assumed that pluralism represents an especially naive set of propositions about how political power is perfectly, or nearly perfectly, distributed within Western liberal democracies.[1] In this sense, pluralism has for some become something of an Aunt Sally, to be knocked down through juxtaposing the idealised equal distribution of power assumed in pluralist theory with the actual inequalities in the distribution of power found in Western liberal democracies.

Such a version of pluralism would assert that pluralists believe that all citizens have a chance to become politically active through individual and group action. The individual has his views represented in policy-making not only through the representative mechanism of elections but also through the participatory mechanism of group politics. Interest groups, such as those consisting of businessmen, trade unionists, citizens who promote the interests of the homeless or the mentally handicapped, may further the views and interests of citizens in policy areas which affect them. The process of decision-making is simply the outcome of conflicts between different groups, with governmental institutions acting simply as the arbiter between these conflicting groups or, at most, acting as merely one of these groups. No one group tends to dominate in this process of group interaction because of the plurality of political *resources*, referring to the diverse bases of group power. If a group does not have a lot of money, it may instead call upon public sympathy to sustain its views in the policy-making process. Furthermore, the electoral mechanism ensures that the government does not persistently decide in favour of one group above others since the overt bias in favour of one group will alienate the government from the rest and will lead to the government losing office come the next time it faces its electorate.

As one particularly crude characterisation of pluralism puts it:

In this widely accepted view [of pluralism], no one group always dominates to the exclusion of others. Interests such as industrialists and workers, businessmen and consumers, housewives and unionists, students and pensioners check and balance each other in the pursuit of their own ends. For pluralists, Government acts as 'honest broker': independent of any particular interest, the Government responds to pressures from different sides. The outcome of the policy process is an even gamble, all win some bets and lose others, in contrast to the elitists' view that the odds are stacked in favour of the house.[2]

The problem with such a characterisation of pluralism is that it bears little resemblance to what pluralists actually say pluralism means, and consequently it is hardly surprising that even the most cursory of empirical investigations can show such a naive version of pluralism is untenable as a description of the distribution of power in Western liberal democracies.

If pluralism is not adequately defined as this naive characterisation of the distribution of political power, what, then, is pluralism? The term 'pluralism' appears to have become something of a residual category applied to all non-Marxist and non-elitist studies of political phenomena.

As such it might characterise mainstream political science—the bulk of the contributions to the major political science journals, for example, could fall into this category. However, it is clearly unsatisfactory, if not impossible, to attempt to synthesise the explicit and implicit assumptions and methodologies of such a broad range of social science research, from studies of political development to policy studies and examinations of electoral behaviour, and offer this as the pluralist approach to political power. In this chapter we offer an interpretation of the main assumptions of pluralism which have implications for the study of power in governmental decision-making. This chapter sets out the debate surrounding pluralism as it emerged in the 1950s and 1960s in the context of the community power debate in the United States. This debate has wider implications for the study of political science since it emphasised major features of the process of governmental decision-making—the plurality of values of participants in policy-making, the plurality of actors involved, the emphasis upon perceptions rather than 'objective interests' and the fact that policy outcomes seldom reflect the values and preferences of one group. These features of pluralist approaches are explored in turn. Finally, the chapter points to some of the weaknesses of pluralist approaches to understanding the distribution of political power.

## THE COMMUNITY POWER DEBATE

The term 'pluralism' has, at least in empirical political science, become most closely associated with the study of power in American urban government and, in particular, with the community power debate of the 1950s and 1960s. Pluralism as a description of where power lies in American cities can best be understood in the context of the studies which it set out to criticise—elite theories of community power.[3] The most influential of the elite studies was Floyd Hunter's 1953 book on Atlanta Georgia, which asked those, such as journalists, group activists and businessmen, who might be expected to know how decisions really are made in the city, to name the most influential individuals within the community.[4] This method of locating those with power, the 'reputational method', was presumed to allow one to see behind the democratic facade of the formally democratic institutions of American government and locate those who really held political power. The study yielded a group of forty men who were the most powerful in Atlanta, and these were treated by Hunter as Atlanta's political elite. This elite group was dominated by representatives of the powerful commercial and industrial interests in the city.

Pluralism, in the context of the community power debate, can be regarded as an alternative description of the distribution of political power and as an alternative methodology for analysing the distribution of power. Pluralists, such as Dahl[5] and Polsby,[6] argued that the reputational approach was inadequate as a means of identifying the locus of political power. There were three interrelated problems with the reputational approach. First, as we have seen, the term 'power' is a complex one and requires cautious definition. This need for careful definition is ignored completely when one simply asks a panel of experts to name people with political power—one has not told them the criteria that they should use for judging whether an individual has power, and neither does one know whether the individuals have used even similar criteria for ascribing power to the individuals whose names they submit. Second, when one uses the reputational approach one is likely to derive a list of those with a *reputation* for power which might or might not be a justified one. Third, the particular reputational approach used by Hunter presupposed that which remained to be proven—that there is a group of forty people in whose hands power in Atlanta is concentrated—by devoting all his efforts to finding out the names of people who appear to belong to this elite.

In contrast to the reputational approach, Polsby argues that the pluralist approach is more rigorous and makes no such *a priori* assumptions about the distribution of power in urban political systems.[7] 'Power' is defined as an ability to influence policy outcomes (see Dahl's often quoted definition in Ch. 1) rather than simply as having a reputation for power. Consequently, the study of the distribution of power should be analysed by looking at actual decisions and finding out which person(s) or group(s) was (were) most responsible for shaping the final outcome of the decision-making process.

Pluralist approaches have stressed the need to look at actual decision-making. Consequently, Dahl's 1961 study of New Haven looked at decisions taken in three areas—education, electoral apportionment and urban development—to see who tended to dominate and why.[8] The conclusion to Dahl's study stressed that it was impossible to identify a single powerful elite which dominated policy-making in each of the three areas, as Hunter's elitist model had suggested. Decision-making tended to be a complex process which involved bargaining between a plurality of different actors, and even in each of the specific policy areas the resulting decisions could not simply be seen as the result of the preferences of one elite group or actor. In the context of the community power debate, a pluralist methodology implied analysis of observable decision-making processes, and the conclusion was that power and influence in American urban politics was far more widely distributed than the Hunter power-elite thesis suggested.

The community power debate has continued into the 1970s and 1980s with both elitists and pluralists refining their methods and theoretical arguments.[9] Since this chapter is concerned with describing what pluralism is, this is not the place to comment in detail upon the relative strengths and weaknesses of pluralism and the critiques of pluralism as it is debated in the American community power debate. The wider significance of the community power debate does not rest upon the fact that the conclusions of the community power studies can be applied directly, sometimes by the authors of community power studies themselves,[10] to other levels of government. Rather, its significance lies in the fact that the pluralist position in the community power debate represented a particularly coherent expression of a variety of strands within political science which were well established before Dahl or Polsby's involvement in the community power debate. Indeed, Dahl locates the questions that he poses in New Haven in the context of a tradition of inquiry dating back to de Tocqueville.[11] Moreover, these strands have persisted through to more recent studies of policy-making. What are these strands?

Marxist theories have tended to assume a link between economic and political power; whether this is a more (as with instrumental Marxist approaches) or less (as with structural Marxist approaches) direct link is debatable. The notion that there is a realm of public or political authority which can and should be separated from economic relationships is a pervasive one throughout Western political thought. Aristotle argued that the *polis* allowed free men to take public decisions, for the good of the citizens and not simply for the private material advantage of the most powerful.[12] Hobbes's distinction between the relationship between individuals in the state of nature and between individuals under a commonwealth suggests that political authority can be exercised independently of the relationships of power between men that result from physical, intellectual, economic and social inequalities.[13] Hegel, to take another example, distinguishes between the public authority of the state as distinct from the relationships that prevail in civil society.[14] Indeed, the theoretical and philosophical, if not the empirical, distinction between relationships of political authority and relationships to be found within the economy is so pervasive throughout Western political thought that it is one of the specific contributions of Marx to political thought that he denied the existence of this separation.

Modern theorists of power have maintained the principle that the bases of political power are not to be found within the economic sphere—at least not in the economic sphere alone. Dahl, for example, in *Who Governs?* argues that:

A list of resources in the American political system might include an individual's own time; access to money, credit and wealth; control over jobs; control over information; esteem and social standing; the possession of charisma, popularity, legitimacy, legality; and the rights pertaining to public office. The list might also include solidarity: the capacity of member of one segment of society to evoke support from others who identify him as like themselves because of similarities in occupation, social standing, religion, ethnic origin or racial stock. The list would also include the right to vote, intelligence, education and perhaps even one's energy level.[15]

This view reflects a widely shared one in pluralist political science that 'since power is a type of influence . . . a power holder may owe his power to his wealth, ability, reputation, popularity or, in general, favorable position with regard to any value'.[16]

The idea that political power can result from a variety of factors, in addition to economic wealth, can be found in many studies of policy-making in Western nations. The influence that local government units, for example, in the United States and Britain possess through the 'inter-governmental lobby' (i.e. through national pressure groups of local government and local government professionals)[17] rests upon their ability to provide central or federal government with valuable information, to mobilise legislators to support their cause and their position and expertise as major providers of welfare state services.[18]

Moreover, just as important as stressing the plurality of political resources, which form the basis for the exercise of power, pluralist approaches tend to stress the contingency of transforming the *potential* for political power offered by the possession of such resources into the *actual* exercise of power. It is not enough, for example, for a president or prime minister to be popular, or for an interest group to have money, status or a cohesive organisation; each must employ *strategies* to bring its influence to bear. In this sense, power is not something that individuals and groups do or do not have automatically through occupation of a particular social or economic position, rather it is something gained through the skilfull deployment of political resources in order to achieve particular objectives.

Neustadt's analysis of presidential power highlights the importance of the strategies employed by the president of the United States and the contingency of presidential influence.[19] As with other holders of potential power, the strategies open to presidents are limited through a variety of factors—the president is constrained through his formal constitutional powers, the degree of popularity he enjoys and the limitations imposed by relations with other countries, for example. Within such constraints, political power, the 'power to persuade', is based upon the president's formal authority as well as his prestige and legitimacy within the Washington community and the nation as a whole. Yet the strategies that the present pursues in his relationships with other political actors are crucial in defining his power: 'A President, himself, affects the flow of power from these sources, though whether they run freely or run dry he will never decide alone . . . Accordingly his choices of what he should say and do, and how and when, are his means to conserve and tap the sources of his power.[20] Similarly, Heclo and Wildavsky's classic study of the relationship between the Treasury and spending ministries in Britain highlights that the Treasury's ability to secure spending decisions that it wants is contingent to a large degree upon the strategies employed in bargaining with spending ministries (and vice versa).[21]

Power, then, in pluralist analyses, is not a simple property that is given to one group and denied to another on the basis of economic or social position. Economic and social position, of course, can be important bases of political power, yet they are not the only ones. Moreover, the link between economic and social position and political power is made even less direct by virtue of the proposition that strong political resources can coexist with weak political influence through the deployment of inappropriate strategies of influence.

## THE PLURALITY OF ACTORS IN THE POLICY-MAKING PROCESS

Like Marxist and elite theory, pluralist theory does not assume that those such as presidents, legislators or ministers, who occupy the formal positions of political authority, are necessarily those with political power. As the literature on interest groups suggests, those without formal political policy-making authority may be highly influential in policy-making, while those endowed with this authority have little power.[22] Where Marxists and elitists diverge from pluralist approaches is that they argue that the influence of outside pressures on government decision-making is limited to those exercised by specific economic or social classes. Pluralist approaches, on the other hand, stress that the types of pressures on government come from a wider array of different types of interests. While pluralist writers cannot be interpreted as suggesting that there is a perfect or even extensive distribution of political power through the mechanism of interest participation in government decision-making,[23] what pluralists do argue is that more groups are involved in making decisions than is suggested by Marxist and elitists, who claim that a particular class or group has a monopoly of influence.

The importance of a diverse body of interests in policy-making was highlighted by the work of Bentley and Truman on group theory. Bentley's group theory postulated that the study of politics was the study of the conflict between groups, although his work did not refer to organised interest groups only but to groups with shared views, interests or experiences.[24] This did not prevent his approach from becoming associated (with some justification) with a theory of interest groups.[25] Truman's work focused more explicitly upon organised groups, the increasing number and importance of which he regarded as a result of governmental growth:[26] the 'trend towards an increasing diversity of groups functionally attached to the institutions of government is a reflection of the characteristics and needs, to use a somewhat ambiguous term, of a complex society'.[27] Moreover, analysis of the actions of these complex groups is essential to an understanding of policy-making in government: 'The behaviors that constitute the process of government cannot be adequately understood apart from the groups, especially the organised and potential interest groups, which are operative at any point in time'.[28]

One example of the importance of the complex interaction between groups for an understanding of policy-making is shown in Heclo's study of 'issue networks' in Washington.[29] Heclo points to the rapid expansion of the number of groups and their representatives in Washington in the 1970s. Although interest-group representation is nothing new in Washington, the huge expansion in the 1970s is only 'a mere outgrowth of old tendencies . . . in the same sense that a 16-lane spaghetti interchange is the mere elaboration of a county crossroads'.[30] These groups have transformed the process of policy-making from rather closed networks of autonomous groups composed of members of the legislature, the executive and groups associated with the 'iron triangle' imagery[31] (referring to a stable set of relationships between a small number of powerful groups, federal agencies and Congressional committees) to a fluid set of 'issue networks', in which 'a large number of participants with quite variable degrees of mutual commitment . . . move in and out of the networks constantly'.[32] These networks are at the heart of policy-making in the United States and are even important in understanding how the US president makes appointments to senior levels in the Federal government.

Similarly, Richardson and Jordan stress the role of a diverse array of groups in policy-making in Britain.[33] In Britain, they argue, there is a 'style' of policy-making which leads central government ministries to consult a wide variety of groups when proposing to make policy changes. For example, in 1980 the British government consulted no fewer than 500 groups in drafting its legislation based upon the Finniston Report on Engineering, even though many of these groups had a negligible impact upon the government, sixteen of them are regarded by Richardson and Jordan as 'key' groups.[34]

None of these approaches suggest that group politics is without substantial defects. Truman points to the fact that the group process excludes a variety of social groups unable to participate in it,[35] a feature of pluralism emphasised by Schattschneider's discussion of the 'mobilisation of bias'.[36] Schattschneider argues that certain types of groups are 'organised into politics and others are organised out of it'. Similarly, Wolin makes explicit the relationship between group bargaining and the exclusion of particular groups by arguing that since legitimacy is something that has become associated with groups, 'public authority has no source of power peculiarly its own'.[37] Instead, public authorities become the representatives of 'residual constituencies that . . . have not been wholly absorbed into the dominant groups', such as the ethnic and racial minorities, farm workers, unorganised industrial workers and those who are almost totally dependent upon the welfare state; 'In other words, public authority has the constituency of the power-less'. Moreover, the fragmentation that group participation creates in the policy process has been held partly responsible for the 'challenge to governance'[38] faced by most Western nations since the 1970s.

## VALUES AND PERCEPTIONS RATHER THAN OBJECTIVE INTERESTS

Marxist theory and, to a lesser degree, elite theory argue that the basis for assessing political power lies in the assessment of the degree to which particular groups can produce policy outcomes which are in their interests. As the discussion of power in Chapter 2 showed, pluralist approaches have explicitly rejected the notion that one can derive a causal explanation of policy outcomes based upon the congruence of the policy outcome with the interests of a particular group or class—that the congruence between the policy outcome and the interests of a group offers strong evidence to support ascribing power to the group. Rather, pluralist approaches stress the need to establish that a group or individual consciously wanted a particular policy outcome and took successful measures to secure it. Thus, in the case of Dahl's study of New Haven, the power of the mayor can only be assessed on the basis of his own particular preferences for urban development and how he managed to secure these preferences in the decision-making process.

Marxist and elitists of course argue that expressed or perceived political preferences can be distinguished from 'objective' interests. But this is because of the influence of the dominant or ruling class propagating a 'political formula' (Mosca) or 'false consciousness' (Marx). Yet in these approaches such perceived interests are the products of a power relationship rather than, as in pluralist approaches, the basis for understanding such relationships. In Marxist and elite theory, where perceived interests differ from objective interests, one can find evidence of the power of the dominant class to shape the values of those over whom power is exercised. Pluralists, on the other hand, normally eschew the concept of objective interests insofar as it suggests that group goals can be deduced from objective data about the social or economic nature of the group.

If political goals and values are not determined by social and economic relationships, where do they come from? One possible answer to this question comes from the application of psychological analysis to political studies. This tradition itself can be traced back a long way in political theory. Hobbes, for example, bases his analysis of the nature of the state upon a few simple axioms about the bodily needs and the personal desires and aspirations of men. In the modern empirical study of politics, the emphasis upon psychological factors in explaining political behaviour is more frequently associated with Graham Walles, whose *Human Nature in Politics* showed that the political behaviour of individuals was just as likely to be the result of 'irrational' beliefs as of a 'rational' calculation of the benefits and penalties that may follow from such behaviour.[39] In part, these beliefs may be acquired through childhood 'socialisation', being transmitted from parent to offspring.[40]

Although childhood socialisation has been important in electoral studies, it has had little application in decision-making studies. More frequently used to explain the source of the preferences of participants in decision-making are implicit references to adult socialisation in the broad sense: that members of organisations tend to adopt many of the values that dominate within that organisation. Selznick's study of the Tennessee Valley Authority and Kaufman's study of the Forest Ranger in the United States[41] both stress the importance of the transmission of sets of values from dominant members of the organisation to the remainder of the organisation as an important feature of the functioning of the organisation—it establishes control within the orga-

nisation and presents sponsors of the organisation in
Washington with a clear image of the organisation's 'mis-
sion'.

More recently, the concept of 'going native' in the
Washington bureaucracy, referring to the tendency of
officials appointed (directly or indirectly) by the president to
adopt the values of the bureaus to which they are appointed
rather than those of the man who appointed them, is a
further example of the importance of socialisation factors as
a source of values. Similarly in Britain, Heclo and Wildavsky
adopt an anthropological tone when they speak of the
British policy-making system in Whitehall concerned with
public expenditure as a 'village community' with a variety of
subtle norms about the type of behaviour which is acceptable and unacceptable, praiseworthy and condemnable.[42]

While one can point to broad influences upon the
formation of individual and group goals, in pluralist studies
goals are more frequently treated as problematic—they
cannot be determined on *a priori* grounds through examining objective circumstances. Indeed, it is very difficult to
determine goals and preferences at all.[43] The stated goals of
actors or groups cannot be accepted at face value since such
statements may be the simple camouflage of more sinister or
at least less acceptable policy goals. Psychological or
socialisation theory cannot provide either coherent or
detailed statements about the goals of actors. It cannot
explain why, for example, President Carter should have
sought to spring the US hostages from Iran in 1980 as the
only logical outcome of his life as a peanut farmer in Georgia
or a president of the United States.

There is a recognition in pluralist studies that the goals
and objectives of individuals are hard to determine with any
degree of precision. Moreover, such goals that can be
indicated are frequently vague, multiple and contradictory.
Statements of what people intended to get out of the
policy-making process are generally something that has to be
established on the basis of careful examination of the
evidence rather than on the basis of assumptions about
interests.

# OUTCOMES SELDOM REFLECT THE VALUES AND GOALS OF ONE GROUP

If elite and Marxist theory assert that important decisions reflect the supremacy of one group in the policy process, pluralist approaches stress the plurality of factors affecting policy outcomes. This is most clearly seen in the concept of 'incremental' decision-making. Charles Lindblom in his article 'The Science of Muddling Through' argued that 'rational' models of decision-making were inaccurate as a description of what policy-makers do and misleading as a prescription of a 'good' or 'proper' way of making decisions.[44] In the 'rational' decision-making model, the policy-maker first specifies the objectives that he is trying to achieve, second musters all the evidence necessary for an analysis of alternative ways of achieving these objectives and, third, chooses the most cost-effective means of achieving these objectives. Unfortunately, policy-makers do not have the resources for such an analytical approach to policy decisions; not only would a comprehensive review of alternative options take up more time and staff than can normally be expected, such an ability to engage in a comprehensive review of policy options presupposes a greater concentration of political power in the hands of a single policy-maker or group of policy-makers than can be found within the American political system. In addition, the approach ignores the fact that decisions are usually made on an 'incremental' basis. That is to say, policy changes more frequently take the form of relatively marginal changes to existing policies. Decision-makers do not have a 'blank sheet' upon which they can inscribe their own policy proposals and supercede what came before. Rather, they accept existing policy instruments as given and make additions or substractions from them.

Lindblom argues that policy-making under incrementalism takes the form of 'partisan mutual adjustment', referring to the practice of making choices among different alternatives not on thè basis of a particularly rigorous evaluation of the 'best' means to achieve a desired 'goal', but through the compromise and agreement of a variety of different

groups. There is no one 'best' policy, merely one that
secures a broad enough basis of support to be agreed upon
and passed.

Studies which can be classed as 'pluralist' do not, of
course, have to make explicit reference to Lindblom or
incrementalism to illustrate the importance of this feature of
pluralist approaches. The notion that there exist a plurality
of influences affecting the outcomes of political processes is
to be found in many of the classic studies of policy-making,
such as the emphasis upon bargaining in the budgetary
process,[45] on the plurality of groups involved in intra-party
policy making[46] and in the legislative process.[47]

## STRENGTHS AND WEAKNESSES

The main attraction of pluralist approaches to the study of
political phenomena lies in their catholicism. As Polsby
suggests in his evaluation of pluralist versus elitist
approaches to power, it is perfectly consistent with pluralist
analysis, as discussed here, to point to evidence of economic
or other elites dominating the policy process.[48] Moreover,
unearthing evidence of such inequality would not cause a
pluralist to challenge the basis of his or her analytical
approach in the same way that evidence of the influence of
non-economically based groups on state decisions has
generated much tortuous re-evaluation of basic theory
among Marxist scholars. Indeed, most of the classic pluralist
writers, such as Truman and Dahl were acutely aware of
inequalities in the distribution of power and the relationship
between these inequalities and social and economic status.
While the *methodology* of pluralist analysis has been
charged with generating a bias against unearthing evidence
of elite or bourgeois domination of the political system, the
implicit *theory* in pluralist studies, as outlined here, is hardly
challenged by such evidence.

A second advantage of the approach is that it is largely
confined to observable empirical phenomena. Studies of
decision-making look at the actual process of policy-making,
the values, goals and strategies of the different participants

rather than postulate abstract, unfalsifiable and unobservable notions of 'objective' interests or 'non-decisions'. As such, pluralist studies can be replicated and, on the basis of empirical evidence, falsified. But in *largely* confining itself to observable phenomena, although through speculating about the role of the unobservable 'anticipated reactions' of one actor to another or considering the values and interests which failed to emerge in the policy making process, it may entertain the possibility of hidden power processes, its main weakness may be that it is a description rather than an analysis of power relationships. This has been at least implicitly recognised by pluralists because, as Polsby suggests, if true, the elitists' and Marxists' contention of the importance of non-observable influences and constraints emanating from one class or group would have important repercussions for the way in which one characterises Western political systems.[49]

## NOTES

1. *See* S. Lukes, *Power: A Radical View* (London, Macmillan, 1974).
2. P. Norris, 'Do the Capitalists Rule?' in H. Elcock, ed., *What Sort of Society?* (Oxford, Martin Robertson, 1982), p. 194.
3. For an overview of the community power debate and its implications in Britain and America, *see* K. Newton, 'Community Power and Decision Making: The American Experience and Its Lessons' in K. Young, ed., *Essays in the Study of Urban Politics* (London, Macmillan, 1975).
4. F. Hunter, *Community Power Structure* (Chapel Hill, University of North Carolina Press, 1953).
5. R.A. Dahl, *Who Governs?* (New Haven, Conn., Yale University Press, 1961).
6. N.W. Polsby, *Community Power and Political Theory* (New Haven, Conn., Yale University Press, 1961).
7. *Ibid.*, pp. 112–23.
8. Dahl, *op. cit.*
9. *See* P. Diesing, *Science and Ideology in the Policy Sciences* (New York, Aldine Press, 1982), pp. 375–81.
10. F. Hunter, *Top Leadership USA* (Chapel Hill, University of North Carolina Press, 1959); R.A. Dahl, *Polyarchy: Participation and Opposition* (New Haven, Conn., Yale University Press, 1971).
11. Dahl, *op. cit.*, pp. 1–2.

12. Aristotle, *The Politics* (Harmondsworth, Penguin, 1972).
13. T. Hobbes, *Leviathan* (London, Dent, 1972).
14. G.W.F. Hegel, *Hegel's Philosophy of Right* (Oxford University Press, 1967).
15. Dahl, *op. cit.*, p. 226.
16. Polsby, *op. cit.*
17. *See* S.H. Beer, 'Federalism, Nationalism and Democracy in America', *American Political Science Review*, 1978, pp. 9–21.
18. *See* D. Haider, *When Governments Come to Washington* (New York, Free Press, 1974); R.A.W. Rhodes, *Control and Power in Central–Local Government Relations* (Farnborough, Gower, 1981).
19. R.E. Neustadt, *Presidential Power* (New York, John Wiley, 1960).
20. *Ibid.*, p. 179.
21. *See* H. Heclo and A. Wildavsky, *The Private Government of Public Money*, 2nd edn (London, Macmillan, 1981).
22. *See*, for example, the discussion of 'pluralistics stagnation' in S.H. Beer, *Britain Against Itself* (London, Faber and Faber, 1982).
23. Dahl, *op. cit.*, pp. 282–301.
24. A. Bentley, *The Process of Government* (Chicago, University of Chicago Press, 1908).
25. H. Eckstein, 'Group Theory and the Study of Pressure Groups' in H. Eckstein and D.E. Apter, eds., *Comparative Politics: A Reader* (New York, Free Press, 1963).
26. D.B. Truman, *The Governmental Process* (New York, Alfred Knopf, 1953).
27. *Ibid.*, p. 52.
28. *Ibid.*, p. 502.
29. H. Heclo, 'Issue Networks and the Executive Establishment', in A. King, ed., *The New American Political System* (Washington DC, American Enterprise Institute, 1981).
30. *Ibid.*, p. 97.
31. A.G. Jordan, 'Iron Triangles, Woolly Corporatism and Elastic Nets', *Journal of Public Policy*, 1, pp. 95–123.
32. Heclo, *op. cit.*, p. 104.
33. J.J. Richardson and A.G. Jordan, *Governing Under Pressure* (Oxford, Martin Robertson, 1979).
34. A.G. Jordan and J.J. Richardson, 'The British Policy Style or the Logic of Negotiation' in J.J. Richardson, ed., *Policy Styles in Western Europe* (London, Allen and Unwin, 1983).
35. Truman, *op. cit.*, pp. 522ff.
36. E.E. Schattschneider, *The Semisovereign People* (New York, Holt, Rinehart and Winston, 1960).
37. S.H. Wolin, 'The American Pluralist Conception of Politics' in A.L. Kaplan and D. Callahan, eds., *Ethics in Hard Times* (New York, Plenum Press, 1981).
38. R. Rose, 'The Nature of the Challenge' in R. Rose, ed., *The Challenge to Governance* (London and Beverly Hills, Sage, 1980).
39. G. Walles, *Human Nature in Politics* (London, A. Constable, 1908).

40. P. Selznick, *The TVA and the Grass Roots* (New York, Harper and Row, 1958).
41. H. Kaufman, *The Forest Ranger* (Baltimore, Johns Hopkins Press, 1960).
42. Heclo and Wildavsky *Private Government of Public Money*, 2nd edn (London: Macmillan, 1981).
43. C.H. Weiss, *Evaluation Research* (Englewood Cliffs, NJ, Prentice-Hall, 1972).
44. C. Lindblom, 'The Science of Muddling Through', *Public Administration Review*, 2, 1959: 77–88.
45. A. Wildavsky *The Politics of the Budgetary Process* 2nd edn (Boston, Little Brown, 1974).
46. R.T. Mackenzie *British Political Parties* (London, Heinemann, 1955).
47. N. Polsby *Congress and the Presidency* (Englewood Cliffs NJ, Prentice Hall, 1964).
48. N. Polsby 'Empirical Investigation of the Mobilisation of Bias in Community Power Research' *Political Studies* XXVII(4) 1979: 530–1.
49. *Ibid.*, p. 541.

# PART III
# Case Studies

# INTRODUCTION TO PART III

In the preceding chapters we saw that there are wide differences between the three major social science theories of power. These approaches to the analysis of power in capitalist society operate with distinct methodological and substantive focuses. Each of the theories can be differentiated in terms of the phenomena they study in order to locate power; by their disagreement over where 'politics' begins and ends in society; how their respective theories are to be substantiated and invalidated; and the degree of freedom possessed by individuals in capitalism to shape and change their societies.

In very general terms, Marxist theorists look for the location of power in the wider social and economic structure of society. There is continuing debate within Marxism over the exact role that the state (or political level) fulfils and whether it has any significant independence from the requirements of the owners of the means of production and the preservation of the system of capital accumulation. In the long term, however, Marxists argue that the scope for human beings to choose freely and to shape their society as they wish is severely circumscribed by the private ownership of the means of production, the necessity of the state to respond to the crises and problems generated by capitalism as an economic system and the inequality of competition between different ideologies. Elite theories do not go so far in limiting the scope for individuals to choose or to shape their societies. They argue that individuals can choose, subjectively, to join, to maintain or to challenge the structure of power which exists. Elite theorists, therefore, stand as something of a 'half-way house' between Marxist determinism and pluralist voluntarism. Most elite theorists also point to the limits imposed upon the freedom of choice of the non-elite through the perpetration by elites of a stratified and inegalitarian access to social, economic, bureaucratic and political resources. Pluralist theories allow for greater scope for individuals, but they also have a far narrower conception of 'the political' in society. These

studies tend to focus almost exclusively on the constitu-
tionally legitimised areas of political action to discover
where power lies. Pluralists are not explicitly concerned with
the economic and social relationships outside the constitutional political system which can exert a constraining
influence on the individuals who are empowered to take
decisions within those institutions (executive, legislature,
bureaucracy and judiciary). Pluralists, therefore, focus more
on the individuals and groups who are centrally located in
the 'black-box' of policy-making in the capitalist state. In
this way, such studies give the subjective wants and goals of
individuals far more centrality as explanations of change.

There is one final point that ought to be made before we
operationalise these theories, and it is one which we alluded
to in our earlier discussions. If all of these theories are value
dependent (in the sense that they are all based upon prior
theorisation of how society is constructed), then it is likely
that they will also have very different prescriptions about
how problems in capitalist society·can be resolved. These
competing perspectives on the range of viable solutions will
flow also from the fact that theories normally carry with
them implicit and explicit notions of how society ought to be
structured. Thus, value-laden choices about what to study
are also supported by value-dependent prescriptions about
what is to be done. Marxists see all capitalist problems as
resolvable but only by replacing this system with a different
one. All solutions within capitalism will be temporary, it is
argued, because the same contradictions simply reappear in
other areas of society. Elite theorists are either optimistic or
pessimistic about the scope for change, depending on
whether they see elite structures as permeable or impervious
to modification or decay. They do, however, believe that
individuals can exert far greater influence over society
within capitalism than Marxists. Finally, pluralists believe
that problems which arise are resolvable if individuals
choose the correct solutions and formulate the right
strategies for change.

In this final section we illuminate these very different
theories and prescriptions through a series of case studies. In
each of these case studies—which deal with major problems

or issues which have prompted analysis from all three perspectives—we briefly outline how Marxists, pluralists and elite theorists analyse the problems; we then show how, and to what extent, they believe these problems can be resolved. As we shall see, in each case the three theories focus on different phenomena to explain the causes of these problems and arrive at very different prescriptions for dealing with them.

# 6 The Military-Industrial Complex

What does the phrase 'the military-industrial complex' refer to, and where did it come from? The original phrase is associated with President Eisenhower who, in his final address as president, warned against the danger of 'unwarranted influence, whether sought or unsought, by the military-industrial complex'.[1] Eisenhower, himself, a former military leader, was pointing to a phenomena which troubled him, and one which others have seen developing in many countries. This phenomena is the increasing penetration of political and economic life by the military since the Second World War. Despite attempts to discuss other countries in terms of the creation of such an industrial-military complex, it is, however, normally the transformation of politics and the economy in post-war America which is the focus of academic analysis of the problem.

Empirical evidence has been presented to highlight this trend. First, there has been a massive increase in the level of military expenditure by the American federal government when compared with figures from before the Second World War figures. The level of expenditure on military equipment and personnel in the inter-war years was around 1 per cent of GDP in both the United States and Britain. In the post-war period, expenditure on the military has been between 5 and 10 per cent of GDP. Within this generally higher level of post-war expenditure there have, of course, been wide fluctuations. Expenditure did fall quite rapidly between 1945 and 1950 as nations reconstructed their war economies, but between 1951 and 1953 expenditure rose again to 10 per cent in reaction to the Korean War and the heightening of Cold War tensions. While expenditure was reduced after this, by the 1960s, with the entry of the United States into the Vietnam conflict, it rose to around 10 per cent of GDP once more. There was a temporary decrease in the early 1970s as a reaction against Vietnam and the eventual withdrawal from armed conflict. Since 1975, however, expenditure on the military has begun to rise again as a proportion of GDP. This was commenced by President Ford (a Republican), continued and enhanced by President Carter (a Democrat nominally committed to peace) and taken to an even higher level by President Reagan into the 1980s.[2]

It is not just the absolute increase in military expenditure and its continuation in the whole of the post-war period which has led people to fear the creation of a military-industrial complex, there are qualitative changes as well. The first to be remarked upon is the close ties which have developed between giant firms and military contractors. This is seen as of particular salience in advanced technological industries, where the costs of research and development are now so high, and the need for an ensured market for products is so important to recoup costs, that government contracting has become of crucial importance to the survival of large corporations. Thus, in the United States, around fifteen companies receive about one third of all prime defence contracts. Some of these companies—like Lockheed, General Dynamics and Rockwell—are now so dependent on government contracts for their survival that they cannot allow political decisions to be made without a continuous pressure to defend their interests being exerted on the political system. This, many writers fear, may lead to corruption and the undermining of the democratic process.[3] Interestingly, this reliance on state funding is not confined solely to industry. Most of the major American universities (whether public or privately endowed) have grown in the post-war period due to large defence related expenditure. A similar conclusion has been made about many of the private research institutes, like the Rand Corporation and the Brookings and Hudson Institutes.[4]

Other developments are also seen as a continuing threat to the democratic nature of the American economic and political system. Not only is there a continuing fear of firms corrupting politicians in the search for contracts, this close

connection between industry and the military is seen as a
threat to the balance of the American economy. Military
expenditure is seen as dysfunctional for the overall performance of the economy because it does not directly contribute
to the balance of payments. Arms sales clearly do but most
military expenditure does not. Military expenditure may
keep people in jobs but much of the equipment produced is
never used and is scrapped or sold at give-away prices so that
the armed forces can have the most up-to-date equipment.
The rationale for this is, of course, the fear that the United
States may lose its military lead and superiority over the
Soviet Union. This trend has been seen as extremely
worrying by those who fear the consequence of the
military-industrial complex and see it as evidence of the
dominance of American foreign policy by military and
industrial advisers. It is argued that these groups have a
vested interest in distorting reality to ensure that America
always appears to be under threat so that they can force the
president and Congress to finance the lavish and unnecessary programmes which they desire. This, it is feared, leads
to a down-grading of the autonomy of Congress, an
unbalanced economy and the creation of a cabal of military
and industrial leaders, who are able to influence the
executive branch of government in an undemocratic way.[5]

There is little doubt that a relationship of this type has
developed in the United States since the Second World War.
Military expenditure is at a very high level, and there have
been numerous reports, both inside and outside government, which attest to the corruption, inefficiency and
massive profits being made in defence contracting.[6] The
problem is, of course, assuming that it is seen as a problem,
what one does about it. But if we wish to do something
about these close and secretive ties between the executive,
the military and industry, we need to know what the driving
force of this development is. The dilemma is that it is not
self-evident what the primary causes of this phenomena are.
Whatever is seen as the main cause will depend on the
theoretical framework which is used to make sense of the
military-industrial complex. In this chapter, therefore, we
will, first, have to outline the different explanations pre-

sented by pluralist, elite and Marxist writers. Having achieved this, we can in our concluding section point to some of the strengths and weaknesses of these explanations and the various prescriptions which flow from them.

## MARXIST EXPLANATIONS

As we saw, there are broadly two schools of Marxist thought—those which rely on an instrumental view of the state-economy relationship and those of a structuralist type, which allow for a degree of freedom for the state and discuss power in terms of hegemony and control. The military-industrial complex has been analysed from both of these perspectives. Although both approaches argue that the only solution to the problem is the ultimate replacement of capitalism by a more socialist and pacifist economic and political system, these two approaches offer different explanations for the increase in military expenditure and the close interrelationship between the military, industry and the state.

The first school of thought can be defined as an *underconsumption and economic determinist* approach.[7] This view holds that what Eisenhower called a military-industrial complex is, in fact, nothing of the sort. There is no military-industrial complex because to define the enhanced role of the military in this way is to assume that the reason for this development is the desire of the military and industry to work together. Presumably, if the military or industry changed their minds about the utility of this approach they could withdraw from it. Instrumental Marxists deny that this is possible. They argue, instead, that this relationship is motivated by the requirements of the ruling class and their desire to maintain profitability and to sustain their political control over society. In this way, following Marx, they contend that if military expenditure and involvement in society and politics has increased, then it must in some way be functional for the survival of capitalism as an economic system.

Baran and Sweezey, writing in the 1960s, came to the

conclusion that the need for high military expenditure is due to the fear by capitalists of post-war stagnation and economic depression. The consequence of this might eventually be rising unemployment and social unrest.[8] Following Marx's thesis about the tendency of the rate of profit to decline, Baran and Sweezey argued that this decline led to a drop in the effective demand in the economy, as more and more money is tied up in research and development and the purchase and maintenance of machinery. This decline in individual consumption was exacerbated by increasingly fierce international competition, which forced companies to replace men by machines to raise their productivity. The consequence was that firms came, increasingly, to produce high-technology goods which individuals could not purchase. Only the state could afford and had the need for such high-technology commodities. This process was further stimulated by the massive increase in state purchase of military and industrial equipment during the Second World War. Before the war the American economy had experienced a severe problem of underconsumption (or lack of demand for the goods which the economy could produce). This problem was resolved only by American involvement in the Second World War. The rate of unemployment was drastically reduced and many of the major post-war corporations in America—General Motors, Boeing, Lockheed, Ford, Chrysler, US Steel etc.— were granted, for the first time, the government contracts for arms and related equipment which ensured that they had an effective demand for their goods. Thus the war gave corporations massive profits and solved the problems of underconsumption. After the war there was a potential problem for the owners of the means of production: if the state reduced military expenditure then the effective demand for the high technology goods—aircraft, tanks, computers etc.—which they were now geared to produce, would decline and the problem of underconsumption and high unemployment might return.

Marxists of this school argue that this forced the American government to fabricate a Cold War with the Soviet Union at the behest of the large corporations.[9] The aim of this was to ensure that America would become a permanent arms economy in which the state would underwrite American corporations through their guarantee of demand for the high technology goods which these corporations had invested in during the war. The evidence to support this argument is the fairly simple fact that when military expenditure was low in the 1930s, unemployment was high and economic growth and profitability was low. Since the 1940s military expenditure has been much higher, unemployment has been low and economic growth and profitability has been high.

This interpretation has come under severe attack from Marxists and non-Marxists in the 1970s. In particular, structuralist Marxists have argued that this approach is historically limited and misunderstands the contradictory role which military expenditure performs for capitalist economies.[10] R.P. Smith has recently indicated how a more structuralist account of military expenditure, which is still true to Marxist principles, can be formulated. Smith begins his analysis with a forceful critique of underconsumption/ determinist accounts.[11] His main thesis is that the empirical evidence does not validate the instrumental account. If the underconsumption thesis is correct, then richer societies should have the highest levels of military expenditure. He points out that since the Korean War those countries with the highest growth rates—Japan, Sweden, Germany and Austria—have had the lowest levels of military expenditure as a percentage of GDP. Furthermore, since the Korean War, military expenditure has, by and large, been falling as a percentage of GDP and material living standards have been rising in most capitalist economies. This only began to be reversed as a trend after 1975. More interesting, for Smith, is the fact that those countries with the fastest rising unemployment levels and the lowest growth rates per annum in the West—Britain and the USA—were also the two countries with the highest level of post-war expenditure on arms. This leads Smith to conclude that the underconsumption thesis is invalid. The Second World War was not, he argues, fought to reduce unemployment. That unemployment fell as a result of war is an undeniable fact, but it was not the primary reason for the decision to fight the war. Similarly, he contends, America did not maintain a perma-

nent arms economy due to the desire to reduce unemployment; it was because of a real perception that the Soviet
Union was a threat to the West. That Marxists may or may
not be correct that this threat is illusory is not the point: the
United States' political leaders felt a threat, and this was the
reason for their involvement in the Cold War. Similarly,
British military expenditure was not generated by any desire
to end unemployment. It was a continuation of her
misguided perception that she was a world power and had to
protect her Commonwealth and maintain an independent
presence in the world.

Smith's critique goes further because he also argues that,
economically, military expenditure is a poor tool with which
to attempt to stabilise a capitalist economy. If states wish to
solve problems of unemployment, then military expenditure
is not a very effective method because it is capital rather
than labour intensive. Furthermore, the time it takes for
military expenditure to result in an operational arms system
can be anything between ten or twenty years. As an
instrument to maintain effective demand in an economy
such long-term spending is highly ineffective. Similarly,
much military expenditure may have a direct destabilising
effect on a country's balance of payments. A massive
amount of British and American military expenditure is
directed to the maintenance of manpower and bases
overseas. Thus money which might have been spent in the
domestic economy contributes, instead, to the level of
effective demand in another country's economy. This may,
according to Smith, stimulate competitor economies against
the home economy or cause domestic inflation as money is
printed to resolve balance of payments and falling demand
problems at home. On the other hand, it may also cause
governments with weak domestic demand and severe
balance of payments problems to reduce demand further
and generate even higher unemployment to the detriment of
the national economy. Smith argues that Britain has been
the classic case of this.[12] Smith concludes his critique by
arguing that if this is true then other forms of expenditure—
in particular, social welfare spending—which pumps money
into people's pockets, immediately raising the effective

demand in the economy, may be a more effective stabilisation policy for capitalist economies trying to eradicate underconsumption.

Having said this, Smith, being a Marxist, has to provide an alternative and more sophisticated account of why military expenditure remains high even if it is dysfunctional for capitalism. For Smith, military expenditure is yet one more example of the contradictions of capitalism—it is both functional and dysfunctional.[13]

Military expenditure is dysfunctional for the domestic economy in the long term because it leads to low investment, lowers overall growth performance and encourages high unemployment and balance of payments problems. In the short term, however, high military expenditure—for example, in the United States during the Vietnam War period—may temporarily boost demand and reduce unemployment. In the long term these benefits are likely to be short-lived. High military expenditure will fuel inflation, reduce international competitiveness, and balance of payments crises will occur as public debt increases. But, if this is so, why do capitalist economies do it? Smith contends that such expenditure is functional but contradictory: it serves the structural requirements of capitalism at home and abroad while at the same time destabilising the performance of the economic structure which it seeks to preserve in the long term.

Military expenditure serves a number of structural purposes. Externally, leading capitalist economies require high military expenditure for the political and strategic defence of the system against any Soviet threat. Similarly, any leading capitalist country which wishes to exert hegemonic influence over the other capitalist economies must be seen to be capable of defending those political and strategic interests which its economic supremacy has given it. Thus for Smith it is not surprising that it is Britain (the former dominant capitalist economy) and the United States (the leading post-war economy) which have felt the need to maintain permanent arms economies. They both came to realise that supremacy within capitalism ultimately requires the use of force or the threat of its use—whether against the Soviet

bloc or inter-capitalist rivals. Domestically, Smith argues
that military expenditure also serves important functions for
the maintenance of capitalism. Well organised and technically proficient armed services can be used as a backstop to
ensure that there is no internal unrest against the existing
order of things. At the same time, militarism, with its
appeals to patriotism and national identity and superiority,
serves a domestic integration function. It inculcates a
national consciousness which undermines a fully developed
and international class consciousness. Respect for the
military and its hierarchical structures also reinforces the
existing authority patterns in society.

Smith concludes, however, that this is one further
capitalist contradiction because the price of an international
military role is the need to destabilise and distort the
domestic economy. This allows competitor countries—
Germany and Japan—to reduce their military expenditure
and to concentrate on domestic industry, thereby undermining the international competitiveness of the leading powers
in the capitalist bloc. As a result, it may become necessary
for these countries to discipline their own working classes as
low economic growth generates domestic unrest. Thus,
though Smith still believes that the military-industrial
complex is a misnomer for a process which is driven by the
requirements of the capitalist mode of production, he does
not argue that it always assists the economically dominant
class. The state has to respond to various pressures which
are contradictory and do not unequivocally maintain and
support the capitalist process of accumulation. This is clearly
a much more sophisticated analysis of the phenomena than
the empirically invalidated instrumental account. It may well
be, however, that this approach misses important explanatory factors which account for why the military-industrial
complex has developed. Some of these alternative insights
can be gleaned from an appraisal of alternative theoretical
approaches.

# ELITE EXPLANATIONS

The leading exponent of this theoretical approach in relation to the military-industrial complex has been C.W. Mills.[14] Writing in the 1950s Mills came to the conclusion that the growth in military expenditure and the close relationship which was developing between the military, industry and the executive in America had led to the creation of a power elite. Rejecting pluralist and other writings as a conscious decision by academics to defend the privileges which this new system of power gave to them through military and industrial contracts, Mills argued that the power elite could be defined in terms of the institutional positions which people commanded in society. Being in some institutional positions ensured that the individuals involved would come to make decisions which would have a major impact upon society. People in these positions did not consciously seek to become part of an elite, rather they were the unwitting members of a structure of institutions—the military, the industrial and the political—which had coincidental needs. As a result, people in these institutions quickly came to take on the roles and goals which these institutions required for their survival.[15]

Mills, like Marxists, also presented an historical account of the transformation of power in American society to explain how and why it was that a new power elite had developed in the post-war world. According to Mills, the United States had been through five epochs.[16] Between the American Revolution and the presidency of John Adams (1776–1801) there was a relative unification of elites. The leader. This epoch was to pass, after Adams's presidency, into similar backgrounds and were very closely interrelated. Washington, indeed, was both a statesman and a military leader. This epoch was to pass after Adams's presidency into a period of romantic pluralism at the beginning of the nineteenth century. In this epoch the military elite was subordinate to the political elite, and the economic elite was divided, pursuing conflictual economic goals due to the massive expansion of the frontier. During and after the presidency of Andrew Jackson (1829–60), a lively and pluralistic competition between the economic and political elite over who should direct the nations affairs was apparent. From the Lincoln presidency at the end of the nineteenth century to the 1920s, Mills argues, an economic elite directed the nation's affairs. While the military were subordinate (having solved the problems of the frontier and the Civil War), the massive increase in corporate power due to industrial concentration and the expansion and unification of the national economy led to the political elite being dominated by corporate power. This was a period of graft and unrestrained corruption. In the fourth epoch, covering the New Deal of the 1930s, Mills argues that there was a stalemate between the political and economic elites. Franklin Delano Roosevelt centralised political power in the executive branch of the government to ensure that there was a competing power to that possessed by the economic elite. By the end of the 1930s, however, the economic elite had begun to recolonise the political institutions created in the Depression. This was because Congress was dominated by the interests of labour and non-monopoly and small business.

The fact that the economic elite was able to colonise the newly centralised executive branch was of crucial importance, according to Mills, for the creation of the power elite in the post-war period. The Second World War forced the United States out of its isolationist past and onto the world stage as the leading capitalist economy. This increased the importance of the office of the president and the executive branch in the national political system. Now the presidency and his executive branch became a political directorate, which increasingly aggregated political power within itself and away from the legislature. The politicians in Congress gradually lost importance in the overall structure of power in America. Since the war had massively increased the productive potential and economic power of the largest corporations, these institutions, as an economic elite, come increasingly to dominate the legislative and, eventually, the executive branches of government. Their aim was to ensure that contracts were given and policies enacted which favoured their interests in making profits. This movement onto the political stage was supported and reinforced by the military. Having massively increased in numbers and importance since 1939, the armed services quickly came to fill the vacuum which existed in the political system as the United States strove to find its post-war role in world politics. Foreign policy was, then, defined by the military in terms which served their own interests; namely, the maintenance of the role and size of the armed forces in society. The Soviet Union was therefore perceived as a threat by both the military and the economic elites because it served both their interests. The military received high expenditure to maintain their new prestigous role in society, and the economic elite were assured of policies and contracts which maintained effective demand and profitability. The result was a military capitalism unchecked by a weak bureaucracy, an ineffective and stalemated Congress and an hedonistic and unthinking mass consumer society. The political directorate increasingly became a tool in the hands of the economic and military elites.

In this analysis Mills rejects both Marxist and pluralist accounts of power. He argues that Marxist accounts assume that the phenomenon occurs solely due to the needs of corporations and their owners. Mills argues that it is more complicated than this; the power elite is a holy trinity of coincidences between apparently dissimilar organisational and institutional interests. The military, economic and political elites have different reasons for existence and different goals, yet they all share one common goal—the desire to give themselves mutual wealth, prestige and power. On the other hand, Mills rejects pluralist accounts because they mistakenly assume that power is only located in the political system. While he accepts that the political system does possess power this, for him, is not where effective power lies. He points out that most of the effective lobbying of politicians occurs in the 'higher circles',[17] by which he means people in the power elite mix in the same social circles and do not need to rely on lobbying within political institutions.

Effective power rests, for Mills, in an elite comprised of *corporate chieftains* (the corporate rich and their chief executives); *war lords* (soldier-statesman like the joint chiefs of staff and the upper echelons of the services); and, a *political directorate* (composed mainly of political outsiders nominated by the other two elites and not peopled by professional politicians).[18] This power elite is an 'interlocking directorate' which has an institutional coincidence of interest, rooted in organisational inertia and self-interest. The result is a permanent war establishment run by a privately incorporated economy operating within a political vacuum. Neither the military nor the economic elite will allow the other elite to suffer or loose its position in this structure because their roles are complementary. The only losers are the American people because they are excluded and, if Mills's theory is correct, they have very little chance of removing this elite from power.

## PLURALIST EXPLANATIONS

Such pessimistic conclusions are rejected by pluralist writers, who believe that the political system can be used to bring about any change in society so long as that is what the majority of people desire. Since these writers retain a belief that the capitalist economic system throws up a responsive liberal-democratic and pluralistic political system, these theorists must always first explain why it is that the military-industrial complex has come about. Within this school of writing there are two broad approaches. On the one hand there are those who argue, in a fairly simplistic way, that if military expenditure is high, it must be because the people want it to be so. The system responds to their desires and, in a nuclear age with the high cost of technology, countries now have to arm against immediate destruction, ensuring that military expenditure must be higher than ever before. Furthermore, the objective threat posed by the Soviet Union and its own nuclear weapons means that the United States has to have a permanent war economy and that the people recognise this and vote for it.[19]

Set against this rather simplistic view of the neutrality and responsiveness of the state to the wishes of electors are pluralist writers who argue that there is certainly a need for greater preparedness, but that the military and the giant corporations in America have far more influence on the political system than they should and that they are a threat to liberal democracy. This threat derives from the way in which these interests are able to force military expenditure higher than is necessary to counter the threat which exists, generate a wasteful arms race and distort American foreign policy goals. Being traditional liberals, these writers—like John Kenneth Galbraith and Senator Proxmire—argue that the military-industrial complex is not an inevitability; it is a cancer on the body politic which can be successfully expunged if the people so desire. This means such writers also reject the notion that it has anything to do with the development and logic of a capitalism as an economic system of production. Let us look more closely at this explantion.[20]

Like elite theorists, pluralist writers deny that a ruling class exists and argue that the cause of the cancerous growth of a military-industrial complex arises from either the desire by the military to extend their power undemocratically or the desire by the bureaucratic structures in industry and the military to defend and extend their own role in society in a self-serving manner. Whichever of these two views is being proffered, pluralists are arguing that the creation of the military-industrial complex is a conscious decision by individuals who are well aware of what they are doing. They are self-consciously striving to subvert the political system to enrich themselves or to strengthen their position in society. The problem is, however, compounded by the fact that the web of this disease spreads ever outward into society and incorporates many different and apparently conflictual sectors of the socio-economic and political systems such that it becomes very difficult to combat its influence.

Pluralists agree with Mills that it is a post-war phenomena and arises due to the United States' need to take on a new world role. The military fill the political vacuum which exists in foreign policy-making, and this brings them into close contact with the industrial firms which prospered out of the Second World War. This leads to a growing military and industrial dependence on government contracting and state expenditure if their existing position is to be maintained. As we have mentioned, fifteen of the major corporations in the United States are seen to receive the bulk of government contracts. These include Lockheed, General Electric, General Dynamics, McDonnell-Douglas, United Aircraft, ATT, Ling-Temco-Vought, N.A. Rockwell, Boeing, General Motors, Raytheon, Sperry Rand, AVCO, Hughes Aircraft and Westinghouse Electric.[21] But for pluralists the problem is that the need to ensure state expenditure on military hardware and personnel does not stop with these giant corporations. Increasingly, other firms are drawn into the web of the military-industrial complex because they realise that government contracts take risk out of business. It is not just that other large corporations (like Grumman Aircraft, Ford and Chrysler) become involved but a whole host of subcontractors, trade associations and local business and community groups become enmeshed. Government contracts become so important for the survival and prosperity of whole communities that local and state politicians follow their more prestigous congressional colleagues into the morass. They are as dependent on retaining and winning votes from local electors through winning government contracts as their industrial and military colleagues are for their profits and prestige, respectively. More worrying, of course, is that this involvement spreads out to incorporate workers and their trade unions and academics and scientists in universities and research establishments. All of these actors become as dependent on a high military expenditure as the Pentagon civil service and the four armed services (army, navy, air force and marines). As a result, due to constant interchange of personnel at all levels, far too much power is given to military buyers and industrial suppliers in the contracting and procurement of military hardware, and American democracy is subverted by a bureaucratic self-interest which masquerades as the national interest.

The definition of the national interest in terms of the interests of a self-serving military-industrial complex leads to a host of political, social, economic and strategic dilemmas for the American people. On the economic and social side, it has been argued, that the money spent on the military might well have been spent more effectively elsewhere.[22] If the money had been spent on social and industrial problems then the American economy might well have grown at a higher rate than it has, and technological innovation might have been more rapid in areas which directly contribute to trade. Obviously, as Galbraith has shown, military expenditure can be a useful short-term stabilisation policy for the economy, but its long term effects are less clear. Galbraith argues that the overall effect is a tremendous waste in unchecked budgets, contracts with massive time and cost over-runs and inefficient and defective weapons sytems which do not assist the American balance of payments. These expenditures may also have generated inflation and wasted talent which could have been used more effectively in resolving more pressing social and industrial problems. The reliance on government contracts may also have contributed directly to the decline in competitive potential of the American economy. Reliance on contracts may 'featherbed' companies and lead them to be less innovative than they ought—one reason, perhaps, for the United States falling behind Japan and Germany in productivity and innovation.

But the problems are also strategic. The bureaucratic world-view of the military requires that there must be a threat to the security of the United States in order to justify continuing high levels of military expenditure. The military bureaucracy must constantly justify itself by 'discovering' military threats to US security, which do not, in reality, exist. Historical examples of this myopia and distortion are the Bay of Pigs Fiasco and the US interventions into the Dominican Republic, Vietnam, El Salvador and Grenada. The problem is, of course, that any attempt to question this military perception of reality is easily questioned as un-Americanism. This, it is argued, hinders rational thought and leads to the avoidance and downgrading of non-military solutions to world problems. As a result, the military have bases they do not require, weapon systems they do not need, to meet threats that do not exist. This leads to the insanity of possessing 'overkill' potential and the ever-escalating costs of the arms race.[23]

Finally, pluralist writers argue that there are political costs. Congress no longer controls either the military or the economy. The military and large corporations control Congress and the president while the American people have to pick up the tax bill to finance it all. In turn, the military's ability to define issues which serve their interests as a threat leads to a heavy reliance on security blankets being imposed on the dissemination of information. This makes informed discussion of foreign and domestic policy by the American people difficult. Corruption, public relations and lobbying work debase Congress and undermine its right to be seen as a legitimate institution representing the American people. Pro-military spokesmen dominate the most important committees dealing with military expenditure, and this is compounded by the fact that the executive branch has given up any attempt to control the military-industrial complex. It spends most of its time tinkering with the edges of budget totals which are largely determined within the corporations and the military.[24]

What is interesting about this view is the fact that despite the subversion of democracy outlined, most pluralist writers maintain an abiding faith in the ultimate democratic nature of the American political system. Despite all the evidence which they have themselves presented to testify to the way in which liberal democratic institutions are bypassed and used to serve the interests of particular interests, these writers still believe the problem can be exorcised within the liberal democratic framework which exists. In particular, they believe that their own writings can create a popular opinion which will vote against this powerful complex. By encouraging people to vote against the complex at elections, it is expected that legislature will then be able to pass laws and regulations and make institutional changes which will expunge this cancerous growth from American society. Some of the more important suggestions for change include new committee structures to allow qualified civilian staff to have information and knowledge to question military assumptions; new congressional committees to review the need for new weapons systems; laws to force people to disclose any bureaucratic and financial interests when dealing with the military and to stop Pentagon officials taking top jobs with defence contractors; and, budgeting systems which would ask for every existing military programme to be fundamentally reappraised every year (zero-based budgeting). More radical proposals include suggestions to allow all military procurement to be undertaken by an independent civilian agency and not by the military; all future defence and foreign policy posture statements to be decided by Congress and not the military; and regular Congressional debate on military priorities and their socio-economic consequences.[25]

Clearly, then, this school concludes that change can come from the people themselves. Thus it is argued that the people should be sure that the presidents and Congressmen they vote for are committed to reducing the role of the military-industrial complex, and that voters should create pressure groups committed to this purpose and the acceptance of policies of arms control with the Soviet Union. Ultimately, this approach argues, this can result in the reform of existing political institutions and the creation of new public policies and regulations which will control the military-industrial complex. They are able to argue this because they believe that the state in capitalist society is neutral and can be used in any way that the people desire. All that is required is that the people have the necessary desire and will to bring change about. This is, of course, a far more optimistic view of the location and nature of power in capitalist society than either of the elite or Marxist theories which we have outlined.

## SUMMARY

It may well be that the reader is expecting the authors to indicate which of these theories best explains the development of the military-industrial complex and how (assuming one believes it to be a problem) it can be eradicated. Unfortunately, as we have been at pains to argue, to do so would be only to impose our own interpretation of reality on the reader. What we can do by way of conclusion, however, is to point out once more the strengths and weaknesses of these various approaches in terms of whether the hypothesis and explanations they employ are rigorous or not.

The first point to emphasise is that there is very little disagreement amongst any of the theorists outlined here about what it is that is to be analysed. The increasing centrality of large corporations and the military in the political and social life of the United States is not in question, nor is the descriptive evidence presented by pluralists of this phenomena. Indeed, it is this descriptive sophistication which is the greatest strength of all pluralist explanations. By looking at the problem from this perspective, a clear and precise picture of the actors involved in military-industrial complex can be gleaned. The problem is that it is not clear whether or not pluralist accounts do anything more than to describe, without explaining, what is happening. There is very little in the way of overall explanation and analysis other than to assume that the complex arises because individuals in the military and large corporations want to protect their own selfish interests. But is this an adequate explanation? The problem with it, so far as we can see, is that if the political system is democratic and the state is relatively neutral then how is it that anyone could use the system in such a way as to ensure that it permanently advantaged them to the exclusion of other actors and interests in the system? Surely those disadvantaged by the consequences of the military-industrial complex would have risen up and used their democratic rights to question it? That this has not come about indicates either that everyone benefits from the system—which pluralist writers show is patently not so—or that the democratic and neutral state is in fact nothing of the sort and that the scope for reform is severely limited.

This conclusion would certainly be supported by elite and Marxist approaches. The evidence provided shows that the military are able to influence thought and action and determine what is the national interest and what is not. If this is so, universal suffrage may very well be no guarantee of freedom of thought and action in capitalist societies. If this is so, one would also have to doubt the veracity of the particular prescription which these writers propose. If the voter is already conditioned to think in certain ways, what hope is there in relying on the people to rise up and cast out the military-industrial complex? Indeed, the record of some of the institutional innovations which pluralists have suggested and which were created in the 1970s, do not appear to have been as successful in reducing military expenditure as pluralists have assumed they would.[26] Despite this criticism, pluralists can point to the fact that the share of military expenditure as a percentage of GDP has not constantly risen since 1945—there were definite downturns after Korea and Vietnam. This, it can be argued, was due to popular pressure against high military expenditure.

There is clearly some truth in this, but elite and Marxist theorists would not be very impressed with it. While they would accept that there has been a movement upwards and downwards in military expenditure, what they find important to analyse is the relatively high levels when compared with other periods. Furthermore, they would point to the fact that downturns have been relatively temporary and have always been followed by a return to high levels of expenditure. This can be taken as evidence to support their view that the political system is now subverted by the relationship between the military and the corporate sector. There are, of course, profound disagreements between Marxist and elite writers as to the causal factors generating this phenomena. Marxists argue that it derives from the needs of the capitalist mode of production, while elite theorists see it as an institutional–bureaucratic coincidence of interest. Let us look at the strengths and weaknesses of these two viewpoints.

The elite theory shares with pluralist writings a very well developed descriptive sense of what has been happening. Mills's account of the power elite contains as much empirical evidence as pluralist accounts. The great difficulty with it is that it makes the assumption that there is a coincidence of interest between all of these actors which will lead them to reject the maximisation of their own special interests in the search for unified position against the rest of society. The problem is that pluralist writings have also shown that there

are continuous and time-consuming battles over budget
decisions and expenditure allocations, even amongst those
whom elite theorists argue are the conspiratorial elite.[27]
Thus, what is beneficial for Grumman Aircraft is not
necessarily in the interest of Boeing. Although the military
may try to give each large corporation a turn in contracting,
these two corporations are in competition and their corporate interests are not always the same. This is, presumably,
why Lockheed found it necessary to ensure that it was
granted contracts around the world by offering financial
inducements to decision-makers in the 1960s and 1970s.
Similarly, while it is true that the military do play a more
crucial role than in the past, it is one thing to say this and
another to argue that the heads of the four services are in
some manner an elite or share similar goals. The internecine
struggles over budgeting between the services is as intense as
the battles between defence and social welfare programmes.
This fact questions any easy assumption about a necessary
elitist coincidence of interest amongst the armed services.
True, they all do want to see that the overall size of the cake
for the military grows, but if any service was to be offered
more while all the other services were offered very much
less, it is doubtful whether the favoured service would say no
in order to defend their colleagues' role in society.

Similarly, empirical evidence concerning reductions in
defence budgets in the 1950s and 1970s indicates that, while
the military-industrial complex can exert far more influence
on the budget than hithertofore, this influence is never
assured. It is a conditional influence, the bounds of which
are dependent as much on the ability to mobilise and win
popular support (which it clearly did not do immediately
after Vietnam, when expenditure on the military fell) as it is
on manufacturing an unholy alliance between numerous
competing bureaucratic, industrial and military institutions.
Having said this, however, elite theory does indicte what is a
central truth of the military-industrial complex. This is the
fact that access to political decision-making in America is
not equally dispersed as pluralist theorists have assumed.
There is no doubting the truth of Mills's view that some
interests in America have a continuing preferential access to

the political system. This power derives, not from any superior individual or institutional competence, but from the strategically important role which these interests have been able to mark out for themselves in American society. The only real problem with this analysis is that it assumes that this is an *unwitting* decision by the individuals involved. The difficulty with this is that if individuals do not choose consciously to subvert democracy—as Mills has argued— why is it that the military and the large corporations as institutions have to dominate the political system and subvert liberal democracy? This is never satisfactorily explained.

It might be thought that Marxist accounts can offer a ready and all-encompassing account which explains away the weaknesses on pluralist and elitist accounts. In a sense this is true, but on closer analysis they are also prone to gaps and inconsistencies. Marxists, particularly those of an instrumentalist persuasion, have no difficulty in explaining the growth of the military-industrial complex. It is a manifestation of the search by the ruling class for a solution to the problem of under-consumption. This is a neat and internally consistent explanation and fully explains *why* it is that the military and industry have to get together. Furthermore, it can also accept that individuals are the unwitting servants of this process; for Marxists, human actors are the carriers of the structural requirements of the capitalist system. The only problem with this neat explanation, as Smith revealed, is that it can be empirically invalidated. The fastest growing economies since 1945 have been those very economies which have *not* indulged in the purchase of nuclear weapons or devoted a disproportionate share of their budgets to military expenditure. Is the Marxist explanation, therefore, totally inadequate? It might be argued that it is, but it is worth dwelling briefly on the insights which structuralist Marxist accounts contain. Like pluralists, structuralists are aware of the dysfunctional nature of military expenditure for capitalism and devote a considerable amount of time to dismantling any simple economist or reductionist account of the growth of the military-industrial complex. Furthermore, structuralist accounts would not demure from the pluralist critique of instrumental Marxist and elite accounts, which show that the political process and the internal workings of the military-industrial complex are highly conflictual. They would, however, question the logic of pluralist prescriptions. It is argued that pluralist accounts miss the fact that thought and action is structurally determined by the requirements of capitalism and that the scope for change through popular pressure in liberal democratic institutions is limited. Thus, while military expenditure may have negative consequences for capitalism, as pluralists argue, it is also functionally necessary and, therefore, impossible to eradicate by political reformism alone.

The functionality of military expenditure resides for structuralists in the contribution it makes to the ideological hegemony of the capitalist system. Thus structuralists, as Lukes argued, are able to take on board the insights of elite and pluralist theories and explain why it is that despite a pluralist system the capitalist ruling class is still able to dominate society even without the use of direct repression.[28] The problem with this view is that, as empiricists have long argued, there is no way of falsifying this analysis. If military expenditure can be both functional and dysfunctional then no amount of empirical evidence to disprove its utility for capitalism will ever invalidate the structuralist account. The structuralist account is true by definition. This means that whether you accept the structuralist account or not is likely to depend on your view of what constitutes an acceptable theory. As we shall see in subsequent case studies, this problem is likely to reappear.

## NOTES

1. Quoted in William Proxmire, *Report from Wasteland* (New York, Praeger, 1970), p. 8.
2. SIPRI Yearbook, *World Armaments and Disarmaments* (Stockholm International Peace Research Institute, 1976). On the impact of Reagan, *see* Stephen Kirby, 'Congress and National Security', *The World Today*, Vol. 37 Nos. 7–8 (July–August 1981), pp. 270–7.
3. J.K. Galbraith, *How to Control the Military* (London, NCLC Publishing Society, 1971); Proxmire, *op. cit.*

4. Galbraith, *ibid.*, pp. 5–9.
5. *Ibid.*, pp. 11–14.
6. General Accounting Office, *Models, Data and War: A Critique for the Foundation of Defence Analysis* (Washington, General Accounting Office, 12 March 1980); Elmer B. Staats, *Ensuring Program Accountability* (Washington, General Accounting Office, 15 November 1979); John Freejohn, *Porkbarrel Politics* (Stanford, Stanford University Press, 1974).
7. Instrumentalist accounts include Michael Kidron, *Western Capitalism Since the War* (Harmondsworth, Penguin, 1970); Paul A. Baran and Paul M. Sweezy, *Monopoly Capitalism* (Harmondsworth, Penguin, 1968); Ernest Mandel, *Marxist Economic Theory* (London, Merlin, 1968).
8. Baran and Sweezy, *ibid.*, passim.
9. This is an important debate within American historiography. Leading writers include Gabriel Kolko, *The Politics of War* (New York, Vintage Books, 1968); Thomas G. Paterson, ed., *Cold War Critics* (Chicago, Quadrangle Books, 1971); Gar Alperovitz, *Cold War Essays* (New York: Doubleday & Co., 1970). For an alternative view, *see* John Lewis Gaddis, *The United States and the Origins of the Cold War* (New York, Columbia University Press, 1972).
10. Leading exponents include R.P. Smith, 'Military Expenditure and Capitalism', *Cambridge Journal of Economics*, Vol. I (1977), pp. 61–76; D. Purdy, 'The Theory of the Permanent Arms Economy', *Bulletin of the Conference of Socialist Economists* (Spring 1973).
11. Smith, *ibid.*, pp. 65–74.
12. *Ibid.*, pp. 69–74.
13. *Ibid.*, pp. 74–76.
14. C. Wright Mills, *The Power Elite* (Oxford, Oxford University Press, 1973).
15. *Ibid.*, pp. 3–29.
16. *Ibid.*, pp. 259–68.
17. *Ibid.*, pp. 3–29.
18. For each of these *see*, respectively, pp. 94–170, 171–97 and 225–41.
19. E.A. Thompson, 'Taxation and Natonal Defence' *Journal of Political Economy* (July/August 1974).
20. Writers in this genre include M.H. Halperin, *Bureaucratic Politics and Foreign Policy* (Washington, Brookings Institute, 1974); S. Rose, ed., *Testing the Theory of the Military-Industrial Complex* (Lexington, D.C., Heath, 1973); S. Melman, *The Permanent War Economy* (New York, Simon Schuster, 1974); Galbraith, *op. cit.*; Proxmire, *op. cit.*
21. Galbraith, *ibid.*, pp. 3–9.
22. *Ibid.*, 10–14.
23. *Ibid.*, 12–13.
24. This argument has been presented forcefully by Aaron Wildavsky, *The Politics of the Budgetary Process* (Boston, Little Brown, 1979), pp. 222–4.

25. Galbraith, *op. cit.*, pp. 15–24.
26. For a discussion of the failures of these approaches *see* Andrew Cox and Stephen Kirby, 'Innovations in Legislative Oversight of Defence Policies and Expenditure in Britain and America', *The Parliamenarian*, Vol. LXI, No.4 (October 1980), pp. 215–29; 'Congressional Reform of American Budgetary Decisions', *The Parliamentarian*, Vol. LXIV, No.2 (April 1983), pp. 64–74; 'Defence Budgeting and Accountability: Britain and the United States', *Review of International Studies*, Vol. 9 (1983), pp. 173–90.
27. Graham T. Allison, *The Essence of Decision* (Boston, Little Brown, 1971) is an excellent account of this, as is Wildavsky, *op. cit.*, passim.
28. Steven Lukes, *Power: A Radical View* (London, Macmillan, 1977), pp. 36–45.

# 7 Regions and Regionalism

In the case studies so far considered it has already been made clear that the particular study itself is, as it were, the product of a set of concerns in politics. The phrase 'the military-industrial complex', though brought into the public eye by Eisenhower, is associated with critical elite theorists such as Wright Mills who bear responsibility for identifying and defining the problem. As the discipline develops, the amalgamation of groups of practitioners having particular issues as central becomes clearer, so that one might even talk of specific 'schools' within the discipline. One of the most important aspects of the existence of such groups is not so much their capacity to uncover fundamental truths as their willingness to raise new serious issues and in the process to shed light on older ones. In so doing they begin the process of explaining a phenomenon, reducing it to intelligibility; of course, that process entails a closing of options, a setting of limits to reality, since understanding is one of the ways in which we control and circumscribe our environment. Just as the term 'the military-industrial complex' has a resonance given to it by a particular school of elite theorists, so the problem of the growth of government is associated with pluralist theories. In other theories it might not as such be a problem, though there may be similar identifications in theories having other central concerns. Naming the problem is a crucial step in explaining the phenomena at issue, because even the name—'overloaded government',[1] 'the technobureaucratic elite',[2] and so on— may place the phenomena within a specific and specifically limited theoretical construct of which the initial apparently innocent name is part. The loose bundle of phenomena, including such disparate occurrences as unruly behaviour of large crowds at sporting events, destruction of or damage to

155

public property by juveniles, disturbing trends in crime statistics and overcrowding in prisons, is frequently referred to as the problem of 'law and order' and by that designation is placed within a particular set of priorities and linked generalisations about the proper structure of society, typically one in which the respect for law and the maintenance of public order have a particularly high value. A different complexion might be put on the same phenomena if instead we referred more particularly to the problems of 'criminal justice' and 'penal policy'.

In this chapter we are dealing with a set of phenomena for which there is not a clearly identified name and which therefore presents different faces in different theories. We have chosen to refer to it as Regions and Regionalism since this is the most generic and uncommitted term available, but there are also references to the same phenomena under the headings 'territorial politics',[3] 'centre-periphery relations',[4] and 'central local-government relations',[5] all of which imply slight or major shifts in theoretical perspective. References to specific aspects of the same phenomena can be found with the terms 'the politics of dependency', 'internal colonialism' and 'regional nationalism'. The lack of sharp focus in this field is a serious obstacle to comparison of analyses and to proper explanation. Sometimes writers wish to discuss under these headings the political claims of regionally limited groups for greater autonomy from a national authority; sometimes the subject is the general relative deprivation of peripheral regions; for a time, particularly in the late 1960s and early 1970s, the term was almost synonymous with attempts by central authorities to use peripheral, hitherto neglected areas as dynamoes of national resurgence, either in the political field, as in Italy, or in economic development, as in France.

The explosion of the term 'regionalism' in this way should lead one to be suspicious of usages of it which slide from one focus of attention to another, eliding explanations in the meanwhile. This academic flexibility of the term is reflected by the many different policy areas regionalism covers in practice. Sidney Tarrow comments about France in the 1970s, paraphrasing Wildavsky, 'If regionalism was every-

thing, then . . . it might be nothing'.[6] This remark has an
enticing obscurity to it, a flavour of 'Confucius, he says . . .';
actually, as with many Chinese proverbs, the point Tarrow is
making is a straightforward and simple one, that regionalism as policy resists categorisation and control within a
particular administrative subject-area and has tended to
develop branch-lines covering a wide range of policy
intervention. So in France, says Tarrow, 'regionalism . . .
came to cover an increasing variety of problems and policies,
from the regionalization of the plan to the reform of
territorial administration to the provision of rural roads and
the urban planning'.[7] In this expansion of the policy side of
regionalism, it resembles the policy aspects of planning,
which should not be surprising since where regionalism as
policy has had most impetus, it has originated from central
planning concerns. But regionalism in this 'everything and
nothing' sense is not just a territorial dimension to central
policy-making; like planning, regionalism could not be
regarded as just one policy among many but rather, in
principle, as meta-policy, the implicit or explicit framework
for other interventionist policies. In this sense of the term,
regionalism is a view from the centre looking out and suffers
from similar tensions to those faced by would-be planners.
There is a sense, indeed, in which all planning is implicit
regionalism, though the reverse is not true.

This argument about the policy aspects of regionalism
could be extended to cover different theoretical approaches
to the basket of problems to which we have been referring.
Other case studies have illuminated in particular ways
general theories about politics, and certainly some of the
approaches to regionalism which we will be considering do
this. But the tendency for the theoretical concerns also to
shift focus and expand is evident in regionalism seen as
theory. Indeed, in a certain kind of theory, centre–periphery
relations are not just a particular case, they constitute the
framework within which all social interaction takes place.

# PLURALIST EXPLANATIONS OF REGIONALISM

Most often associated with the school of functional sociology, these ideas have as axiomatic a pluralist integrative approach to political development, in which the centre is synonymous with authority; and in so far as societies fail to conform with the model of integrated consensual authority, they are not properly modern. Edward Shils, one of the foremost exponents of this school, puts it thus: 'When, as in modern society, a more unified economic system, political democracy, urbanization, and education have brought the different sections of the population into more frequent contact with each other and have created even greater mutual awareness, the central value system has found a wider acceptance than in other periods of the history of society.'[8]

The centre in this explanation should not, as Shils observes, be understood in a geometric sense or even in a geographical sense; in fact, the term 'centre' stands for the value systems by which society is ordered and thus may have only the weakest of links with particular concrete manifestations of elite values in politics, economics, culture or other aspects of societal interaction. 'The centre' in this theory should therefore be understood, though Shils does not use this term, as a metaphysical entity.

It is therefore misleading to describe Shils as having an elitist concept of the bureaucracy as a universal class, as Tarrow does.[9] Functional sociology may be Weberian in its origins, but Shils, with his emphasis on integration and the sacred nature of societal values, reads much more like a Durkheimian. That this is an important variant of pluralist theory can be seen from Shils's outline of the network of elites supporting and governing his society. Shils wrote with confidence of the universal value of this centre–periphery model, in a way which might now appear as a paean to a particular vision of the American way of politics:

The larger society appears, on a cursory inspection and by the methods in current use, to consist of a number of interdependent sub-systems—the economy, the status system, the polity, the kinship systems and the institutions which have in their special custody the cultivation of cultural values. Each of these sub-systems itself comprises a network of organisations which are connected, with varying degrees of affirmation, through a common authority, overlapping personnel, personal relationships, contracts, perceived identities of interest, a sense of affinity within a transcendent whole and a territorial location possessing symbolic value.[10]

Note the lack of direct empirical support and the abstract character of the argument; Shils himself admits to his approach being 'tentative and provisional . . . an attempt to elucidate things . . . of great importance but which are very obscure'.[11] Even if marred by partiality and vagueness, this work is easily recognisable as theory, as explanation, not mere descriptive generalisation. The confidence of the American sociologist in the early 1960s might seem misplaced in the more cruel climate of the late 1970s, after Vietnam, Watergate and international economic crises, but still the pluralist vision is extrapolated outside America and achieves the status of international historical trend. what misreading of West European politics could produce the following assimilation of the urban radicalism of the 1970s in Western Europe to the pluralist ideal of small-town politics in the United States?

Citizen involvement requires the opportunity and incentive to act, which in turn can exist only if political structures offer many points of relatively easy access—which means strong local government. As little as a decade ago, this view might easily have been categorized as American, drawing on a particular fusion of James Madison with Alexis de Tocqueville. Nowadays it seems clear enough that such views have spread quite widely in Europe as well. Complaints about bureaucracy, impersonality, and inefficiency, demands for cultural autonomy and for new types of participation have all sustained a very widespread attack upon existing structures everywhere, in particular upon centralization and hierarchical control.[12]

In the case to which Gourevitch is referring, it seems, in a pluralist description, that the existing formal authority is actually less modern than some of the peripheral strata. This, according to Shils, is a not unusual pattern of development nor need it necessarily be troublesome in the

long term.[13] Peripheries in relatively advanced societies
which have undergone the process of homogenisation
described by Shils may be susceptible to investigation by
pluralist methods, if only because the overwhelming predominance of a specific value-system ensures that peripheral
conflict is usually limited to items which do not impinge on
the central elite values. But where societies have areas,
sectors or elites still undergoing this process, or where the
advanced society shows signs of vulnerability in its central
value-system, pluralist methods may fail to fully explain
persistent conflict because of their limited assumptions of
causality and, in particular, because of their unwillingness to
look at other manifestations of power in society, such as the
market, coercive forces, legal-rational institutions and the
structural impact of value systems themselves; Shils has little
to say, as he acknowleges, about the ways in which these
may structure relations between centre and periphery. Even
his generic ethic-based theories about modes of integration
in advanced societies are constrained by his normative
distinction between what he terms 'the ideological mode of
integration' and 'pluralistic integration'.[14] In these ways,
conflict which for whatever reason cannot be integrated
through the action of the central elites is a large residue in
functional pluralist approaches.

The most troublesome cases are provided where the
problem is identified by pluralists as one of incomplete
integration into the central value-system resulting in a state
of backwardness in the outlying regions which may be
permanent. Though this relative deprivation of the benight-
ed outliers may, in the pluralist perspective, show itself in
economic dependency, lower income, poorer quality of life,
social disadvantages or in lack of political influence, there is
no doubt that the ultimate causes are socio-cultural,
appertaining to values, ethics, modes of belief, which
obstruct the modernising capacities of the central elites from
dispersing throughout the society. These problems can occur
in societies which are already developed and modern as well
as in developing nations. It should be clear that in pluralist
theory 'regionalism' is then rather a misnomer since the
territorial location and conformation is utterly irrelevant. In

the inter-war period the physical distance of descendents of Italian immigrants in New York and Chicago from the geographical bases of the economic, cultural and political central elites was of no consequence; in the pluralist explanation of the failure of such groups to integrate into modern American society, their cultural isolation was much more important.

An influential work on this question of isolated groups which fail to modernise was written in the late 1950s by the sociologist Edward Banfield. Banfield journeyed to the hinterland of southern Italy to try to find out what it was about the original culture of Italian immigrants that so retarded their sociological development. His book, whose title *The Moral Basis of a Backward Society*[15] speaks volumes even on its own, is still referred to in some quarters nearly thirty years after the research as an authoritative statement on this problem. It is worth considering in more detail for this reason alone, but it also represents a categorical summary of the pluralist perspective on regionalism. Though pluralists may not call the problem 'regionalism', at this point their concerns certainly converge with those of others who do.

The conditions met by Banfield, and other researchers in similar fields dubbed 'backward societies', are certainly different from those in the societies from which they have come. Social, economic and political conditions in the southern Italian hinterland were different even from those in Banfield's original focus of attention, the immigrant ghettoes of the urbanised north-eastern United States. But they were also so far removed from conditions elsewhere in Italy that Banfield's attention centred on this intra-national gap, and noting the many efforts which had been made by successive Italian governments to deal with 'the Southern Question', he asked why these peripheral 'backward societies' were, as he put it, 'ultra-stable', apparently trapped in dependency and poverty. Though many other features certainly were recognised by Banfield as relevant, the characteristic of these societies that he adopted as the key to explanation was the absence of concerted collective action by the peasants for improvement of their own position. The methods that he chose to investigate this phenomenon were mainly social-psychological, enquiring into the motivations and psychological reactions of individual peasants rather than into the concrete structures and conditions of their lives. As a result of his findings (or rather of those of his wife who accompanied him, since Banfield himself did not speak any Italian), Banfield derived the following as his explanation. The southern Italian peasant, he said, acts as if following this rule: 'Maximise the material short-run advantage of the nuclear family; assume that all others will do likewise.'[16]

Whether this ethic is actually held by the individual peasants concerned is irrelevant; presumably they would be unable to specify the grounds for their own actions in this way, but what matters is that their behaviour actually appears to follow this rule, and this has to be sufficient explanation. The term coined by Banfield for this ethic is 'amoral familism'; that it is 'amoral' is implicit in the exclusive pursuit of short-run material advantage ascribed to individuals in such societies, so that they lack any capacity to sacrifice immediate gains in favour of long-term advantage, and they are unable to associate any good to society as a whole with possible good to themselves or their family. The individual with this ethic does not engage in any cooperative activity for goals beyond the immediate interest of the nuclear family.

Whatever one may think of its application to the particular case, there can be little doubt that Banfield has at the very least described in an ideal form a society in which thrift, enterprise, trust and cooperation are impossible, and therefore one in which political and economic development along liberal democratic and capitalist lines are grossly inhibited. This is a forceful if limited restatement of the pluralist argument that a crucial condition for peripheral development is the appropriate political culture fostering the activities of capitalist elites.

Banfield recognises that other factors contribute to this problem, though the precise relationship between these and the immediate explanation is not delineated. The general material conditions, involving a high death rate, unpredictable climate, poor terrain, unstable land-tenure provisions and the absence of the extended family, are all referred to as forming part of the causal chain, though Banfield appears satisfied to stop his specific explanation at the ethical level. Therefore 'power' in the peasants' vocabulary is equivalent to 'arbitrariness', while in the sociologist's it appears to be analytically reduced to 'making others accept one's own values'.

Since the analysis is at the level of individuals, the solution should be also, but Banfield was perhaps surprisingly pessimistic about the prospects of any effective solution at any level. Certainly he did not regard large-scale state intervention as having any effect except in the very long term, since the causal conditions are located ultimately in cultural attitudes, not in the factors on which state intervention operates. But neither does he fall back on the traditional liberal solution of improving educational provision, since he has no illusions about the difficulties of inculcating the civic virtues necessary for proper development.

Banfield's work, though a classic of its kind, is recognised even by pluralists as too limited in scope to provide a full explanation of the phenomenon of long-term peripheral deprivation. A development of Banfield's explanation is provided by Johan Galtung on the basis of his own research in a similar environment.[17] Galtung is much more concerned than Banfield to place the individual within the variety of social structures in which social interaction takes place, though ultimately his explanation, like Banfield's, is behaviourist in its terms and suppositions. In particular, he criticises Banfield for ignoring structural or (more properly) ecological factors, such as density of population, rates of illiteracy and level of Communist voting. But Galtung concludes that the main problem is that the target of loyalty, which is the family, is ill-adapted to operating at the level on which new institutions will emerge. Politico-economic development occurs with the emergence of collective action in cooperative associations—not only limited companies but also political parties, trade unions and social organisations based on trust and enterprise. Whereas Banfield largely ignores economic linkages, Galtung makes a clear connection between market forces and political development, arguing that the traditional ethics described by Banfield actually obstruct the proper working of the modern marketplace. In this perspective the centre is much more concrete and material than in the more ideal culture supposed by Banfield, so that problems of geographical distance, cultural isolation and economic marginality can all be recognised; but the combination of causes—cultural lag together with structural factors—is not an easy one, since the two levels of causality implied do not immediately present themselves as mutually complementary. In generic terms, both Banfield and Galtung reiterate the familiar theme that the fundamental problem is the lack of enterpreneurs both in economics and in politics able to show the peripheral masses how to make the system work for them. So areas which might otherwise be productively integrated into developed societies are constrained by an unchanging ethos dominated by traditionalist elites, subject to economic and political dependence on the centre. Typically, as in southern Italy, high birth rates and inflexible landholding systems can lead to persistent land-hunger and social unrest which demand the attention of the central elites, but if pluralist arguments are accepted, the unrest resulting from the inadequate diffusion of liberal authority is not a problem that can be solved in the short term. As a safety-valve mechanism, as well as in the effort to use the peripheral labour resources productively, liberal economists such as Vera Lutz have recommended the encouragement of emigration to areas of labour-scarcity,[18] but this may also produce problems of integration in the long term.

## MARXIST THEORIES OF REGIONALISM

An entirely different version of this problem is put forward by Marxists. The general form of the argument can be found in Paul Baran's *Political Economy of Growth*, though that work is part of the Marxist school of writings on the Third World and dependence rather than specifically about intra-national centre–periphery relations.[19] On the pluralist argument that the entrepreneur is the moving force behind economic development, Baran argues that the periphery, though marginal, may be fully penetrated by capitalist values and capitalist economic roles; the nature of the integration into international capitalism means that structural constraints, such as external control of peripheral investment and production decisions, ensure that industrial development is limited and vulnerable. It is therefore either a tautology or a fallacy to state that lack of entrepreneurial talent is the reason for poor growth. It is tautological if all that is being said is that where there is no industrial capitalism, there are no industrial capitalists, and vice versa; and it is fallacious if it is intended as a substantial proposition meaning that the limited growth in some Third World economies is due to the absence of innovators, intermediaries, risk-takers and the like. Baran argues that such economic actors are present in all forms of development, though certainly not always as capitalist entrepreneurs. What has to be explained is why in the long-term stagnant economies the innovators do not turn their hands to productive capital accumulation (or, for that matter, to the mobilisation of poitical forces, though this would not be Baran's argument). Risk-takers and innovators in underdeveloped economies tend to be found either in highly speculative enterprises such as property development and money lending or in the liberal professions, the traditional home of the unproductive intermediaries.

One of the first Marxist writers on the problem of the Italian south was a founder of the Communist party of Italy, Antonio Gramsci. Gramsci argued, like Banfield did some thirty years later, with a direct political aim, but in Gramsci's case the problem was to develop a political strategy for the Communists adequate to the conditions in the rural, clerical-dominated and agricultural south, as well as to the conditions in the much more urban, secular and industrialised north of Italy. Gramsci saw the dichotomy between the two not as a centre–periphery relationship but rather as an aspect of the way in which the interests of monopoly capital used the state to keep the undeveloped areas repressed and passive; Gramsci describes the south variously as 'a semi-colonial market', a 'source of savings and taxes' and a 'pool of cheap docile reserve labour'.[20] But it must not be thought that this domination is exercised only through the repression of dissent by police, though this certainly is important. Gramsci's most original contribution to Marxism lies in his analysis of the ways in which the state transforms coercive force into a structured more consensual domination to which he gives the name 'hegemony'.

Gramsci is therefore arguing that class cleavages can and do take spatial forms, such as urban capitalist middle-class versus rural semi-feudal peasantry. However, he does not as Tarrow seems to argue, ignore class contradictions within the territorially based proletarian community;[21] in fact he pays particular attention to the complex class structure of the depressed areas, identifying as crucial within them the role of the rural intelligentsia, the commercial interme-diaries and the local clergy.[22] The rural intelligentsia, together with the religious authorities, have a major part to play in translating the values of the external forces into an acceptable ideology within the terms of the exploited areas.

Unlike the pluralist approach which when dealing with macro-political issues directs its attention towards attitudes, ethics, belief systems and individualistic cultural compo-nents, this Gramscian Marxist perspective investigates the linkages between economic structures (such as landholding), national development (such as the effect on artisan or fledgling industry of suddenly imposed competition with more advanced areas) and the instruments of intellectual control through which the economic domination is legiti-mated. The exploited areas (in this case the south of Italy) remain underdeveloped and poor because the more adv-anced sectors, which control the state, direct and dominate the underdeveloped areas in a way which blocks any attempt at organisation and cooperation with them. The most active elements of the intelligentsia are won over by personal privileges to the prevailing ideology as well as being subject to the prevalent intellectual control while the peasants are tied to the land by economic hardship imposed through short-term, small-unit landholding contracts (such as sharecropping), which discourage capital investment. By the fragmentation of units inherent in this system, the development of large-scale capitalistic enterprises which might compete with the advanced sectors is discouraged.

Gramsci's analysis is taken up by the Italian sociologist Alessandro Pizzorno and applied particularly to the 'Amoral Familism' thesis of Banfield.[23] The pluralist approach is repeatedly criticised (and not just by Marxists) for its neglect of 'objective factors', and Pizzorno adds to this with his charge that Banfield is both superficial and culturally inaccurate. The problem with states of this kind is not that they exclude all organised groups, as the doctrine of Napoleonic administration says they should, but that they exclude unequally and grant access and favours to certain privileged groups. Though Banfield's research is partially accurate if read merely as description, it does not explain fully the lack of concerted action by those excluded from privilege, and it is at least misleading, if not inaccurate, in its neglect of the pre-modern political organisation of these areas, which is based on personal patronage networks centred on landholders. This traditional organisation characterised by individualistic, vertical clienteles militates strongly against the horizontal group-formation typical of modern politics. It is certainly a surprising omission on Banfield's part not to take full account of the importance of patronage and clientelism in their own right as determinants of political action.

But the most important element in Marxist analysis of centre–periphery relations is the concept of historical marginality. This is an unusually clear and simple notion to come from Marxist theory, though in its factual basis it is also highly contentious. Pizzorno argues that the modern underdevelopment of the south of Italy can only be understood in terms of the historical relationship of area to the locations of power and productivity by which it has been dominated and to which it has been marginal. It is always uneconomic for capitalism to develop areas it calls 'backward', and the areas themselves lack the capacity to create and sustain their own growth.

In one form of the argument, which is found in Pizzorno,

the periphery has a very limited role in residual economic activities, usually in those associated with peasant farming, characterised by small-scale, low-technology, fragmented units operating close to subsistence. Most commonly, the units will only use family labour, but if wage-labour is employed, there is likely to be a large differential between wage rates in the periphery and those paid in the centre. The lower productivity of peripheral units and the low proportion of wage costs in total costs means that the relatively cheap labour does not give the periphery a significant price advantage over more advanced units. As well as suffering greater vulnerability to international trade cycles, the periphery also suffers a loss of labour to the more advanced areas.

This argument is particularly applicable to southern Italy and to other sub-national areas of southern Europe. A more general argument takes up the reference by Gramsci to the 'semi-colonial market' and develops the concept of 'internal colonialism', which has had widespread application to areas as different from one another as the peripheral regions of Great Britain, the black homelands in South Africa, Alaska and the Amerindian areas of Central and South America.[24] There is more than a little that is suspicious about a term which can be used in so many different contexts, and Hechter's original thesis has been criticised for being unhistoric and too-abstract. There are in fact several different categories of territorial cleavage to which the term has been applied, but the major development by Hechter on Pizzorno's line is the increased emphasis on the penetration of the periphery by the centre; the periphery is seen as dependent in the sense that industrialisation takes place in a manner which leaves it dependent on the centre for investment and management control. This might now be more applicable to areas like southern Italy, where massive state intervention since the 1950s has resulted in a patchy, vulnerable and fragile industrial growth and in considerable changes in the political culture of the region, than it is to Scotland, the Basque Country or Northern Ireland, where, as Tom Nairn observed in the 1970s,[25] the peripheral regions have relatively industrialised, middle-class cultures. In the

British case at least, the problem of national or ethnic difference was masked for a long period by development occurring in the peripheries at the same rate and in similar ways to development in industrial England.

The pluralist answer to these arguments would not be to deny the existence of conflict; on the contrary, one of the great virtues of the pluralist model in the eyes of its proponents is the emphasis on the positive benefits of conflict and diversity within a society. But pluralists, like Shils, would put any conflict, even the most profound, into the context of societal integration, to the extent that 'one cannot speak about society without at the same time making statements about the integration of society. That is what a society is'.[26] Where the Marxist identifies penetration of the periphery by capitalist values and roles as an aspect of the contradictions within capitalism, the pluralist sees diffusion of central vlues as a force overriding the immediate disagreements:

Conflict would seem by definition to be incompatible with integration . . . In reality, however, conflict and integration are incompatible only with respect to the particular actions and intentions constitutive of the conflict, and the particular ends sought by each of the parties to the conflict . . . The parties to a conflict remain, moreover, parts of a single society by virtue of their acknowledgement of a common name, by their participation in certain common divisions of labour and allocation from which they cannot extricate themselves except by secession, emigration or anchoritic or cenobitic withdrawal.[27]

But the traditionally minded researcher might be forgiven for asking what these two distinct approaches have to do with politics, for both of them in their own ways have argued major political components of regions and regionalism out of court. The pluralist discussing large-scale societal issues of this sort does not argue for decisional methods or observation of group interaction but rather for the supposedly inevitable, though always incomplete, diffusion of central values, so that understanding political power is a matter of charting the spread or decline of these values. The Marxist, on the other hand, sees political power as an epiphenomenon determined by structural economic relationships.

There remains, however, a wide range of views covering more obviously political aspects of the phenomena which could only be described together as 'elitist' if we accept that term as a residual category.

## ELITE THEORIES OF REGIONALISM

The initial interest of political researchers into the question of what to do with the regions came about, it must be said, not out of concern for neglected political interests in the periphery (what Tarrow refers to as 'regionalism as peripheral defence')[28] but because of a trend thought to have been observed in modern politics which seemed to go to the heart of the functioning of modern political systems. This was the idea, popularised in Shonfield's *Modern Capitalism*[29] but covered in a very large number of other works also, that a shift was occurring away from territorially based representation towards representation based on functional cleavages, with a consequent decline in the power of the territorially based representative assemblies known as parliaments and an ever-increasing role for corporatist organisations able to negotiate for organised functional interests at the national level. Associated with this corporatist trend, which seemed to decrease the power of the traditional peripheral politicans, was the development of regionalism as a policy mode, to which we referred earlier. There is not space to discuss here even briefly the many controversial issues raised in the literature on corporatism,[30] but in so far as territorial politics are concerned, it must be observed that even if there was or is a trend towards greater centralisation of political representation, this does not at all mean that there might not also be a functional deconcentration towards the periphery in specific cases. Central administrators, in other words, may find it necessary to use peripheral agencies to implement their decisions, either setting these up *ad hoc*, using existing administrative bodies, or even integrating elected officials.

Even if there is a general trend towards greater centralisation of representative decision-making in the industrialised

West—and in fact it is not unequivocally clear that this is so—that would not be a good reason for proclaiming the demise of regionalism as an issue. A characteristically political perspective would argue for a more articulated view of the complexity of centre–periphery relationships than either pluralism or Marxism can provide but would also warn against imposition of a single political model such as corporatism.

In the context of regions and regionalism, the political aspects of the problem lie in the types of representation of group interest, the ideological bases of relevant decisions, the forms of policy and its implementation. Those who adopt neither the Shils model nor the Marxist one cannot, as we have said, be readily categorised on this issue. However, a major assumption of those who reject both these models tends to be, as in Tarrow and Suleiman,[31] that in so far as group interests are expressed or mobilised through institutions that survive in the long term, those institutions develop their own rationality and specific conformations and have definite resources and limitations. This is so whatever the formal or legal scope of the institution, and it implies that any institution which serves as a channel for the articulation and aggregation of group interest in centre–periphery relations has a certain amount of autonomy, however limited that may be. The other major assumption made from this approach is that the territorial cleavages formed by the centre–periphery divide are not superimposed exactly on other social and political cleavages; on the contrary, the existence of cleavages within the centre and within the periphery may compel the central and peripheral elites to seek alliances—to pursue a coalitional strategy, in Tarrow's terms. The differing forms of these strategies will fundamentally alter the direction and scope of central interventions and peripheral responses.

Taking other factors into account, such as ideologically based preferences and the need for linkage between central and peripheral implementation agencies, Tarrow argues tht both the pluralist and the Marxist approaches pay insufficient attention to the political leverage which the periphery may exercise over the centre, and to the possibility of

communal interests being voiced in peripheral areas in ways
which can have real effect on the centre. But it should also
be emphasised that the limitations on peripheral leverage
are severe.

In general, the more directly political approach argues
that the manner in which the state may compensate for the
misery of the periphery is crucial and warrants serious
investigation since under certain circumstances it may be
possible for state intervention to operate with beneficial, net
long-term effects. For instance, Tarrow hypotheses that
where a generally populist strategy is adopted by a broad-
based urban-rural coalition able to call on a strong administrative apparatus, social policy may have a general redistributive impact in raising the standard of living in the
periphery. It might be argued, of course, that it is no good
thing for any state to be involved in redistributive welfare
policies—in which case the periphery must presumably be
left to fend for itself. Another less weighted but no less
effective criticism is that those areas which most need really
effective state intervention are the least likely to produce the
conditions in which intervention can work, the most obvious
reason for this being that deprived peripheral regions are, as
Banfield noted, not locations attrative to administrative and
political elites of the kind needed to implement the reforms.
It is much more likely that the distribution of state benefits
will occur through narrow informal political networks
supportive of the ruling central coalition. Alternatively,
effective intervention premised on strong central control
may be channelled in ways which are similarly narrow, even
if the aims of the central planning elites are closer to being
met. Tarrow finds a similar pattern in his study of
centre–periphery relations in France and Italy

By means of his administrative strategy, the French mayor gains more
from a more efficient system, but to do so he must accept the technocratic
values of the policy elite. By means of his political entrepreneurship, the
Italian mayor gains less from a clientelistic system, but he has more of a
chance to use the resources he gains for goals that correspond to the policy
values of his party.[32]

# CONCLUSION

It must be observed that only with difficulty and in a highly tentative manner can one find common ground between the theories discussed here; in this conversation the participants are talking past one another. Unlike the debates over the military-industrial complex, the general and wide-ranging nature of the arguments in this chapter reflects disagreement about what the problem is and different approaches to what constitutes a theory. The different theories are therefore not pointed directly against one another. This is, however, a revealing case study in that disagreements show up the different modes of explanation clearly. But the theories are not strictly comparable, and their strengths and weaknesses are not necessarily obvious.

As readers who have pursued this work from its outset will be aware, our argument is that one of the persistent strengths of pluralism is its capacity to produce consistent and detailed descriptions of particular aspects of reality. At its best, pluralist-orientated research provides us with an idealised description, in this case of the backward region, which puts certain features in very high relief; in Banfield's study, these features are mainly related to individual attitudes. From these is derived an explanation which rationalises the individual's actions in terms of universalisable rules of behaviour, which constitute a general ethic and which provide the logical ground for his or her action. Within the terms of the ethic the individual's action is rational; the ethic is therefore the logical explanation for the action, in a limited sense. But this explanation is achieved only at the cost of excluding a very wide range of other factors, and offers us no coherent, integrated answer to the question 'What causes the peasant to observe this ethic?'—a question that cannot really be answered in this methodology. At the same time, this ethic-based explanation fits well into a particular corner of the general theory of social integration offered by Shils, though the gap between the very general theorising of Shils and the over-particular and superficial descriptions of Banfield is a result of the great difficulty this variant of pluralism has in achieving its

declared aim of sustaining empirically based theory and
empirical research guided by theory. There is an irony in the
unverifiability of Shils's theory which might be fairly
condensed to 'Who says society says integration'. This
difficulty is shared by many such theories, of whatever
provenance, which rely on an idealised notion of culture to
carry the burden of explanation. However, the Marxist
position is no more verifiable even if it constitutes a more
rounded explanation. A major problem with traditional
Marxist analysis is that by laying all sins at the door of
capitalist development, it fails to explain what keeps the
periphery in a long-term relationship with the centre, since
there appears to be little in the relationship for either
partner. Gramsci's theory of hegemony is a partial answer to
this; but there remains unanswered the question how
development occurs at all in peripheral areas. In Italy some
development in the south has occurred, though it is of a
fragile and unbalanced nature, and it is not seriously
suggested that this area is yet capable of self-sustained
growth. This development is dependent largely on state
intervention, sometimes relying on direct compulsion on
state-owned enterprises; efforts to oblige large Italian-based
multi nationals like Fiat and Olivetti to follow suit have been
much less successful. Neither the historical marginality nor
internal colonialism arguments fully explain the action of the
state in depressed areas; the fragmented nature of the
responses of capital in such areas does not encourage holistic
explanations.

The elitists offer us explanations less ambitious than either
of the grand theories, explanations which borrow un-
ashamedly from other conventions and which have obvious
gaps and limitations. They do not purport to explain fully
why peripheral areas are in the condition in which they find
themselves, nor do they regard one dimension (in this case,
the political) as offering the complete explanation. But
whereas the other approaches relapse into pessimism in the
face of these permanent blots on their theories, the elitist
line of argument is much more hopeful, largely because of its
emphasis on the ways in which interaction between key
elites provides room for manoeuvre for peripheral actors.

Such peripheral elites may operate in a variety of different spheres—ideological, economic, party political, administrative—and their range enables them to extract support, admittedly within limits, from more specialist central elites. But they do see the problem as a political one, identifying the political dimension as one involving choice, decision-making power, boundary setting and coalitional strategy.

The different levels at which power operates are therefore crucial to one's definitions of the problem of regionalism and to one's mode of explanation. The very serious policy implications of decisions in this field make theory a major component, even if unacknowledged, of errors and successes that are suffered or enjoyed by the population of peripheral areas.

## NOTES

1. *See* R. Rose, 'On the Priorities of Government: A Developmental Analysis of Public Policy' in *European Journal of Political Research*, 1976, pp. 247–89, and the case study on this issue in chapter 8.
2. J. Hayward, *Governing France: The One and Indivisible Republic* (London, Wiedenfeld and Nicholson, 1983).
3. S. Tarrow, P.J. Katzenstein, and L. Graziano, eds., *Territorial Politics in Industrial Nations* (New York, Praeger Publishers, 1978).
4. S. Tarrow, *Between Centre and Periphery: Grassroots Politicians in Italy and France* (New Haven, Yale University Press, 1977).
5. R.A.W. Rhodes, *Control and Power in Central-Local Government Relations* (Aldershow, Gower Publishing/SSRC, 1981).
6. Tarrow, Katzenstein and Graziano, eds., *op. cit.*, p. 100.
7. *Ibid.*
8. E. Shils, *Centre and Periphery, Essays in Macrosociology* (Chicago, Chicago University Press, 1975), p. 11.
9. Tarrow, *op. cit.*, (1977), p. 19.
10. Shils, *op. cit.*, p. 3.
11. *Ibid.*, p. viii.
12. P.A. Gourevitch, *Paris and the Provinces, The Politics of Local Government Reform in France* (London, George Allen and Unwin, 1980), p. 2.
13. *See*, in particular, Shils, *op. cit.*, pp. xli–xliii, 406–516.
14. *Ibid.*, p. xxx.
15. E. Banfield, *The Moral Basis of a Backward Society* (New York, Free Press, 1958).

16. *Ibid.*, p. 33.
17. J. Galtung, *Members of Two Worlds* (New York, Columbia University Press, 1974). It must be emphasised that though on this issue his adoption of Banfield's terminology and of some of his methods marks his conclusion as clearly pluralist, his general position is idiosyncratic and distinctly more radical in its tone than either that of Banfield or Shils.
18. V. Lutz, *Italy: A Study in Economic Development* (London, Oxford University Press, 1962).
19. P. Baran, *The Political Economy of Growth* (Harmondsworth, Penguin, 1973).
20. A. Gramsci, *La Questione Meridionale* (Roma, Editori Riuniti, 1974).
21. Tarrow, *op. cit.*, (1977), p. 25.
22. A. Gramsci, *Quaderni del carcere, vol. IV* (Torino, Giulio Einaudi editore, 1975), pp. 2035–40.
23. A. Pizzorno, 'Amoral Familism and Historical Marginality', in *International Review of Community Development*, 1966, pp. 55–66; also in M. Dogan and R. Rose, eds., *European Politics: A Reader* (Boston, Little, Brown and Co., 1971).
24. *See* M. Hechter, *Internal Colonialism: The Celtic Fringe in British National Development* (Berkeley, University of California Press, 1975); T. Nairn, *The Break-up of Britain: Crisis and Neo-nationalism* (London, New Left Books, 1977).
25. Nairn, *ibid.*, pp. 199–207.
26. Shils, *op. cit.*, p. xliii.
27. *Ibid.*, pp. 82–3.
28. Tarrow, *op. cit.* (1977), pp. 97–122.
29. A. Shonfield, *Modern Capitalism* (London, Oxford University Press, 1969).
30. *See* P.C. Schmitter and G. Lehmbruch, *Trends Towards Corporatist Intermediation* (London, Sage Publications, 1979).
31. *See* Tarrow, *op. cit.* (1977 and 1978) and E.N. Suleiman, *Politics Power and Bureaucracy in France: The Administrative Elite* (Princeton, Princeton University Press, 1974).
32. Tarrow, *op. cit.* (1977), p. 248.

# 8  Growth of Government

The term 'government', like so many of the basic concepts in political science, is open to a variety of interpretations. For instance, government may be seen as a set of institutions, whether this be all public sector institutions, or a limited set of them, such as Cabinet, Parliament or Congress and the Civil Service. Or it may be seen as a process—the act of 'authoritatively allocating values'.[1] The issue of the meaning of government is not simply a semantic one. If we are to point to government growth, then different conceptions of the term might lead to different measures of growth.[2]

In fact, if one understands government growth to refer to the increase in the degree to which government affects the nature of the society in which it operates, it is possible to derive a variety of measures according to the different ways in which a government can influence its environment. Perhaps the most important way in which government affects its environment is through passing laws. In this sense, government growth means passing more laws which affect an increasingly large number of aspects of our lives. The number of laws on the statute book increases cumulatively since governments repeal relatively few laws.[3] While precise indicators of the numbers of laws depend upon more precise definition of what are considered as laws (there is a variety of different types of order, statute and regulation), one crude indicator for the expansion of legislation in the United States is that the *Federal Register* grew from 2,355 pages in 1936 to 60,221 pages in 1975; another indicator for Britain is found in the *Index to the Statutes*—the index listing legislation for the period from 1235 to 1935 takes up 788 pages, while that for 1936 to 1982 takes up 978 pages. However, to measure in laws is unsatisfactory since this treats all laws as equal. A law which regulates the ability of a local authority to display venereal disease posters in public places is given the same weighting as a law which expands the welfare state substantially through the provision of free school education or establishes a free health service.

Another way that government can intervene in its environment is to employ people to do the intervening for it—manpower. Thus the growth in government could be measured in terms of the number of people that government employs. This has increased from 7 per cent of the workforce in 1929 to 19 per cent in 1980 in the United States, while the figures for Britain are 11 and 31 per cent, respectively.[4] However, such a measure can be criticised on the grounds that much of the state's activity, that covered by the term 'income maintenance', is left out of the definition of government activity, as is the important role that government plays in financing, according to a strict definition, non-state activities (e.g. incentives to firms).

The most common means of measuring the growth of government is suggested by a third way, that the government can affect its social, economic and cultural environment—spending money. The level of expenditure and expenditure growth is usually expressed as a percentage of a measure of the total economic activity of a particular country, such as Gross National Product. In Britain, public expenditure ran at 44.6 per cent of GNP in 1983, while in the United States this was 34.2 per cent. Moreover, these levels show a substantial increase in expenditure over time: in 1900 the percentage of GNP spent by the government was 15.0 in Britain and 6.9 in the United States.[5]

Whatever measure that one uses, government has grown rapidly during this century. Moreover, the nature of government intervention in its economic, social and cultural environment has changed. Rose points to a developmental model of the growth of government which suggests that governments usually begin by adopting what he terms 'defining functions'.[6] Defining functions, such as defence, internal law and order and tax collection are the *sine qua non* priorities of the state. Without these functions the state would simply cease to exist. Once the state has provided internal and external order, it begins to expand its functions outside the defining field into 'resource mobilisation'—creating the right conditions for the economic prosperity of the country through the development of roads and communications. Finally, when the country is sufficiently economically developed, the state can pursue social welfare priorities, such as education and social services.

In both a quantitative and qualitative sense, government has grown. An increased public workforce engages in a wider range of activities and an increased portion of the population is dependent upon the state for benefits; both are paid out of an increasing share of economic resources devoted to the public sector. How can this growth be explained? One popular explanation is the 'displacement effect hypothesis' of Peacock and Wiseman.[7] This hypothesis suggests that governmental expenditure grows by a series of relatively sharp leaps caused by some form of emergency or crisis. In a crisis, such as a war, a government is forced to increase expenditure sharply, in this case for military mobilisation and consequently revenue. Assuming the government does not lower its revenue, there will be some additional revenue at its disposal once the crisis is over. This additional revenue is then spent on non-emergency state activities; that is, it is displaced. After each crisis the level of state activity increases. The problem with this explanation is that it does not explain the growth that has occurred outside the crisis periods.

Another popular explanation was offered by the German economist Wagener when he proposed his 'law of increasing state actions'.[8] What Wagener's Law suggested was that the expansion of public services reflected the 'exigencies of industrialisation'—as a nation industrialises it develops needs for collectively provided goods such as roads, sewers transport, and so on. While the merits and demerits of this argument have been explored extensively, one major objection to it is that it begs the question of who identifies and defines the 'need' for an expansion in public intervention, and how a perceived need results in specific policies that produce an expanded state sector. As in the other chapters, this chapter looks at three broad approaches to explaining the growth of government.

# MARXIST APPROACHES TO THE GROWTH OF GOVERNMENT

Marxist accounts of the growth of government do not concentrate specifically upon the issue of government growth, rather their discussions of increasing public spending are usually couched in terms of a more general explanation of the role of the state. Corresponding to the earlier discussion of the forms of Marxist thought, there are two major Marxist perspectives on the growth of government. One, an instrumental perspective, argues that the state is an instrument to maintain the capitalist mode of production, and the other, a structuralist perspective, contends that the growth of state intervention may be generated by social and political pressures as well as the economic requirements of capitalism but that ultimately the scope for manoeuvre for the state is constrained by the requirements of the capitalist mode of production.

Instrumentalist theories locate the expanding role of the state in terms of two contradictory needs. First, the state must meet the ever-increasing requirements for effective demand generated by the capitalist mode of production. Second, the state must also legitimise its role in preserving and reproducing an exploitative and inegalitarian system of production through the provision of welfare benefits. These contradictory roles create a fiscal and legitimacy crisis for the state, which will ultimately be overthrown by the working class.[9]

The role of the state in creating effective demand emerges from the tendency of conditions of relatively open market competition to develop into increasingly monopolistic and oligopolistic market relationships. As monopolistic/oligopolistic companies came to control domestic markets, they looked to the state to follow colonial policies as these companies sought expansion overseas. The cost of inter-imperialist rivalry and wars, as well as the cost of administering the colonies, eventually came to be seen as wasteful and this, with the eocnomic crisis of the 1930s, led to a problem of low profitability and under-consumption; in other words, a decline in effective demand.[10] The decline in effective demand also affected the legitimacy of capitalism since it created mass unemployment and poverty at home and anti-imperialism abroad. The pressures of demand management and legitimacy therefore produced social democratic welfare policies at home. We saw in Chapter 6 how Marxists argue that military spending is one solution to underconsumption; at the same time Marxists would also argue that Keynesian demand management and social welfarism is another instrument for creating higher effective consumer demand, which also serves to create further false consciousness among the working class and defuse threats to the legitimacy of the state.[11]

These two developments are for Marxists contradictory since they ultimately undermine capitalism in the form of crises of legitimacy and fiscal insolvency. This is brought about by the spiralling levels of taxation upon the private sector. Taxes on the private sector produced by a social welfarist strategy raise costs and decrease competitiveness. In order to seek to maintain profits, government must create extra demand, spending goes up and taxes follow. This spiralling is further fuelled by the rising expectations among the working class for higher levels of spending. The consequence of this process is the 'fiscal crisis of the state'.[12] The only effective options for the state are to reduce concessions to the working class or increase taxation further; the first solution would undermine state legitimacy and the second creates an unresolvable crisis of legitimacy.

Obviously, this school of thought has its strengths in common with Marxist insights in general. In particular, the instrumental approach locates government growth in a broader pattern of social and economic development. However, it has been challenged on a number of grounds. First, the approach says very little about the precise actors involved in the growth of government. It does not matter who designed, opposed, supported or acquiesced in the development of welfare state policies—they were all behaving in a manner determined by the logic of capitalism. This tends to make analysis of practical power reductionist or simplistic.

Second, the approach leads to non-falsifiable explanations, meaning that no evidence that can be marshalled could possibly fail to fit in with it.[13] Perhaps the most glaring example of this problem of non-falsifiability can be found in the manner in which Marxists have been able to argue that state spending is functional for capitalism: increases in state spending are functional since they increase effective demand and legitimacy, yet so are decreases in state spending since they increase the profitability private sector firms.

Partly in recognition of these problems, a modified structuralist account of the development of the state has emerged. This approach draws heavily from the insights of Gramsci, Lukacs and Adorno.[14] Habermas sought to develop an argument which introduced the individual actors within the political system to a Marxist account of the state.[15] He argued that the legitimacy of the inegalitarian capitalist system was maintained by ideological conditioning (false consciousness), repression (real or anticipated) and instrumentalism (the material benefits of capitalist systems, including social welfare benefits). The problem for capitalism, however, was that in allowing the state to intervene so extensively, economic crises had become internalised within the state, and this undermined the state's legitimacy. This is close to instrumental accounts of the role of the state, but Habermas argued that these economic crises would only threaten capitalism if they were unresolved. The ability of the state to resolve these crises would depend on the state's ability to raise revenue and mobilise public support. If it did neither, then a legitimacy crisis would occur.

The crucial point here is that individual perceptions about benefits and the legitimacy of state actions to overcome economic crises were equally as important as the crises themselves. This introduces a new avenue of analysis into Marxist writings; it opens the possibility of recognising that social and political systems may not operate solely on the basis of objective laws but may have a degree of freedom driven by the individual, group and elite perceptions.

This point was developed by Miliband in his distinction between economic power and state power.[16] He argued that social, political and bureaucratic elites have their own sources of political power which allow them to act relatively autonomously or independently of the requirements of capital. While these actors might try to protect capitalism, the ability of the dominant fractions or parts of capital (monopoly and finance capital) to use the state as they wished was always problematical. The dominant capitalist fraction requires a power bloc which will control the state in its own interests, but because people always perceive their reality subjectively, the ability of those in control of the state to deliver the goods is always in question.

This is particularly so in the growth of government. From this perspective, the growth of government may well owe something to the need by capital to socialise demand and legitimate the mode of production; on the other hand, political power is relatively open and the growth of government may be driven by pluralistic bargaining, rising expectations and through effective working-class parties seizing power due to a fortuitous combination of forces in the political struggle over and around the state. Of course, not even structuralists would suggest that such political power would allow the working class to overthrow capitalism.[17] Workers parties and pressure groups may seize power and expand the role of the state, but if this is pushed too far, it will be constrained by economic power in the form of economic crises (currency crises, lack of private investment, decline in profitability).

Structuralist accounts therefore seek to accommodate the insights of elitist and pluralist writers and synthesise these with a broader historical understanding of the development of capitalism. But in doing so they raise further problems of their own. Not the least of these problems is that raised by Poulantzas that the concentration upon the pluralistic influences within the state (introducing the 'problematic of the subject'), calls into question the whole basis of a specifically Marxist analysis, and structuralist analysis may thus become indistinguishable from pluralist or elitist analysis.[18] Another related problem is in the general vagueness of the relationship between the constraints of capitalism and the scope for state autonomy and pluralistic policy-making processes—none of the structuralist approaches offer clear criteria according to which we may define the limits of each. This leads to a third problem, that of falsifiability again. Virtually nothing that the state does can contradict the theory. Government growth might be a result of the requirements of capitalism. On the other hand, if it is impossible to find any evidence of the congruence between government growth and the requirements of capitalism over a certain period, then this could be explained as a result of the autonomy of the state from the requirements of capitalism.

## ELITE APPROACHES TO STATE GROWTH

The approaches which have been here categorised as elite approaches do not suggest that a small clique were responsible for a decision taken at some unspecified point in the past that government should grow. As far as we are aware, nobody is suggesting this. However, some authors suggest that governmental elites, by which is meant the permanent officials within a government bureaucracy, are responsible to a significant extent for the growth in government.

The notion that officials or 'bureaucrats' have a vested interest in the expansion of the public sector is a well accepted one; it is reflected in C. Northcote Parkinson's Law that 'work expands to as to fill the time for its completion', as does manpower, and a persistent theme in the popular British comedy series *Yes Minister* was the importance to top bureaucrats of maintaining large numbers of officials to do nothing particularly useful. This popular insight was transformed into a general theory of bureaucracy by William Niskanen, an economist.

Concentrating upon the growth in government budgets as an indicator of the size of government in the United States, Niskanen argues that officials have a vested interest in maintaining large budgets. For a bureaucrat, 'salary, perquisites of the office, public reputation, power patronage [and] output of the bureau . . . are a positive function of the total *budget* of the bureau during the bureaucrat's tenure'.[19] This assumption of 'budget maximisation' is constrained by the expectations of its sponsors—primarily congressional committees—responsible for approving expenditure. The relationship between the bureau and its sponsors is such that the constraints on budget maximisation are likely to be weaker than the factors operating in its favour. First, because the sponsors of the bureau's expenditure are likely to appreciate the benefits of extra expenditure without responsibility for the costs, and second, because 'advocacy of spending programs tends to be concentrated, and the opposition is diffused'.

The approach adopted by Niskanen is very strongly tailored to the United States condition. Moreover, the empirical basis for his hypotheses about the budget maximisation assumption and the complicity of sponsors in the growth of government has been severely challenged on two main grounds. First, on the theoretical grounds that the complicity between congressional committees and the bureaucracy may produce lower than anticipated budgets, and second, that such a model ignores the institutional and political realities of the executive branch in America—above all, the Presidential Office of Management and Budget and the plurality of other actors in the policy-making process.[20]

## PLURALISTIC APPROACHES TO GOVERNMENT GROWTH

A variety of authors have pointed to the importance of what may be termed 'intra-governmental' influences upon expenditure growth. Those employed by the state do argue for an expanded state role in their sphere—doctors argue for more health spending, as do teachers for more educational spending. However, few would argue that this has a determining influence on the size of the public sector or that such a diversity of actors can be described as a single 'elite'. Rather, authors such as the US Advisory Commission on Intergovernmental relations and Rose and Peters in Britain tend to stress the plurality of causes of growth in public expenditure.[21]

Rose and Peters argue that there are three broad groups of actors who have traditionally been in favour of higher spending, at least since 1945: the *producers* of public goods and services, including leading politicians; the *consumers* of public spending, including voters and welfare recipients; and the *suppliers* of public goods and services—public officials and professionals dependent upon the state for their income. The producers of public expenditure have helped increase public spending since the competition for votes has led politicians to promise more and more spending; moreover, since governments come into office with a vast amount of spending commitments inherited from previous governments, their ability to reduce these commitments substantially is limited through the length of time that would be required to make such reductions, and further, they are unlikely to court unpopularity through doing so.[22] As Aaron Wildavsky has stated, 'political addition is easier than political subtraction'.[23]

The consumers of public expenditure have contributed towards the growth of public expenditure not only through expecting the government to spend more on them but also by increasing in number. People are living longer, and a greater proportion of the population in 1984 consists of older people (11.3 per cent aged over 65 in the United States and 14.8 per cent in Britain) than it did in 1945 (7.5 per cent and 10.1 per cent in the United States and Britain, respectively). Government expenditure, through provision of better living conditions and health care for the elderly, has itself contributed towards this. Older people are more expensive for the state to care for—not only are they eligible for state pensions, which account for 13 per cent of public expenditure in Britain and 22 per cent of the federal budget in the United States, they are also the most costly group for public health services since they are likely to require expensive operations and long stays in hosptial. Government programmes such as old age pensions, and services such as education, commit government to expenditure which varies due to factors outside its control—demographic changes. As Rose and Peters show, for many major government programmes, demographic changes relevant to government expenditure between the end of the Second World War and the middle of the 1970s all tended to commit the government to higher levels of spending.[24]

Supplier groups, that is to say the welfare professional organisations such as teachers' groups and social workers' groups, also have an interest in the expansion of government expenditure. This need not necessarily be for the pure career-orientated reasons suggested by Niskanen—whether teachers or social workers have suggested policy changes that increase expenditure for pure self-interest or through the genuine altruistic belief that a greater supply of their services will benefit their society, such groups have occupied central roles in the expansion of their services.[25]

The growth of government reflected these upward pressures on expenditure. Yet these upward pressures became irresistible in the period of the economic prosperity that followed the Second World War. Rose and Peters regard this period as one of 'treble affluence'; first economic growth was large so that, second, government expenditure could increase without, third, reducing through taxation the real wages of individuals. Consequently, government could grow without encountering any substantial opposition from those whose taxes would pay for this growth. As Heclo states:

Economic growth, with its virtually automatic increases in tax revenues, tended to make social policy expansion almost costless in political terms. In the era of austerity, consolidating the welfare state had required strong political backing, something that was a long time in coming until depression and war eventually mobilised these forces. In an era of affluence, passive acquescence could suffice; politically the welfare state could expand on the basis of more for everybody . . . Those who saw an 'end of ideology' in this period were, in a limited sense, right. Welfare state politics could lie in repose while the engine of economic growth did its work.[26]

Not only did government growth require little positive commitment, the acceptance of a form of Keynesianism, termed by Rose and Peters as 'one-eyed Keynesianism', seemed to be telling politicians that public expenditure growth was a good thing.[27] The message distilled from Keynes's theories by politicians was that governments should increase public expenditure to generate economic growth through stimulating demand. The Keynesianism of

post-war governments in the West was 'one eyed' because it
ignored the corollary of this: that when the economy is
growing fast, expenditure reductions can prevent it from
'overheating'.

Perhaps the only major systematic attempt to explore the
validity of contending approaches to explaining the growth
of government is provided by the United States Advisory
Commission on Intergovernmental Relations (ACIR) study
of the growth of government in America. After carefully
exploring a variety of different theoretical approaches to
explaining government growth, the study looked at seven
different policy areas—public assistance, elementary and
secondary education, higher education, environment, unemployment, libraries and fire protection—and examined who
or what was important in the process of governmental
growth. The study concentrated on three major groups of
influences: internal policy actors, including Congress, the
president, interest groups, the bureaucracy and courts;
external policy actors including public opinion, elections,
political parties and the press; and environmental influences, including demographic change and crises.[28]

The conclusion reached after analysing the seven policy
areas was that no one influence could be seen to have caused
the growth of government. There was only one influence
which was important across all seven policy areas—the role
of Congress. Congress, through individual 'congressional
entrepreneurs', usually initiated regulation as rather small
and modest programmes many of the programmes that later
grew to add substantially to public expenditure and regulation. The initially modest programme would then be
supported by a variety of groups—other Congressmen and
pressure groups—and there would be pressures for expansion of the programme: a 'spiral effect'. One of the ACIR
examples of this is the Area Redevelopment Act. This act,
aimed at combating unemployment in depressed areas, was
sponsored by a single Democratic Senator, Paul Douglas,
and was provoked by the hard core unemployment in south
Illinois, his home state. After six years of persistent
agitation, the ARA became law. The ARA programme
itself was short-lived. It did, however, 'create a demand for

infusion of development funds into increasingly more jurisdictions. As a result, by 1979, ARA's successor, the Economic Development Administration (EDA), encompassed fully 84.5 per cent of the nation's population in its 2,230 designated areas'.[29]

The dynamic of a small beginning, usually in Congress, creating a further set of demands for an expanded programme among inside players, especially from interest groups, applied across most of the ACIR case studies. Surprisingly, among the inside players the bureaucracy did not occupy a particularly important role. The outside influences, courts, public opinion, and so on, tended to be supportive rather than causal; they offered a series of 'green lights' to governmental growth, while demographic trends were of importance in some policy areas (public assistance and education) and wars and crises were important in public assistance, higher education and unemployment.

## CONCLUSION

Of course, the ACIR study cannot be taken as unambiguous falsification of Marxist and elite theory approaches and support for pluralist approaches. The ACIR case studies, as discussed in the ACIR report, do indeed conform to the models of pluralism outlined in Chapter 5. Yet, as was made clear in the community power debate, methodology is closely related to the nature of the conclusions reached. As such, the ACIR study shares much in common with the pluralist community power studies, a form of decision-making study of important and diverse policies. It does not claim to explore a methodology for assessing the more difficult areas of non-decisions and the analysis of constraint which is suggested in Marxist approaches to the topic.

What, then, can one make of the various explanations for the growth of government? Clearly, explanations which locate this growth primarily in the notion of a conspiratorial and self-interested bureaucratic elite seem to be the least fruitful forms of analysis. In particular, the idea that a complex modern bureaucracy is capable of a coherent, cohesive and conspiratorial approach seems highly dubious, not least because of the fragmentation found within public orgaisations and the diversity of groups, legislative and interest groups, with which they interact. In fact, internal conflicts may exist within the bureaucracy as different sectors within it compete for scarce resources. Perhaps the most that one can say of the bureaucracy is that it is a force for inertia in public spending since, once created, agencies programmes and projects are very difficult to dismantle.[30] This means tht bureaucratic actors are but one among a plurality of forces maintaining the growth of government rather than primary cause of its growth.

Furthermore, as we have seen in the discussion of Marxist accounts, monocausal explanations do not provide particularly convincing arguments. The traditional Marxist view that high public spending ensured effective demand and legitimated the capitalist state has come under increasing empirical questioning as, in recent times, those who could be termed capitalists and their supporters have called for spending reductions. The fact that this has not yet led to a fundamental delegitimisation of the state's role has led some Marxists to develop a more sophisticated awareness of the divergent forces operating upon the growth of government. These more structuralist accounts recognise, along with pluralists, that politically there is a myriad of pressures forcing governments to grow in size and for public spending to increase. The only major difference between such accounts and pluralist accounts is that pluralists tend to describe the specific political pressures without attemtping to relate them to broader theories of the relationship between state, society and economy. The pluralist account is descriptively sound, therefore, but may be open to the charge that it ignores this broader vision of socio-economic and political change. On the other hand, pluralists may accuse the structural Marxist accounts of dressing up pluralism with a rather turgid form of Marxist verbiage. Moreover, if the state's role results from a variety of subjectively perceived wants, as the structuralist perspective appears to argue, then it is open to question whether such an explanation is consistent with the basic axioms of Marxist theory which imply that social, economic and political development are the result of the largely impersonal unfolding of the objective laws of history.

## NOTES

1. D. Easton, *The Political System* (New York, Knopf, 1953).
2. *See* R. Rose, 'What, if Anything, Is Wrong with Big Government?', *Journal of Public Policy*, Vol. 1, No. 1 (1981), pp. 5–36.
3. *See* R. Rose, *Understanding Big Government* (London, Sage, 1983).
4. *See* R. Rose, *et al.*, *Public Employment in Western Nations* (London, Cambridge University Press, 1985).
5. *See* S. Fabricant, *The Trend of Government Activity in the United States since 1900* (New York National Bureau of Economic Research, 1952); A.T. Peacock and J. Wiseman, *The Growth of Public Expenditure in the United Kingdom 1890–1955* (London, Allen and Unwin, 1967).
6. R. Rose, 'On the Priorities of Government: A Developmental Analysis', *European Journal of Political Research*, Vol. 4 (1976), pp. 247–89.
7. Peacock and Wiseman, *op. cit.*
8. Discussed in the P.D. Larkey, C. Stolp and M. Winer, 'Theorizing about the Growth of Government: A Research Assessment', *Journal of Public Policy*, Vol. 1, No. 2 (1981), pp. 176–8.
9. D.K. Fowley, 'State Expenditure from a Marxist Perspective', *Journal of Public Economics*, Vol. 9 (1978), pp. 221–38.
10. P. Baran and P. Sweezey, *Monopoly Capitalism* (Harmondsworth, Penguin, 1966), passim.
11. J. O'Connor, *The Fiscal Crisis of the State* (Norfolk, Va, St Martin's Press, 1973), passim.
12. *Ibid.*, p. 120ff.
13. Larkey, Stolp and Winer, *op. cit.*, p. 201.
14. For a discussion of these views, *see* R. Jessop, *The Capitalist State* (Oxford, Martin Robertson, 1982).
15. J. Habermas, *Legitimation Crisis* (London, Heinemann, 1976).
16. R. Miliband, *The State in Capitalist Society* (London, Weidenfeld and Nicolson, 1970).
17. N. Poulantzas, 'The Problem of the Capitalist State', *New Left Review*, Vol. 58 (1969), pp. 67–78.
18. N. Poulantzas, 'The Capitalist State—Reply to Miliband and Laclau', *New Left Review*, Vol. 95 (1976), pp. 63–83.
19. W.A. Niskanen, *Bureaucracy and Representative Government* (Chicago, University of Chicago Press, 1971), p. 22.
20. Larkey, Stopl and Winer, *op. cit.*, pp. 187–90.

21. Rose and Peters, *op. cit.*, US Advisory Commission on Inter-governmental Relations (ACIR), *The Federal Role in the Federal System: The Dynamics of Growth. An Agenda for American Federalism: Restoring Confidence and Competence. A–86.* (Washington DC, ACIR, 1981).
22. Rose and Peters, *op. cit.*, p. 108–14.
23. Aaron Wildavsky quoted in R. Rose and E. Page (eds.) *Fiscal Stress in Cities* (London, Cambridge University Press, 1982) p. 31.
24. Rose and Peters, *op. cit.*, p. 122.
25. *See* ACIR, *op. cit.*, p. 16.
26. H. Heclo 'Towards a New Welfare State' in P. Flora and A.J. Heidenheimer (eds.), *The Development of Welfare States in Europe and America* (New Brunswick and London, Transaction Books, 1981), p. 397.
27. Rose and Peters, *op. cit.*, p. 135–41.
28. ACIR *op. cit.*
29. ACIR *op. cit.*, p. 15.
30. Rose and Peters, *op. cit.*, pp. 114–20.

# 9 Policy-Making in Local Government

The community power debate in the United States, with its concentration upon the politics of urban government, focused attention upon fundamental issues about the nature of power and its distribution, as well as upon the measurement and analysis of relationships of power. The community power debate caught on in Britain only insofar as different theories and methodologies of assessing power were concerned. There were a few attempts at 'community power' studies as such, which sought to replicate the sorts of methods used in the United States, and the results of these few attempts were largely disappointing since they tended to end with the rather trite conclusion that it was the local authority and its members and officers who were the most influential people in local politics.[1]

Nevertheless, the question of who makes decisions within local services in Britain is undoubtedly an important one since a large proportion of state activity is channelled through local authorities. The 548 local authorities of the United Kingdom are responsible for 28 per cent of public expenditure and 39 per cent of public employees are local authority workers.[2] The services delivered by local authorities in Britain include police, fire, civil defence, public health, building control, refuse collection, housing, education and social services. Local authority functions vary within Britain,[3] and the 26 district councils in Northern Ireland have relatively few functions, the most important of which are leisure and recreation and refuse collection and disposal.[4]

Despite the fact that Britain never produced many community power studies, it is still possible to identify the characteristics of the three approaches to the study of power suggested by pluralist, elitist and Marxist theory in analyses

193

of policy-making within British local government. The nature of British government highlights a problem of community power studies in the American context too; local authorities, whether American cities or British counties or districts, cannot be regarded as independent political systems in the same way that one might regard nation states as independent political systems. Central government in Britain, and state government in America has formal direct authority over local government units in a way not found in relationships between the national governments of different countries. Consequently, any analysis of who makes decisions in local government in Britain must take account of what Dunleavy calls 'non-local sources of policy change'— national government officials, groups and professions.[5]

This chapter will focus upon each of the three perspectives of elite, pluralist and Marxist approaches at two levels: first, at the processes of policy-making within the political system, and second, at the level of the relationship between this local political system and national influences upon local services.

## PLURALISM

One of the dangers in using three perspectives for analysing power is that in seeking to define how one perspective has been applied, one sets up a straw man which does great injustice to perceptive scholars of the subject. Such straw men have been constructed in the case of theories of 'democracy' in local government in general and of 'pluralism' in local government in particular. Dearlove's characterisation of 'orthodox' views of local government democracy suggests that pluralism in local government involves 'the idea that the interest group world is one of reasonably perfect competition, where the rules of the game ensure fair play and the equal access of all to the favourable decision of those in government'.[6] Such pluralism is alleged to exist in the context of an 'electoral chain of command' in which the electorate elects the councillors, and the councillors tell the council employees what to do. Through these mechanisms the orthodox view, Dearlove suggests, envisages wide mass involvement in council decisions and actions.

Of course, it is not hard to challenge this view. Such is the nature of straw men. Councillors are elected as representatives of parties and, in comparison with national issues and the fortunes of the political parties at national level more generally, local issues play a relatively small part in the local election process.[7] Officers, that is to say, full-time council employees, have an important policy-making role, sometimes minimising the influence of even the most important elected councillors.[8] Few participate in elections, fewer in local pressure groups, with group participation largely concerning middle-class citizens with more time, inclination, money and participatory skills than working-class citizens.

However, another characteristic feature of straw men is that the closer one looks at the writing of authors cited as its main representatives, the less the alleged features of their writing fit the caricature. Few analysts of local government policy-making believe that local government decision-making works in the rather idyllic way suggested by the straw man. One major textbook on local government politics in the pluralist mode is well aware of the limitations of the local electoral mechanism and the paucity of genuine public participation in local policy-making, as are local government democracy's greatest advocates.[9]

What does a real pluralist approach to how decisions are made in local government look like? As suggested in Chapter 5, two characteristic features of pluralist approaches is that they regard a variety of non-economically defined groups as relevant actors who can exert influence upon the policy-making process. Who might these actors be? They are different groups of actors found among councillors, officials, national governmental institutions and the local public. Each of these four categories of actors can be found subdivided with the result that a great plurality of actors are involved in local policy-making.

Councillors are organised into parties. It has long been a controversy in the study of local politics whether politics actually does make a difference to local government decision-making. The conventional means of assessing the difference that parties make to local decision-making has been to look at the levels of local spending and see whether high spending is correlated with Labour party dominance in the council.[10] While the statistical evidence does not provide a conclusive answer to the question of 'Does politics matter?', an unambiguously positive answer can be given if one takes the response of Labour councils in Britain to the Tory demands for cutbacks in local spending. This is one clear instance of party control of local councils making a difference to policy outcomes. Indeed, in the case of some cities, such as Manchester, Liverpool and London, it was a change of leadership within the Labour groups of the councils, from centrist councillors towards more radically left-wing councillors, that has proved decisive in shaping council financial relationships with central government.

In addition to a degree of unity among councillors of the majority group provided through party membership, the working organisation of the local authority tends to fragment council leadership. Most of the work of British local councillors takes place in council committees. These may cover a whole service, such as education, social services or housing, or they may be committees which refer to a particular aspect of all services, such as finance and manpower committees. The tendency for councillors to be concerned with the issues affecting their committee—indeed, actively to promote and safeguard the areas covered by their committee—at the expense of other areas of council policy led to the criticisms of 'fragmented' decision-making within local government in Britain.[11] The recommended solution to this was 'corporate management', which sought to create institutions which would allow councillors to debate broad strategic issues that went beyond individual committee jurisdictions. The fact that this corporate management initiative failed can be interpreted as evidence of the strength of the committee system as a fragmenting force.

The failure of corporate management also provides evidence of the different divisions among the local government officials. Local government officials are organised into departments, frequently, but not invariably, coinciding closely with the committee structure of the council. Criticism of the 'departmentalism' of council employees was also at

the heart of the Bains Report, which made recommendations for corporate management. Departmentalism refers to
the tendency of chief officials to be concerned solely with the
affairs of their department at the expense of more general
interests of the council. The importance of departmentalism
can be seen most clearly in the process of local budgeting in
which different departments compete for funds.[12]

There are a variety of national institutions which are
involved in local policy-making. Perhaps the most important
of these is national government, which has the constitutional
ability to pass legislation affecting local government (its
structure, the functions it may undertake and how it may
raise revenue, for example) and in addition provides local
authorities with moneyu in the form of grants and advice,
and expertise in the form of circulars and technical reports.
There are a variety of divisions within central government
which reinforce the image of a plurality of actors involved in
the policy process. As the Central Policy Review Staff made
clear, central government is plural not singular.[13] Issues
affecting local government may involve discussions or
negotiations between two or more separate central government ministries. The introduction of the Block Grant under
the 1980 Local Government (Planning and Land) Act
involved discussions between the Treasury and the Department of the Environment, and the reform of the rent subsidy
system in the period 1981–83 involved the Treasury, the
Department of the Environment and the Department of
Health and Social Security.[14] As Griffith showed, different
ministries, or even different parts of the same ministry, have
different types of relationship with local authorities.[15]

There are a variety of other national institutions which
may affect policy-making within individual local authorities.
The local authority associations (the Association of Metropolitan Authorities, the Association of County Councils, the
Association of District Councils and the Convention of
Scottish Local Authorities are the most important of these)
are formed by the councillors of British local authorities to
provide advice and guidance to central government and
member authorities, negotiate wages and articulate and
promote common interests of its members, often through

exerting influence on central government. There are national professional associations, such as the Chartered Institute of Public Finance and Accountancy (for finance officers) and the Society of Local Authority Chief Executives (for chief executives, formally the most senior post in local authorities), which also seek to influence central government.[16] In addition, such national professional bodies can influence the behaviour of their members through the deliberate attempt to disseminate 'good practice' or through the less deliberate adoption of professional values which become part of the stock of values and predispositions of those within the profession.[17]

Within the public there are a variety of forms of possible participation. Local citizens can participate individually through voting for the councillors of their choice, through direct contact with a local councillor or official, or through availing themselves of the participatory mechanisms, developed across a variety of different services.[18] Citizens can also participate through groups, and different localities give rise to a plurality of groups. As Newton shows in Birmingham, there are 4,500 voluntary groups in Birmingham of which around 1,000 have the capacity to influence local policy-making.[19]

The case of local government certainly offers the possibility of identifying a plurality of actors who might be involved in local policy-making, with these actors belonging to groups which are not defined on the basis of economic classes. In addition, the values of these groups and what they seek to achieve in the policy process cannot be easily framed in terms of class-based economic objectives. Central issues of local politics, such as improvement subsidies to home owners, the location of schools and roads, appear to be issues which produce constellations of support and opposition which cut across class lines. A road widening scheme, for example, might threaten the property of both middle-class and working-class residents. In addition, the actions of national groups, such as the role of the Association of County Councils in opposing attempts by central government to limit the discretion of local authorities to raise rates, does not appear to fit in neatly with any class-based analysis of political conflicts, since the Conservative dominated Association in this respect shares the same objectives as the Labour-dominated Association of Metropolitan authorities.[20]

Pluralist studies are characteristically agnostic about the outcomes of policy-making processes. While they rarely suggest that the outcomes of the policy process tend towards equitable treatment for all, as gross characterisations of pluralism often suggest, the focus of their concern is upon how and why particular decisions fall the way they do rather than in searching for confirmations of expectations about who tends to dominate in the process.

## ELITE APPROACHES

The difference between pluralist and elite approaches is largely one of emphasis than one of great substance. Pluralist studies are well aware of the fact that a number of features of local politics in Britain limit the number of individuals and groups who may be effectively involved in local policy-making. Such factors would include the apparent inability of important issues decided at the local level to serve as the basis for publicly visible conflicts, in contrast to the position in the United States; the low levels of participation in elections and in participatory institutions designed to involve the local population in decision-making; the tendency for group activity to be dominated by the larger middle-class and business groups and the important role of officials in local policy-making. Conversely, writers such as Pahl, Dearlove and Saunders who have here been included in the elite approach are well aware that groups and individuals from outside the elite groups on which they focus their analysis may influence local decision-making.[21] Before this can be discussed, we need to outline why the approaches of these three writers can be included in the elite category.

Ray Pahl's work on 'urban managerialism' starts from the assumption that key resources are delivered to individuals on the basis of criteria over which those who provide them can exercise their discretion. Thus, for example, building

society managers have discretion over the people to whom
they offer loans, housing officials have discretion over who
they take on as council tenants, and planners exercise
discretion over the location of shops, offices, housing,
schools and roads. The fact that such people, 'urban
managers', have discretion gives them *de facto* control over
the distribution of goods and services, giving them great
power. Pahl's elaboration of a 'pure managerialist' theory
suggests that because:

existing state legislation in the fields of planning, housing, social welfare,
and so on, permit wide discretion on the part of the local controllers . . .
access to local resources and facilities is held by the professional officers of
the authority concerned. Such gatekeepers share a common ideology . . .
manipulate their elected representatives so that the political composition
of the council makes little difference to the policies pursued and, hence,
there is a common impact on real incomes of the population as a whole.[22]

In the American context, a similar notion was developed
under the rubric of 'street-level bureaucracy'.[23] Moreover,
these managers themselves may be part of national professions and share common values with urban managers of the
same resources nationwide through, for example, similarities in training, background or socialisation. One of the
main tasks of urban sociology, according to Pahl, was then
to explore the values of urban managers. If they had
discretion in distributing wanted goods and services, then it
is important to examine the criteria according to which such
discretion was exercised.

Pahl's concentration upon urban managers to the virtual
exclusion of features of the local environment which serve to
limit the scope for discretion by the urban managers has
been one of the major sources of criticism of Pahl's work;
planners may make plans to knock down houses, but they
cannot carry them out if there is opposition from the
political leadership of the council; housing managers generally allocate houses according to points systems which they
themselves have not devised; and building society managers
do not have unlimited funds to lend and do have national
guidelines surrounding the grant of loans.[24] All of these
things are subsequently conceded by Pahl, who then goes on

to open out his discussion of urban managers to see them in relatively pluralistic framework as one influence among many others in the distribution of resources in the city.[25]

Perhaps of greater influence in British political science is the work of Dearlove and Saunders on Kensington and Croydon, respectively. The results of these influential works bear much in common with pluralistic studies since they ultimately see policy outcomes as the result of the interaction between a plurality of groups and values, yet they emphasise the ability of relatively small groups to influence these outcomes disproportionately. Dearlove, for example, considers the relationship between councillors and officials of the Royal Borough of Kensington and Chelsea and finds that the access to policy-making processes is highly skewed. Although, in principle, groups have equal access and influence within the local political system, there is a systematic bias in favour of groups which are supportive of the Conservative ideology of the local council. Groups such as residents associations, or voluntary social organisations which themselves offer some form of service receive a sympathetic hearing from councillors and therefore have no need to take recourse to patterns of action involving direct appeals to public support, such as demonstrations and petitions, taken by those groups not favoured by the Conservatives, such as groups of council tenants or ethnic minorities. In turn, the mode of activity of the less favoured groups makes them less acceptable to councillors and officials since such direct appeals are regarded as unconventional and a challenge to the concept of the local council as a form of representative democracy. Consequently, certain types of local groups are severely handicapped in their chances of influencing local government decision-making.[26]

Saunders's study of Croydon is consistent with the notion that local government elites have the chance to decide on who has influence in the local political system. One of Saunders's main focuses is the relationship between councillors and business groups. He starts his study by discussing the commonly held view that local businessmen do not 'piss around with local politics', that somehow local government issues are too trivial for business to become involved in.[27]

He then goes on to examine the close ties, social and ideological, between the business community and the councillors.

The relationship between business and the council is one of partnership, not manipulation, and this reflects the fundamental agreement between the two over policy priorities. Far from being the passive tool of business interests, the local authority has operated autonomously of outside political pressures, but in doing so it has not acted in isolation from them. In other words, it has sought to integrate business interests into the local political system, either informally (through the 'social circle') or formally (through consultation), with the result that these interests have provided a continuing source of guidance and direction for its own policy initiatives.[28]

The elite approach to understanding local government decision-making in Britain is probably best conceived as a particular view of inequality in access and influence within a system that remains pluralist in its basic features—the groups that have privileged access to local decision-making are not necessarily, but may be, economically defined, they tend to dominate in the policy process rather than determine its outcome, public pressures may under certain circumstances be more important than the policy preferences of these groups, and such groups may sometimes be defeated by other groups or at least be forced to make large concessions to them.

## MARXIST APPROACHES

One of the main justifications for a discussion of the institution of local government as a discrete institution within the governmental apparatus is that what goes on within this institution—the process of policy-making between different groups—makes some sort of difference to policy outcomes. Such a view, that local government political processes make a difference, is difficult to reconcile with one of the distinctive features of instrumental Marxist theory, that the state can be usefully conceived of as a whole and that it acts as a whole in the interests of capital. Given such potential for irreconcilability, it is therefore understandable that the best instrumental Marxist theories regard the focus upon the internal dynamics of one state institution in isolation, local government, as largely irrelevant to the development of capitalism and the state's role in this development. However, some studies, notably Cockburn's, *The Local State*,[29] have sought to combine an institutional focus with an instrumental Marxist perspective.

Cockburn begins with a strong affirmation of the unity of the capitalist state:

> The state nationally has its headquarters in London, but it comprises nationwide and permanent institutions. The armed forces, the judiciary and the police are found in local barracks, courts of law and police stations. In the same way, government departments dealing with education, housing and health, while they may have large offices in London SW1, carry out their work in and through schools and education offices, housing estates and local housing departments, hospitals and local health authorities. These are often technically the responsibility of a local council or other local or regional authority. Their officials nonetheless are state employees . . . When I refer to Lambeth Borough Council as 'local state', it is to say neither that it is something distinct from 'national state' nor that it alone represents the state locally. It is to indicate that it is part of a whole . . . In spite of its multiplicity, however, the state preserves a basic unity. All its parts work *fundamentally* as one.[30]

This would appear to be rather close to the notion that one would associate with instrumental Marxism—the conception of the state as a single actor operating within the interests of capital. However, the problem emerges in Cockburn's analysis when she comes to explain the development of policy within a single local authority. In tracing the development of neighbourhood councils in the borough, she discusses the influence of the labour party, the decision of the Finance and General Purposes Committee, the role of key officers, local groups and associations and unorganised members of the public. In telling the story of the neighbourhood councils, in fact, only Cockburn's terminology would distinguish the analysis from a conventional pluralist discussion of policy-making. The analysis abounds with discussions of choices and decisions made throughout the process with no evident overall constraint imposed by the balance of class forces or the demands of capitalism. We hear, for example, that the people of Lambeth 'had woken up to a new sense of their own power', and the officers and councillros learned 'to survive and handle the activism of neighbourhood councils'.[31]

Cockburn's analysis, then, offers some justification for the belief that an institutional focus is largely incompatible with an instrumental Marxist theory. Structuralist Marxist theory has been far more sophisticated in analysing urban political processes. Indeed, some of the most important developments in Marxist social theory have come through the incorporation of urban social processes into a view of modern capitalist society. This development of Marxist theory in an urban context is particularly associated with the work of the Spanish sociologist Manuel Castells and the insights that his work has given to scholars in Britain such as Peter Saunders and Patrick Dunleavy.[32]

While it is beyond the scope of this book to offer a comprehensive outline of the development of Castells's work and its criticisms, Castells's influence derives in large part from his analytical distrinction between production and consumption issues in modern capitalist society.[33] While traditional Marxist theory has concentrated upon the role of the state in issues of production—profits and capital accumulation, for example—the state also maintains the capitalist system through providing services to individuals (e.g. housing and education) which can be termed as a form of intervention in issues of collective consumption. As capitalism develops, it generates cities and specifically urban problems. Capitalist entrepreneurs cannot profitably provide all consumption goods and services such as housing to the labour force needed to reproduce labour power, and consequently such goods and services are provided by the state. Collective consumption itself generates conflicts between certain groups of recipients of state consumption goods and services and the capitalist state. Consequently, collective consumption processes largely define the nature of urban social conflicts, which characteristically have as their focus local or subnational agencies of government. The local level of government can frequently, therefore, be seen as supporting the capitalist system through providing collective consumption. Moreover, in the provision of collective consumption the state generates new forms of social cleavage, in addition to the production-based cleavages of the bourgeoisie and the proletariat, surrounding demands for particular levels or forms of collective consumption.

The relationships in the production sphere, of course, shape the collective consumption processes in two ways. First, they generate the problems of collective consumption, and second, they constrain the range of options open to decision-makers in the urban political arena. These two factors, which make the 'autonomy' of local political institutions from the constraints of production-based interests only 'relative', can be shown in the context of Castells's analysis of the British new towns policy.

Castells argues that the post-war emphasis upon dispersal policy in Britain was in part a reaction to the serious inner city congestion and the imbalance in jobs between different regions within Britain. The drift to the south-east of England was generated, Castells argues, by the requirements of monopoly capitalism developing with few state-imposed constraints.[34] This, in turn, generated pressures and demands to relieve inner city deprivation and high levels of unemployment in particular regions. As early as the beginning of the twentieth century there was a movement (as with the garden cities movement of Ebenezer Howard and the Town Planning Institute) for the planned dispersal of city populations outside the inner city areas. Despite these pressures, little was achieved by the end of the Second World War. The reason for increased activity after the war was that war damage so reduced housing stock that some form of reconstruction policy was necessary, and this led to the 1944 Abercrombie plan for the decanting of people and jobns out of London and to the new towns in the surrounding counties.

However, although the war damage constituted a necessary condition for new towns policy, it was not a sufficient condition. According to Castells, the decisive element was the 'political conjuncture, with the upsurge of working-class political awareness and the electoral triumph of the Labour party, which reinforced the pressure for change, and required satisfaction . . . in order not to radicalise the class struggle'.[35] The Abercrombie plan did not, however, produce a significant shift in patterns of capital investment. Its offer of incentives to locate in the new towns did little to curtail the broader trends of economic development in the south-east. Castells draws heavily on the fact that although the London region expanded by 1.7 million people between 1946 and 1956, the new towns only took 19 per cent of this growth (and mainly through skilled and unskilled labour) to support his argument that the effects of this reformist move were marginal upon the more powerful development of British capitalism. The state, therefore, whether conceived of as local government, the central state or both, only has relative autonomy from the production processes; the problems it faces and the way in which it reacts are shaped by them.[36]

Similarly, in terms of social consumption, the role of the state in providing urban public services demonstrates that the state has to deal with problems generated by capitalist economic development. Moreover, its options, such as providing more or less urban services, are also constrained by the implications that these options would have for capitalist production in terms of the reduced profitability of firms following increased taxation.[37]

In British local government studies, perhaps the most important implications that Castells's approach has had is through its influence upon the development of theoretical perspectives which develop the notion of collective consumption and tend to move further away from a relationship between consumption and production; this relationship being widely acknowledged as problematic in Castells's theories. Because they move further away from the production issues, they can scarcely be termed Marxist. Patrick Dunlevy argues that local government politics can be seen as dominated by issues of collective consumption.[38] Issues like these, such as housing, education, health and transport, generate consumption cleavages which structure urban political conflicts. These cleavages not only structure the goals and values of mass citizenry (through the influence on voting behaviour) but also the goals and values of the service providers, the professionals within the welfare state. It is these professionals—who at central, regional and local level, through their formal organisations and through the less tangible influence that they may exert through shaping the agenda and context of policy-making (see his discussion of 'ideological corporatism')[39]—who are becoming increasingly important actors in policy-making over issues of collective consumption.

Peter Saunders seeks to link processes of collective consumption with processes of production through his notion of a 'dual state'. The dual state approach follows on from a number of the problems Saunders identified in Marxist analysis.[40] It argues that the state is not only concerned with groups defined by relations of production but also with groups defined by relations of consumption. Briefly, the dual state argument suggests that there is an 'ideal typical' division within the state apparatus between social investment functions (broadly operationalised as decisions affecting capital accumulation) and social consumption functions (usually welfare type policies). Social investment is a function of regional and central government and is subject to 'corporatist' modes of interest mediation. Social consumption is a function of local government and is subject to more 'competitive' or 'pluralist' forms of interest mediation.

## CONCLUSIONS

From this discussion of the various approaches to policy-making in local government in Britain, it is clear that one theme from our case studies reappears. This is the way in which crude pluralist, elite and Marxist explanations have been gradually extended and made more sophisticated by a process of academic interchange.

Pluralist writers have been made aware of the inegalitarian and restricted nature of participation in local policy-making. Elite theorists, who have assisted this insight in their discussions of agenda setting and various key issues at the mercy of 'urban managers', have, however, faced serious critical appraisal. Pluralist writers have questioned the ability of urban managers to control and dictate policy-making in local government on a consistent basis. On the other hand, Marxist writers have raised important questions such as 'Who manages the managers?' By this, Marxists imply that while there may be a bias in the policy-making process over who decides, it is also important to ask in whose interests do policy-makers decide? It is this question which traditional pluralist and elite writers did not directly confront, and this could be one of the major benefits to be derived from a Marxist perspective.

As we have argued, however, traditional Marxist explanations which attempted to operationalise this insight through an analysis of the instrumental role of the local state for capitalism have not been very successful. They have been able to maintain their view of an instrumental and repressive state only by reading into a basically pluralistic process hidden conspiracies and intentions. For this reason, in recent years a more sophisticated structuralist Marxist approach has been developed. This approach recognises the pluralist bargaining process involved in local policy-making but seeks to defend the notion of the state's functionality for capitalism by dividing issues between production and consumption. By developing the notion of the dual state, the pluralism of local politics around issues of housing, welfare and education can be understood. At the same time, the functionality of the state rests upon the twin ideas that consumption issues are ultimately constrained by the production system, while production issues in local government will always be dominated by local and national business interests.

The strength of this dual state approach is that it allows one to conceptualise the nature of the economic constraints within which local policy-making must operate, while at the same time showing an awareness of the empirical reality of pluralistic bargaining and the role of non-economic elites in that process. Whether the fact that such a theoretical approach can be termed as a truly Marxist one or just a more sophisticated pluralist approach is open to question. It is to these wider theoretical and epistemological questions that we now turn in our final chapter.

## NOTES

1. *See* Ken Newton, 'Community Politics and Decision-Making: The American Experience nad its Lessons', in K. Young, ed., *Essays on the Study of Urban Politics* (London, Macmillan, 1975).
2. R. Rose *et al.*, *Public Employment in Western Nations* (London, Cambridge University Press, 1985).
3. *See* E. Page, *Comparing Local Expenditure. Lessons from a Multi-National State*, Glasgow, University of Strathclyde Studies in Public Policy No. 60, 1980).
4. *See* W.D. Birrell and A. Murie, *Politics and Government in Northern Ireland* (Dublin, Gill and Macmillan, 1980).
5. P. Dunleavy, *Urban Political Analysis* (London, Macmillan, 1980).
6. J. Dearlove, *The Reorganisation of British Local Government* (London, Cambridge University Press, 1979).
7. *See* Kenneth Newton, *Second City Politics* (Oxford, Clarendon Press, 1976).
8. *See* C. Collins *et al.* 'The Officer and the Councillor in Local Government' *Public Administration Bulletin*, 28 (December 1978), pp. 34–50.
9. J. Gyford *Local Politics in Britain*, 2nd edition (London, Croom Helm, 1984); G.W. Jones and J.D. Stewart, *The Case for Local Government* (London, Allen and Unwin, 1983).
10. N. Boaden, *Urban Policy-Making* (London, Cambridge University Prses, 1971); K. Newton and L.J. Sharpe *Does Politics Matter?* (Oxford, Clarendon Press, 1984).
11. *See* Dearlove, *op. cit.*
12. R. Greenwood, C.R. Hinings and S. Ranson, 'Changing Patterns of Budgeting in English Local Government', *Public Administration*, Vol. 61, No. 2 (1983), pp. 149–68.
13. Central Policy Review Staff, *Relations Between Central Government and Local Authorities* (London, HMSO, 1977).
14. M.J. Hill, 'The Implementation of Housing Benefit', *Journal of Social Policy*, Vol. 13, No. 3 (1984), pp. 297–320.
15. J.A.G. Griffith, *Central Departments and Local Authorities* (London, Allen and Unwin, 1966).
16. R.A.W. Rhodes, 'Can There Be a National Community of Local Government', *Local Government Studies* (1983).
17. P. Dunleavy, 'Professions and Policy Change: Notes Towards a Model of Ideological Corporatism', *Public Administration Bulletin* (1981).

18. N. Boaden, M. Goldsmith, W. Hampton, P. Stringer, *Public Participation in Local Services* (London, Longman, 1982).
19. Newton, *op. cit.* (1976).
20. Rhodes, *op. cit.*
21. R. Pahl, *Whose City?* (Harmondsworth, Penguin, 1975); J. Dearlove, *The Politics of Policy in Local Government* (London, Cambridge University Press, 1973); P. Saunders *Urban Politics: A Sociological Interpretation* (Harmondswotth, Penguin, 1979).
22. Pahl, *ibid.*, p. 278.
23. M. Lipsky, *Street Level Bureaucracy* (New York, Russel Sage Foundation, 1979).
24. P. Saunders, *Social Theory and the Urban Question* (London, Hutchinson, 1979).
25. Pahl, *op. cit.*, pp. 288–303.
26. Dearlove, *op. cit.* (1973).
27. Saunders, *op. cit.*, *Urban Politics*, p. 298.
28. *Ibid.*, p. 324.
29. C. Cockburn, *The Local State* (London, Pluto Press, 1977).
30. *Ibid.*, pp. 16–17.
31. *Ibid.*, p. 157.
32. *See* Saunders, *op. cit.*, *Social Theory*.
33. M: Castells, *The Urban Question* (London, Edward Arnold, 1977), passim.
34. *Ibid.*, pp. 276–83.
35. *Ibid.*, pp. 280–83.
36. *Ibid.*
37. O'Connor, *op. cit.*, passim.
38. P. Dunleavy, *Urban Political Analysis* (London, Macmillan, 1980).
39. P. Dunleavy, 'Professions and Policy Change: Notes Towards a Model of Ideological Corporatism', *Public Administration Bulletin*, 36, 1981: 3–16.
40. See Saunders *op. cit.*, *Social Theory*.

# PART IV
Conclusions

# 10 The Future of Theories of Power in Capitalist Socialist

Having outlined the debate over the nature of power and operationalised three major approaches commonly used in the social sciences, in this final chapter we conclude our discussion by pinpointing some of the problems with each theoretical perspective in terms of whether any of the theories used here is adequate in explaining power in capitalist societies. Having concluded that no one theory is totally adequate on the basis of the criteria we outline, our discussion concludes with an appraisal of recent attempts to resolve the problem. In looking at these recent developments, we point to recent convergences amongst contending theories which, perhaps, offer a way forward for those interested in pursuing the matter.

## THE UTILITY OF THEORY

In Chapter 2 we outlined, briefly, some of the major epistemological debates revolving around the proper delineation of the concept of 'power'. As we saw, no final agreement was reached concerning its proper definition. Rather, we outlined the fact that 'power' remains an essentially contested concept, which has given rise to competing theories of power in capitalist societies. It would be fruitless to take this discussion further because, we have argued, an eclectic approach can provide useful insights for those who are prepared to remain open-minded and utilise the range of theories available to explain a particular problem or event. Indeed, we would hope that the benefit of this eclectic approach has been revealed by our application of theories to similar problems in the four case studies presented. We would contend that these case studies reveal that each theory has strengths as well as weaknesses and that only by utilising each can the researcher hope to comprehend fully the nature of the problem involved.

While this may be so, it is perhaps useful in conclusion to summarise the main strengths and weaknesses of each theory in terms of a test of theoretical utility. This will be achieved by first outlining the criteria we believe are necessary for a sound theory, and then by testing each approach against this.

In establishing criteria for the adequacy of a theory in the social sciences, we can begin from one of several different perspectives. The most commonly used is the positivist approach, in which theories are adequate, broadly speaking, in so far as:

1. The research on which they are based is replicable.
2. They provide a consistent and clear causal explanation.
3. They can be used to predict future events.
4. They do not presuppose acceptance of ideological or normative principles or definitions.
5. They can be subjected to refutation by the production of counter-factuals.

These criteria pose many problems for social scientists, as we discussed in Chapter 1. The most general problem is the dichotomy between fact and value which they presuppose, but there are other difficulties also, such as the difficulty of replication, the unavailability of existing theories to guide research and the lack of a consensus over methods and terminology which might allow the cumulation of explanations into general laws.

A second approach is that associated with phenomenologists, such as Winch, and with social historians such as Max Weber. Though these have different notions—both about normative principles and about methods—they share an approach to causality which is based on the idea of 'meaningfulness'; that is, their social causes are radically different from natural science causes because of human intentionality. The proper object of social science research is human action, and all human action is distinguishable from all other kinds of actions or movement by reason of the meanings given to it by the intentions of the actors and the social framework within which it occurs. A strict set of criteria for this method acceptable to all would be difficult to draw up, but it is easy to see that methods based on meaninglessness would reject all five of the positivist criteria.

A third approach has one of its best-known expositions in the writings of Karl Popper. Popper came from a natural science background but developed as a sceptic about the possibility of verifying even natural science propositions. Maintaining that there is a unity of knowledge to natural and social sciences, he turned this previously positivist idea around so that the difference between the two was not in gradations of strength of certainty but in gradations of uncertainty. At the same time, he allowed for the evident fact of human progress in knowledgeable control of the environment by an evolutionary epistemology in which the certainty of one generation of theories has its own value but is eventually to be superseded by the certainty of future generations; improvement occurs through the constant process of subjective plural assaults on theories of limited but positive usefulness. This process is much more successful in the natural sciences than in the social sciences; the level of predictive capacity achieved by natural scientists is logically impossible in the social sciences because, among other things, of the nature of the subject to be studied.

We discussed in Chapter 1 the way in which the social sciences developed with methodological paradigms borrowed from other disciplines. Those who offer discourses on our methods are, by and large, academics who have never actually engaged in empirical research in social science. Metaphysicians, linguistic philosophers, political philosophers, natural scientists turned historians of knowledge (with an addendum on social science)—all of these have discussed our methods without attempting to operationalise theory and empirical research. Their writings have been uniformly pessimistic in their conclusions.

In a work of this sort it is not possible to resolve all the questions raised by the need to develop criteria of adequacy for theory. Our aims are more modest and perhaps more practical. Instead of trying to construct theories about theories, a more worthwhile effort might begin by asking 'Adequacy for what purpose?' Theories can be adequate in a variety of personal, social and academic ways. We seek theories to help us understand; but though many are motivated by the wish to get to the bottom of things simply for the sake of getting there, other motivations, not necessarily less worthy, are also present—we want to convince colleagues, we want to convince policy-makers outside universities, we want to get things across to students, and not least, we need theories to guide our research. Supposedly objective standards of truth, imposing verifiability, replicability, predictive capacity, freedom from value judgements, and so on, are not necessarily relevant as absolute norms to the purposes of research-orientated theory-development. And it may be that by paying attention to what are usually regarded as the lesser purposes of theory, researchers might also serve the greater purpose.

The immediate and major objection to this frankly instrumentalist approach is that what it produces is not adequate to any serious purpose, but rather is sloppy, partial, ill-informed and approximate. To meet this criticism it should be established clearly from the outset that pursuing a less ambitious objective does not absolve one from the observation of basic rules of investigation and does not entitle one to regard all opinions as equally valid and equally invalid. Criticism of social theory can occur at different levels. Popper, for example, analyses the development of knowledge in terms of three different worlds: the first world being that of sense-observation; the second, that of scientific theory in its social context; the third, that of objective truth; he also argues, more controversially, that it is possible to achieve scientific laws through the use of reason, but the more limited point is easier to take that knowledge occurs in a series of frameworks, a point not dissimilar to Wittgenstein's language-game analysis.

The process of explanation has different levels of operation engaged in a constant interaction. Granted that it is impossible to speak properly of a 'theoryless reality', any empirical data, however broad, presupposes a prior orientation, a framework or language-game within which it makes sense. But much data in the social sciences is open to use in several different language-games, with different questions and different explanations. Consider census data, for example: periodically governments spend large amounts of money collecting information in specific categories about the inhabitants of their territories. The theory that produces policy of that kind would be very difficult to specify, and the census data itself is used by researchers from widely differing theoretical backgrounds—for instance, by commercial interests for market research and by social planners to guide government intervention of a kind that might be entirely irrelevant to the members of the Chamber of Commerce. The different values, theories and usages to which original data may be put can often contradict one another—a noteworthy example is Domhoff's use of data originally collected by Dahl in New Haven to attack Dahl's original thesis, arguing that Dahl had failed to take proper account of counter-indications in his own material.

At an initial level of operation, therefore, anyone using the material has to be concerned with verification of empirical data; one has to be able to have confidence that the census data corresponds to the actual occurrence of the phenomena in the appropriate categories, that the research interviewees really did act in a particular way, that the soldier's widow really did utter the heart-rending and politically charged words attributed to her in a popular newspaper. Whatever the theoretical implications of the decision to collect data of that particular kind, and whatever may be the varying usages to which it can be put, the data is useless unless it corresponds to reliable phenomena.

This does not mean that hypotheses in the social sciences have to be falsifiable in the strict sense. We have seen that Marxist explanations can often be convincing, stimulating and replete with insights, but they are not usually falsifiable in the positivist sense. Empirical data which appears to contradict the explanation is moulded in to later theoretical developments through new concepts and new definitions. The data is verifiable in the sense that it corresponds to a really existing state of affairs, but the explanation into which it is drawn is not falsifiable. There is another sense, of course, in which Marxists would say that their explanations have scientific value, and that is the sense in which science consists not in the positivist separation of theory from reality but in the revolutionary unity of theory and practice in the process of history.

For most researchers in the social sciences, the question of falsifiability of explanation does not normally arise, precisely because of the difficulties inherent in the scientific understanding of social processes. Much more important are the plausibility, coherence and completeness of the explanations, and the reliability of the data for other users. As a general guide for research, the following rules of investigation could keep the researcher to the strait and narrow path.

1. *Selection*: the research must select as suitable material for explanation only empirical data, corresponding to specifically-observed phenomena and reported in an accurate clear manner;
2. *Operations*: the development of knowledge in the social sciences as in the natural sciences occurs through the continuous operation of accumulation of insights, which occur within already-existing frameworks of explanation;
3. *Relevance*: the existence of different disciplines within the social sciences is a necessary constraint on explanation—explanations which are relevant in one discipline may not be so in another. Researchers must therefore direct their questions to specific purposes;
4. *Parsimony*: explanations must refer only to data and theories coherent internally, and not to other material drawn from other research which has different suppositions, definitions and levels of reliability;
5. *Complete explanation*: this is a complementary rule to the previous one. Just as researchers must account only for coherent data, so they must account for all such data, not omitting inconvenient material.

These rules do not provide us with a test for the adequacy of theory, and the preceding discussion does not pretend to resolve the question of how social science researchers may properly be said to explain. The idea of a general theory in the social science is, to say the least, an unconvincing one at present; it is against this background that we now go on to discuss the explanations provided by the partial theories covered here.

Taking pluralist theories first, we saw that the main focus of study is on observable conflicts of interest within the defined political decision-making process. Power is conceptualised in terms of the ability of A to force or persuade B to do something which A prefers when there is a clear and observable conflict of interest. The methodology utilised is various, ranging from research based on reputation, history and the frequency of individual or group participation in the policy-making process to research based on any issue or problem considered by an individual researcher to be worthy of analysis. Little distinction is made between issues in the policy process; if conflict of interest is observable, then the research studies the problem in terms of the stance taken by the observable participants; if interests or wants are not manifest within the policy process, then they are not regarded as significant in the analysis of power.

A number of clear benefits accrue to pluralist approaches. The perspective is based upon common sense in that it concentrates on conflicts of interest which are empirically verifiable and clearly observable. This is then a logical approach which is capable of empirical verification and falsification. If the researcher argues that no one group in the policy process dominates all decision-making all of the time, then this argument is capable of empirical falsification by replicable research. It is also a descriptively sound approach because it is heavily reliant on observable empirical observation.

Set against this, however, are a number of weaknesses. By ignoring latent interests which cannot be seen in the policy process due to factors such as agenda setting and by failing to recognise a distinction between types of issues, this approach suffers from a somewhat limited explanatory utility. Similarly, the approach has been criticised for being atheoretical because the researcher has no abstract theoretical conceptualisation of power against which empirical observations of reality can be tested. Willer and Willer have argued that the methodology used is a form of 'systematic empiricism'.[1] By this they mean that pluralist workers make generalisations based upon the probability of observations recurring. This they contend is not science or proper theory because it is neither abstractive nor predictive. Pluralist theorists are able to develop laws—the Law of Dispersed Inequalities for example—which are based on the probability of the recurrence of events, but the probability of recurrence is not the same as an adequate theorisation, explanation and prediction of social or political reality. Thus, since empiricists take individual preferences as their starting point, they are unable to explain fully the nature of power in society because they have no way of explaining why individuals have particular preferences; they must take them as given and cannot explain why individuals have the 'wants' they express subjectively.

This has been a major drawback in pluralist writings which tend to ignore concepts like the mobilisation of bias, non-decision-making, agenda setting, the role of ideology and suppresion of preferences through the unconscious operation of social and political values and institutions. In this respect, while pluralist accounts are clearly the richest descriptions to be found of the detailed relationships within the political decision-making process, they have not been as capable as other theories in terms of prediction and explanation. While it is clearly empirically falsifiable as a perspective, it has not been able to refute satisfactorily the range of counter-arguments presented by elite and Marxist theories. This is not to say that such an approach is therefore invalid, rather it is to caution researchers to its limits as well as strengths.

But does elite theory perform any more satisfactorily? As with pluralist theory the answer is both Yes and No. As we have seen, elite theorists go beyond the narrowly circumscribed decision-making process in their attempt to define the locus of power in capitalist societies. While not eschewing concern for political actors, elitists do not assume that observable conflicts of interests in the institutions of the state are the only area in which power is to be found. Rather, they take the structure of society—in its social, political and economic spheres—to be the proper focus for analysis and assess the ability of individuals possessing social, economic and political resources to ensure that what they want is normally accepted by society.

Clearly, this perspective takes the analysis of power into areas not normally traversed by pluralist writers and raises additional insights and concepts for analysis. Concepts like 'the mobilisation of bias', 'agenda setting' and 'non-decision-making' offer valuable insights into the processes by which societies are maintained and change. Since these concepts have been arrived at by observable, empirical research and they have not been adequately refuted by pluralist writers, then in terms of adequacy elite theories can be seen to have a wider scope than pluralist perspectives. Having said that, however, such studies do have a number of serious weaknesses. First of all, it must be doubted whether elite theories are based upon wholly falsifiable criteria and whether they are therefore empirically sound. One of the major weaknesses here is the fact that most elite writers have decided which individuals constitute an elite prior to research. Research then becomes an attempt to find evidence to substantiate the existence of an elite. The problem here is that this approach may suffer from researcher bias in terms of the specification of the elite and in the search for evidence to corroborate this *a priori* assumption. While elite writers contend that their theories are capable of empirical verification, there is a tendency for them to defend their explanations against counter-evidence by the argument that the issues studies are not significant for their elite. In other words, the concept of 'key issues' allows the elite theorist to deny the validity of counter-factual information.

Further criticisms have been levelled at this approach by Marxist scholars who argue that elitists fail to explain the persistence of elites. Elite writers tend to rely on the assumption that if you are in an elite, you will want to maintain your position. One problem here is that not everyone from the same socio-economic background will necessarily have the same values and goals. It can be argued, therefore, that by relying on the thesis that elites cohere to protect their privileges is merely descriptive. Such an approach does not fully explain why individual preferences are formed or sustained. Finally, by taking a 'snap-shot' of the stratification of society at any time in history, elite theorists have very great difficulty in analysing or predicting why societies cohere and change or how elites are replaced.

On the grounds of scope, and for expanding our awareness of the social, psychological and economic forces which shape political action, elite theories have made a valuable contribution to the analysis of power in capitalist societies. They do, however, suffer from weaknesses in relation to subjectivity and non-falsification, as well as having limited predictive and explanatory utility.

Marxist theories, as we saw, do not draw any distinctions between economic, social and political sources of power. The focus of analysis is on the totality of social relations in which the connection between the economic and political is seen to be inextricably intertwined. Early formulations—in particular those associated with instrumental accounts— were clearly based on a logical theoretical reasoning which started from an analysis of the means of production and the objective relationship of owners and servants to these productive processes. The great strength of this theory, we argued, was that it allowed for analysis, explanation and prediction of historical events. The difficulty, however, was that while instrumental accounts met the test of logical coherence and had a wide analytic utility, empirical research has questioned the initial assumptions that a ruling class (owners of the means of production) is always in a position to use the state repressively to control and shape the actions and thoughts of the subordinate classes. This questioning of Marxist assumptions was clearly based upon pluralist writings which pointed to the democratisation of capitalist societies and the pluralistic bargaining processes within capitalist political systems.

These problems have been met by Marxist writers in a number of ways. First of all, theory has been adapted to explain away problematic developments like social welfarism and democratisation. Thus welfare and voting rights are seen by some Marxists as but a further example of the capacity of the ruling class to develop a 'false consciousness' amongst the working class. Rather than being real gains for the working class, these reforms are seen as further measures to maintain the legitimacy of capitalism. Now, it is argued, crises within capitalism can be blamed by the ruling class upon welfarism or the government of the day rather than upon the system of production. Furthermore, since voting rights are seen by individuals as conferring equality politically, this contributes to sustaining the legitimacy of a system of economic inequality. People believe that the vote allows them to change things even though the private ownership of production severely constrains the capacity of government to do as they or the electorate may prefer.

Obviously, this reformulation of early Marxist writings is consistent with the initial theory, but it has led to the valid claim by pluralist and elite writers that Marxist accounts are simply not falsifiable. If one accepts the theory then any empirical evidence which refutes the basic assumptions can be rejected by Marxists as an example of 'false consciousness' or clever ruling-class manipulation to hoodwink the working class by the process of ideological conditioning. In this sense Marxist accounts are based on logical and coherent theoretical argument, but they do not contain a counter-factual which would render them capable of formal falsification. Despite this severe weakness in terms of our test of adequacy, Marxist accounts can be seen as useful in terms of the scope and breadth of analysis. They also possess a predictive utility and within their own terms are internally logical and coherent. Whether or not they are descriptively sound and empirically consistent depends upon whether one accepts the initial premises or not. That they raise interesting concepts and insights for the further analysis of power—the importance of latent interests, the role of social conditioning and ideological hegemony in shaping attitudes and preferences and the need to study the constraints which economic power places on the use of political power—is not, however, in doubt.

What is in doubt, as we have emphasised throughout, is whether theories which operate on very different epistemological foundations can ever have been made commensurable, so that a universally accepted theory of power can be agreed upon. What this discussion has tried to reveal is that each theory, while providing useful insights into the way capitalist societies are structured and changed, is not on its own capable of fully explaining the complex reality of power in capitalist society. This takes us back to our initial discussion in Chapter 2. There we argued that, while a fully adequate theory may be illusory, to analyse problems from different and contending theoretical perspectives serves a useful heuristic function. We hope that our discussion of theories and their application has shown the value of such an approach. Even if it does no more than force people to question their uncritically held assumptions about power, then it will have served its purpose.

## A CONCLUDING REMARK ON THE COMMENSURABILITY OF POWER AND CONSTRAINT

We have argued throughout that given the continuing disputes over the meaning of 'power', it is best to treat it as an essentially contested concept. Our reason for doing this was to allow our readers to judge for themselves whether pluralist (first dimensional, elite (second dimensional) or Marxist (third dimensional) accounts provide better explanations of the nature of power in capitalist societies. It may well be that the reader has made up his or her mind on the subject by now. On the other hand, some readers may be more sceptical and believe that all of the theories have something to offer about how decisions are taken in capitalist societies and who benefits from these. If either of these conclusions has been reached, then the book will have served its purpose. It may be, however, that some readers wonder whether it is possible to arrive at a more inclusive and holistic account of power which obviates the need to look at the concept from competing theoretical perspectives.

There would appear to be two broad views on this question. On the one hand, there are those who argue that 'power' can be empirically defined and is not subject to essential contestability, but only if Marxist theory is first rejected as a useful tool of analysis. On the other hand, some writers argue that 'power' can be defined fairly rigorously in empirical terms but that to ignore the insights to be derived from Marxist analysis is to weaken our analysis of who benefits from the decisions taken by strategically placed individuals in capitalist societies and why. This does not mean that power must remain essentially contested but that ways to bring together two concepts drawn from different theoretical perspectives must be found. These are, respectively, the concepts of *power* (with its connotations of who decides) and *constraint* (with its connotations of the limits within which individuals have freedom to choose).

One leading exponent of this latter view has argued that Lukes's attempt to provide a single, all-embracing explanation of power (discussed in Ch. 2) is fundamentally flawed because he oscillates between constraint and contingency.[2] We saw that Lukes rejected first and second dimensional accounts in favour of a third approach based on Marxist insights. It has been argued that this solution has merely clouded the issue because Lukes does not tell us what the exact relationship between the individual (as a free decision-maker) and the economic and social structures (constraints) is. While Lukes argued that individuals in capitalism were shaped by the requirements of the mode of production, in certain circumstances he mentioned that they could choose freely—they had a 'relative autonomy' to pursue their own 'real' interests.[3] In this way, Lukes argued that Marxist theories could be subject to empirical verification. When men chose freely, then theorists could analyse why it was that they did not always choose to act in ways consistent with their empirically verified 'real' interests. In such circumstances it would become apparent that the freedom to choose would be limited by the institutional and ideological constraints of the society. This, it was argued by Lukes, would tell us more about power than empiricist accounts which confined their analyses solely to the expressed wants and desires of individuals.

While this view would seem to be consistent and a way out of the essentially contested impasse which power had fallen into, on closer scrutiny it is not. As we saw in Chapter 3 (pp. 71–76), Marxist theories moved in the direction outlined by Lukes but found that they had to introduce into their analysis individual motivations (the problematic of the subject). Thus, while instrumental Marxist accounts have been superseded by structuralist accounts, which allowed for a degree of relative autonomy for individuals to choose freely, these explanations still had to maintain that in the long term (or the last instance) the structural determinism of the requirements of the mode of production would shape human action. It has been argued that this approach is logically inconsistent. If a theory allows for space for individuals to choose freely, then it cannot also accept any notion of structural determinancy. Conversely, if theory implies determinancy, then it must deny the possibility of free choice for individuals.[4]

This insight can lead in any of two directions. First one may argue that this logical inconsistency can only be resolved by focusing on who decides (who has power over whom in political decision-making) and rejecting the issue of constraints altogether. The second approach is to agree that 'power' is not an essentially contested concept but to argue that while some theories concentrate on power (who decides), other theories are concerned with constraints (how choice is limited and shaped). Since both of these concepts illuminate the structures and workings of capitalist societies, attempts must be made to make these two concepts commensurable within a new theoretical approach.

One recent critique of Lukes's position has pinpointed quite accurately the major dilemma with the structuralist account of power. Since Marxist explanations of power are ultimately located within a specific economic theory, which is also logically connected with a specific theory of social revolution, ideology and class consciousness, these inter-connections force consistent Marxists to adopt a determinist account of power which denies the autonomy for individuals to choose freely.[5] Thus, it has been argued, Marxists are wrong to believe—given their own theory—that they could ever locate an individual or a group of individuals who would ever be in a position to choose in a manner which was not fettered by the conditioning imposed through the structure of capitalism and its ideological imperatives. Thus structural Marxists oscillate between constraint and contingency, when in fact they really believe that constraint is more important as an explanation of power than the ability of individuals to choose freely. It is not surprising, given this fact, that structuralists argue that 'power' is an essentially contested concept. But, does this mean that power must remain an essentially contested concept? It has been argued that power can be empirically verified and need not be essentially contested. The only way that this can be achieved is, however, by rejecting out of hand Marxist accounts of power as irrevocably ideological and misguided and confining any analysis of power to the first and second dimensional accounts which are capable of empirical falsification.[6]

This view has been developed many times by empiricists who seek to deny the utility of Marxist explanations of power. It is worthwhile, however, considering for a moment whether this solution is necessarily the best way forward. While there is little doubt that Marxists must be forced to accept that thought and action is determined by the requirements of capitalism if they are not to reject their own theory out of hand, to say this is not to deny that Marxists accounts can provide valuable insights into the workings of capitalist societies. Our case studies have shown that all three theoretical approaches provide useful questions and illuminating insights which would be lost if any of the theories were rejected out of hand. Indeed, somewhat contradictorily, one empiricist critic of Lukes, himself, attested to the utility of third dimensional accounts. He argued that a modified structuralist account 'has greater descriptive reach than either its liberal or reformist rivals'[7] and that 'it is by no means impossible to defend the scientific standing of the Marxian theory of power, given an appropriately loose understanding of 'science'. A Quinean view, for example, suggests that it is quite legitimate to 'save' key theoretical concepts . . . by adjustments elsewhere in the theory'.[8]

It is somewhat surprising, therefore, that this critic should argue that social scientists ought to avoid the 'dubious epicycles of Marxian social theory'. An alternative approach might be to try to develop a neo-Marxist explanation. This has been attempted by Jessop, who has maintained that 'power' need not be an essentially contested concept so long as it is confined conceptually to the specification and description of who is successful in wining out in observable conflicts of interest between key decision-makers in society.[9] This is a view with which empiricist critics of Marxist theories of power would be able to agree becasue it confines the notion of 'power' to the production of intended effects by individuals who can act freely to pursue their own subjective interests. Jessop, however, does not end his analysis here. Jessop is concerned that the insights provided within Marxist theory should be brought together with the insights developed by empirical observations of who decides. He suggests the adoption of a *relational* or *conjunctural* analysis of power. Jessop's view is that the analysis of power in society cannot be confined merely to 'the production of intended effects', important though these may be. Jessop defines power as 'the production of effects, within the limits set by the "structural constraints" confronting different agents'.[10] This definition allows Jessop to accept that individuals choose how they will act, but it does not limit his analysis to the assumption that all we need to know is what individuals want—as pluralist and elite theorists do. Nor does it force him to argue—with Marxists—that human beings are merely the carriers of the self-reproducing structures of capitalism and therefore devoid of any autonomous choice. On the contrary, Jessop maintains that we need to know both the structural constraints and the peculiar nature and aspirations of any particular actor involved in a key social and political decision to fully comprehend the 'exercise of power'. It is impossible to predict outcomes, he argues, in the absence of these two factors.[11]

But as Jessop is well aware, while this may resolve the problem of the essential contestability of 'power', it only does so by making 'power' a relatively meaningless or secondary concept. 'Power' becomes (as pluralists and elite writers have always wanted it to be) merely an empirical description of who is successful over whom, it does not tell us *how* intended effects are achieved. In order to tell us how, Jessop argues that it is first necessary to define what is possible for human actors to achieve. Thus the analysis of the limits and constraints facing human beings as they decide and struggle is, for Jessop, logically prior to the study of the actions of the actors involved.[12] This is not, however, to argue for a simple-minded acceptance of reductionist and determinist analyses of power in capitalist societies. Jessop maintains that what Marxist theorists have often overlooked is the fact that, while they may be able to define the intersts which people must have given their objective positions in society, in any given period (conjuncture) these objective conditions are always subjectively perceived and acted upon by the individuals involved. There is no necessary reason why there should be any correspondence between the objective laws of motion of capitalism and the actions and understanding of these by human beings. Thus, if people can ignore what is in their best interests and continually act against them, then, Jessop argues, marxist theory must take account of this. This means, on the one hand, that Marxists must accept the pluralist and elite conceptions of 'power', while, on the other, retaining their own insights based on their understanding that 'politics is the art of the possible'. Conversely, empiricist social scientists should not ignore the analysis of what it is that determines what is possible.

By this method Jessop seeks to 'provide the means to integrate Marxist perspectives with other points of reference and principles of explanations so that concrete, complex phenomena can be adequately theorised and explained'.[13] Whether or not he achieves this is of course debatable. While his approach does seem to accommodate empiricist desires to delimit the concept of 'power', in doing so, Jessop makes it into a concept of secondary importance in the analysis of capitalist society. Whether this is a problem is open to question, what is less contentious is the fact that Jessop's solution may have created more problems than it resolves. One major criticism stands out. If the goal is to provide an explanation of change in capitalism which allows Marxist concepts to be integrated with empiricist theories, it is not clear that Jessop has been successful. Jessop's position

seems to be that the constraints which face individuals when
they choose to exercise power are determined as much by
their subjective perceptions and misperceptions as by the
objective requirements of capitalism as an economic system
of production. If this is so, then what utility does the Marxist
approach have over empiricist accounts? Other than to
provide a reified theoretical guide by which social scientists
can indicate which societies and decision-makers best
understand or most misperceive what the analyst believes to
be their true intersts, it is not clear what special practical
utility this modified Marxist approach has in Jessop's
formulation. In this sense, it may well be that in trying to
render power and constraint commensurable, Jessop has
questioned the utility of Marxist explanations, while at the
same time making 'power' a concept of secondary importance for the analysis of capitalist society. Nevertheless,
while this resurrection of constraints as a key concept has
not resulted, yet, in any adequate theorisation of the nature
of constraints in capitalism, it may well offer a way forward
for a synthesis of various accounts of the nature of power.

In recent years C.E. Lindblom has developed a *critical
pluralist* perspective to counter his initial rather limited
approach associated with incrementalism, which was discussed in Chapter 5. Lindblom's recent work has emphasised
that while many social groups are involved in political
activity, this activity is constrained because the political
agenda is biased in favour of corporate power. Thus, while
the state and its agencies may develop their own relationships with important sectional interests within society,
the bias of policy will favour corporate power nationally and
internationally.[14] This new direction by Lindblom is revealing because it shows his willingness to break out of his
formerly constraining pluralist analytic straight-jacket in an
attempt to utilise the insights of elite and Marxist accounts of
power and constraint. Interestingly, a similar convergence
may be seen in recent structural Marxist accounts with
writers like S.M. Hall[15] and Nicos Poulantzas[16] attempting
to incorporate the insights of pluralist and elite theories into
Marxist discussions of capitalist society.

While this 'new wave' of theorising may not lead to the

development of a 'meta' theory of power, it certainly indicates that there is a convergence of interest by scholars of different theoretical persuasions on the issues of power and constraint. If this leads to cross-fertilisation and a greater understanding of the mechanisms of change and continuity in capitalist society, then it can only be applauded. What is not in doubt, however, is that this continuing discussion will ensure that the concept of power will remain a central issue in the study of politics and the social sciences.

# NOTES

1. D. Willer and J. Willer, *Systematic Empiricism: A Critique of a Pseudo-Science* (Englewood Cliffs, New Jersey: Prentice Hall, 1973).
2. Bob Jessop, 'On the Commensurability of Power and Structural Constraint' (Revised version of a paper first presented to the EGOS Symposium on 'Power', 6/7 May 1976, Dept of Government, University of Essex, Colchester, England), pp. 2–10.
3. Steven Lukes, *Power: A Radical View* (London, Macmillan, 1977), pp. 27–30, 54–5).
4. Jessop, *op. cit.*, p. 10.
5. G.W. Smith, 'Must Radicals be Marxists?', *British Journal of Political Science*, Vol. II, No. 4 (October 1981), p. 421.
6. *Ibid.*, p. 425.
7. *Ibid.*, p. 414.
8. *Ibid.*, p. 425.
9. Bob Jessop, *The Capitalist State: Marxist Theories and Methods* (Oxford, Martin Robertson, 1982), pp. 254–5; and *op. cit.*, pp. 28–29.
10. Jessop, *ibid.* (1982), pp. 252–3.
11. *Ibid.*, p. 254.
12. *Ibid.*, p. 255.
13. *Ibid.*, p. 228.
14. C.E. Lindblom, *Politics and Markets* (New York, Basic Books, 1977).
15. S.M. Hall, 'The Representative-Interneutronist State: 1880s–1920s' in *State and Society* (Open University, Course D209, Block 3, Unit 7, 1984).
16. N. Poulantzas, *State, Power, Socialism* (London, New Left Books and Verso, 1980).

# Index

economic theory of democracy,
18
economics and politics, 12, 15–
20, 24, 26
Eisenhower, President, 130
electoral competition, 94
elites, study of, 8–9, 16–17,
33–4, 41, 67–9, 71–2, 80–106,
108–13, 127–9, 139–42, 170–
2, 184–5, 199–202, 220–1
Elizabethan Poor Laws, reform
of, 56
empiricism, 9–10, 14–15, 20,
23, 26–7, 36–7, 40, 74, 95–6,
120–1, 152, 217, 219, 225,
227
Engels, F., 47, 51, 56–7
Enlightenment, 53
entrepreneurs, 52–4, 61–2
epistemology, 22–3, 71, 73–4,
213–15, 223–4
essential contested concepts,
27–39, 213, 224–31

Fabian Socialists, 12
false consciousness, 76, 116,
223
falsifiability, 217–18
Fascism, 14
feudalism, 51–6
functional sociology, 158–9

Galbraith, J.K., 143–7
Gallie, W.B., 29–30, 37–8
Galting, James, 163–4
Game theory, 5
Gerstenberger, 64
Gourevitch, 159–60
governing class, 83–8
governing elite, 83–8
Gramsci, A., 66–9, 165–70,
174, 182
Gray, John, 37–8
Greek City States, 28

growth of government, 177–91

Hall, S.M., 230–1
Hayward, Jack, 16
Heclo, Hugh, 113–15, 118, 187
Hechter, 168
Hegel, 111
Hirsch, J., 64
history and politics, 20–1
Hobbes, 7, 111, 117
Hobson, J.A., 60–1
Holloway and Picciotto, 64
Howard, Ebenezer, 205
Hume, David, 11
Hunter, Floyd, 96–8, 108–9

ideological hegemony, 66–71,
74, 76, 166–7, 174, 223
ideology, 21–2, 26–7, 40–1, 86,
88–90, 166, 223, 226–7
imperialism, 58–61
incremental decision-making,
119–20, 230
individuals, role of, 127–9
instrumental marxist theories of
power, 47–66
interest groups, 8, 106–7, 111–16
interests (real), 35–6, 38, 101

Jessop, Bob, 65–6, 70, 75–7,
228–31
Jordan, G., 115

Kaufman, 117
Keller, Suzanne, 86, 91–2, 95,
98
key issues, 102–3, 221
Keynesianism, 18, 27–8, 61–2,
181, 187–8

landowners, 51–2, 55–6
Laswell, Harold, 13, 88
latent interest, 101, 219–20, 223
law and politics, 20–1